The Example of Edward Taylor

The Example of

Edward

Taylor

by Karl Keller

The University of Massachusetts Press Amherst 1975

Publication of this book was assisted by the American Council of Learned Societies under a grant from the Andrew W. Mellon Foundation.

Acknowledgment is made to the following authors, publishers, institutions, and individuals for their permission to reprint copyrighted material.

Yale University Press, for quotations from Norman S. Grabo, editor, *Edward Taylor's "Christographia."* Copyright © 1962 by Yale University; and for quotations from Donald E. Stanford, editor, *The Poems of Edward Taylor.* Copyright © 1960 by Yale University Press, Inc. Reprinted by permission of Yale University Press.
Michigan State University Press, for quotations from Edward Taylor's *Treatise Concerning the Lord's Supper,* ed. Norman S. Grabo (1966). Copyright © 1965 Michigan State University Press.
Redwood Library and Athenaeum, for quotations from *The Metrical History of Christianity,* ed. Donald E. Stanford (1962). Copyright 1962 by Donald E. Stanford.
Connecticut Valley Historical Museum, for quotations from, *The Diary of Edward Taylor,* ed. Francis Murphy (1964). Copyright 1964 by Springfield Library and Museums Association.
The New England Quarterly and editor Herbert Brown, for chapter 8 of this study, published originally as "The Rev. Mr. Edward Taylor's Bawdry" in *New England Quarterly* 43, no. 3 (September 1970). Copyright 1970 by The New England Quarterly.
Early American Literature and editor Everett Emerson, for chapter 3 of this study, published originally as "The Example of Edward Taylor" in *Early American Literature* 4, no. 3 (Winter 1970).
Harper & Row and Allan Kaplan, for "Poem" from *Paper Airplane* by Allan Kaplan. Copyright © 1971 by Allan Kaplan. Reprinted by permission of Harper & Row, Publishers, Inc.

Library of Congress Cataloging in Publication Data
Keller, Karl, 1933–
  The example of Edward Taylor.
  Includes bibliographical references and index.
  1. Taylor, Edward, 1642–1729. I. Title.
PS850.T2Z74 811'.1 [B] 74–21240
ISBN 0–87023–174–X

for William Mulder
        University of Utah
and Charles Foster
        University of Minnesota

The nature of nations is the way they were born. Culture is nature.

Giambattista Vico

Contents

Illustrations

Illustrations follow page 78.

Acknowledgments

Indebtedness: Especially to Donald E. Stanford of Louisiana State University and Norman S. Grabo of Berkeley, who laid the foundation for this study and who have given encouragement and advice at many points. But also to Austin Warren of Yale University, Everett Emerson and Mason I. Lowance of the University of Massachusetts, Sacvan Bercovitch of Columbia University, Thomas M. Davis of Kent State University, and David S. Wilson of the University of California at Davis, for advice and sympathetic readings. To Harold F. Maschin of Westfield and Francis B. McMahon of the Westfield Athenaeum, for special materials. And to the San Diego State University Foundation, for two grants to bring this study to completion.

Gratitude: To my wife Ruth for kind encouragement and indulgence. And to all the kids.

Chapter 1

Introduction to a New Poet

Chime my affections in
To Serve thy Sacred selfe with Sacred art.
                    Preparatory Meditations 2.36

Edward Taylor is America's first poet of importance. In him American poetry not only has a beginning but also an example of much that was to be important to it in the centuries to come. Though he could not have thought of himself as a poet of any worth to his own time and most likely had little hope of a poet's reputation after his death, in the eye of the historian-critic-reader of American literature Taylor emerges as a poet of important dimensions. In his depth and variety Taylor participates in the ideas and arts of the mainstream of American culture. It therefore seems very much worthwhile to experiment with a few possibilities for understanding and enjoying Taylor and, through him, some aspects of Puritan life, thought, and art. These possibilities argue a Puritan esthetic worthy of serious consideration. Edward Taylor is its best example. Less than special pleading but more than documentary historiography, this discussion of that example is unique only in locating a serious esthetic *within* Puritanism rather than at its limits.

Taylor needs such an introduction, for the most profound fact about him is his remoteness (1642–1729). Discovered in our own time (1937), Taylor may seem merely to fit a slot in early American literary history. How he is a forebear needs to be understood better. Admittedly, on the conventional scale of canonization, Taylor is a second-string poet, perhaps even a poor poet. But even as an unusual figure in literature, Taylor can be appreciated without being inflated. There are quite a number of unexplored aspects of Taylor's poetry that give one a sense of the man's individuality and the ways he belongs significantly to the tradition of American letters. He is more interesting and more important than one might at first think. A minor writer like Taylor can be known and enjoyed as purely as a major one, and perhaps more easily.

As much as one would like to include Taylor in the pantheon of American poets somewhat better, perhaps H. H. Waggoner errs on the side of veneration when he writes of Taylor:

> He is the initiator of a great tradition. Taylor's anticipations of what was destined to become the main tradition in American poetry—insofar as American poetry is not simply a rather inferior branch of British poetry—are somewhat more apparent in the way he uses language and his attitude toward poetic forms than they are in the substance of his poems.[1]

And Sidney E. Lind errs on the side of denigrating bias when he writes of Taylor:

> Taylor has been given, in a quantitative sense at least, as much consideration as though he were a poet of high merit whose resurrection has added significantly to the cultural hoard of America. Yet he is at best a mediocre poet, as he was doomed to be, whatever his inherent poetic gifts, by reason of his station in life. . . . The scholar or critic who elevates the poet beyond the limits of such a culture is indulging in empty rhetoric, despite skillful expression or full documentation.[2]

But there is a middle ground that is less honorific or pejorative but still realistic about both Taylor's limitations as thinker and writer and the possibilities for interest in his work.

A thorough discussion of Taylor does not so much attempt answers about the substance of his thinking and writing as it raises questions about the relationship of our own motives to colonial letters. This introduction to Taylor presents at one and the same time his interest to us and his determinate differences, or, in a larger sense, our relationship and opposition to Puritan art itself. If this discussion assists one in sensing that connection a little better, then so remote and insignificant a writer as Edward Taylor is of service.

Rather than attempting here to be comprehensive or even conclusive on any topic, my intent is to be provocative in an area of literary study that does not always evoke a great deal of interest: Puritan poetry. Resurrected, it still smells like dry bones. But it does not need to. It has to it, if we look again, some of the flesh of good poetic practice, some of the substance of serious esthetics. I therefore try various kinds of acid on Taylor's work to see what colors it might produce. And though this may leave one without an entirely comprehensive or coherent picture of the man, the hope is that the various approaches may still reveal important aspects of his work—aspects which help to fix him in our awareness a little better.

Taylor came as a surprise when he was first discovered. He has since provided many readers with a modicum of interest in the austerities of Puritan culture. And he continues to offer a few new insights into religion and art in early America. Admittedly there is not much in Taylor to assist one in understanding the sources of current social issues or the intentions of religious and philosophical history in our society, and there may seem not to be much in him to give one pride in the nation's humanistic traditions. He reveals little to us about ourselves. Yet for all that, Taylor can still move one to an interest in early America. He has caught the eye of the best critics of American culture; for example, here is Leslie Fiedler discovering Taylor:

> Taylor is a seventeenth-century poet as alive for us as his English forerunner John Donne. Lines from his poems have already made their way into our new anthologies and, more significantly, into our heads, from which they will not be dislodged. . . . The sole line of American poetry which has an unbroken line of development as old as our country itself is the one that runs from Taylor to Emerson to Dickinson to Frost and beyond.[3]

And Taylor has recently become the stimulus for several works of imaginative literature—for example, of Joyce Carol Oates' *Upon the Sweeping Flood*[4] and poetry by Allan Kaplan.[5]

In other studies, Taylor has already been discussed adequately as apologist, as evangelist, as an example of Puritan life, but inadequately, I feel, *as a poet*. Yet above all he was a man who loved words, loved them as a way of moving himself and others. If God was not exactly The Word to him (that would have been too metaphysical a representation for his mind to hold), he at least believed that for him words were a simulation of as much of salvation as earth-bound man

might experience. When we realize that language was to him sacramental, then we are talking about him as a poet. How he wrote may
be more significant to us in the long run than what he believed,
though to him there may not have been any difference. More important than how his verse reveals his beliefs are the ways in which he
conceived of his faith esthetically, how he imagined his life and his
words to be one life, and how he wrote words as if their sound and
surprise were of service to his salvation. This he called "arts Cramp-
ing task." (2.57)[6] Everything else about him but the poet in him is
standard-brand Puritan of the seventeenth-century Connecticut
Valley.

Poetry came fairly late in Taylor's life. He was forty when he first
wrote something good. By that time he was able to conceive of poetry
not in terms of converting someone to his misery or of glamorizing
his aggressive joy or of probing his enthusiasms, but it was in large
measure finally simply the form his thanksgiving took. He made
poetry out of his gratitude:

> Now when the world with all her dimples in't
>   Smiles on me, I do love thee more than all.
>
> (1.48)

and out of his identification with hell:

>   this world doth eye thy brightness most
> When most in distance from thyselfe. . . .
>
> (2.21)

In almost childlike fashion, he therefore calls his poetry "an Offering
to thy Love," "a song of Love to thee," "a gift of praise," and at the
same time decries all that he writes as "hellish damps." He was not
setting his beliefs to music so much as letting his faith and his fears
lead him to song. "This rich banquet [the sacrament of the Lord's
Supper] makes me thus a Poet," he wrote in one of his grateful
moments. (2.110) Taylor's is the example of a poet who wrote out of
love of God and out of an acceptance of his divinely determined self.
There are few poets who have successfully set such an example.
Except for Whittier, he is the only important orthodox Protestant
poet in the whole of American literature.

Though it is full of the desire for God and a life beyond this one,
Taylor's poetry is a kind of humanistic poetry. Outdistanced in form

and idea, untempted by enterprise and competition with the world, uninterested in the profanity of progress, and uncommitted to appearances, with verse Taylor cultivated the virtues of faith and hope. He was a poet who persevered in his religious thinking, preferring a quietude where things of the soul were alive. He managed without wisdom and without civilization, ridding himself of the superficial, the unreal, the useless, whenever he turned to writing his meditative verse. With his poetry he could reduce his needs to one: a simple faith that might cure him of fear and anxiety. The art of living was to the meditative Taylor a matter of preserving identity by turning inward against the grain of civilization. In his poems time stands still, he is not tied to time, really free of time by virtue of his faith. In the privacy of his meditating, renunciation gave him victory over meaninglessness. There is a Christian humanism here that is unusual.

Perhaps it is the privacy, more than anything else, that gives Taylor's meditative poetry the quality it has. Sure of what he was and what he was doing, he did not need praise. Though he desired approbation, as we shall see, he would not allow the world to be his judge. In his poetry he was a suppliant before only God. Not having to worry about saving his name, he could concern himself with saving his soul. This meant that he felt that in order to exist, one must produce. Detachment was the only solution—that is, achievement without fame—though this seems never to have reached the stage of the saintly, in whom the self-satisfaction of renunciation makes a kind of heroism. Steeped as he felt he was in the truth, there was not anything any man could bestow on him that he did not have already. He therefore did not need to publish his poems.

This does not mean, however, that Taylor did not pursue a destiny. To exploit one's capacities but without having one's merits recognized was to a Puritan like Taylor a definition of life itself. So it was with his poetry. His private, meditative poetry is itself therefore a paradigm of the Puritan's life in the world. Success and fulfillment belonged beyond this life; existing in the hope of recognition, as Taylor does through his poetry, signified something alive. His poetry therefore takes the form of prayers desiring to be appreciated on high, though without certainty of recognition. To Taylor there must have been both presumptuousness and power in such longing. His is a poetry of humility and hope.

But for all of its introspective quality, Taylor's is not a kind of poetry that advances the writer's self-knowledge. In it, instead, he plays the role of the misunderstood lover or outcast. In his execrations he is pitiable. He feeds on his own bile. He turns language into a psychiatric exercise. He permits himself to pursue meaning but not to discover it. And then his state of grace lies in the fact that he can endure disappointment and frustration of his desires to know salvation. Taylor's is therefore a poetry of oppression mixed with relief from the worldly: discomfort and deliverance from the world. His poetry made both a hell and a heaven available to him. It is a poetry that dramatizes Puritan redemption best.

One of the major ironies of Taylor's poetry, however, is that it does not ask one to *like* it. It is not attractive enough to expect that. It would violate the theology in it if it exacted delight; it would violate it if it itself became an object of personal interest. One's interest in it must be intellectual, analytical, remote. It is hardly experienceable poetry, in other than a scholarly, historical sense. It requires a disinterestedness.

Distinterested, we are bound to find in Taylor an esthetic conscience, a self-consciousness, and a conscientiousness, but without finding him knowing at all what about himself and his work would interest *us*. It is quite enough that Taylor should have thought of himself as a private poet only. One thing we can be sure about him is that in public he was *not* a poet. In private, with the door closed, he thought of himself as a poet—amateur poet, but a poet nonetheless. For him that was apparently enough. Like a pianist playing just for himself what nobody else is meant to hear, he made things insufficiently in his eagerness to make anything at all. He is like a number of poets—Emily Dickinson is the best American example —the roughness of whose verse is of as much interest as anything they might have finished finely. The private source of his poetry therefore makes its literary-critical exploitation a minor, if necessary, sacrilege.

The irony of expressing one's inability to express oneself—a major feature of Taylor's poems—is perhaps merely the Puritan paradox of being justified yet human. Which Taylor would see were he us looking back at *him* disinterestedly. On a literal level Taylor's poetry commemorates his fallen condition, for only because he is fallen does he write about his condition, must write about it, and can *only* write about it. Writing about it gives it its existence in a world that cannot substantiate the hell he needs to rise above or the heaven he hopes to rise to. There is little or no reality to what he writes about but writing makes it so. On another level, his verse is what he makes in the face of the Fall. If he cannot go anywhere, he can, like Taylor's bird in its wicker cage (1.8), at least "tweedle," sing, turn himself into sound in the awful silence.

Ironically, too, in his poems Taylor is only a voice. Language reduces him to a discursive function, excluding the world of activity and experience. His sense of presence lies in his ability to talk. The gift of expression eludes him for the most part, and still it is for him a way to apprehend his life. Being tied to language as a mode of action describes the Puritan mired in his system of signification. Perhaps the tragedy of a writer like Taylor is that he expects some kind of transcendence from a language that actually binds him. It may even be that Taylor envisaged language as an organism that perpetually transcends itself. But having chosen language as the vehicle of his meditation, he is therefore limited to it, limited *by* it. Language is the house in which he has chosen to live. That is a definition of Puritan tragedy, for he has chosen to live in an *illusion* of reality, at a remove from action and experience.

His only freedom lies in being playful, playful in sound and with illusion. As Kafka discovered, the absurd is a corner left by God for man to play in. In his little corner, Taylor toys with the language, almost unnoticed. As Emily Dickinson was also to discover, it is what there is left to do. That Taylor turns his toys into praise is to the credit of his faith. He had a conviction that he was alive through the act of writing poetry. In this he is an interesting example.

Beyond whatever delight Taylor found in writing and whatever interest one may take in discovering that delight, there is in Taylor the more awful example of the *cor irrequietum*, the restless discontent of Augustine and Calvin and the Puritan preparationists. This is what one must try to remember him most for. But I'm not sure this is something a reader of Taylor can ever appreciate. When the poetry turns inward, it excludes us. It cannot be poetry *for us*. It cannot move us the way it apparently moved Taylor, and so it may seem to us only mechanical, inconsequential, perhaps silly. But then this is the fate of the private poet.

The privacy, however, does not prevent one from sensing the ways in which Taylor's poetry flavors early American literature. Its vitality again teaches us the vitality of the culture. Taylor was not an anomaly. What we end up saying of him honestly I think we will eventually say of much of the world around him. As I try to argue in this study of Taylor, the flavor he adds came from the fact that the exploration of his own soul showed him how the esthetic was organic to the form and order of Puritan thought. Underneath the wooden exterior of Puritan culture there is an esthetic life.

Chapter 2
This Pilgrim Life of Mine

*None can give a better account of a person than
the person himselfe, and altho' where the
account that a person lays down of himselfe, if
it be matter of Honour, is oft entertain'd with
Suspicion by Wise men, yet where the person
Speaking is a person of approoved integrity,
none but fools will Suspect his account.*

Christographia

From the available biographical information, we can know Edward Taylor only as something very wooden—something like a wooden Indian in Harvard clothes that stands outside the door to the storehouse of early American culture, very stiff, a rigid stereotype, weatherworn and critically abused, yet with just enough color and oddity to attract us to the store where we may buy a little knowledge of colonial culture.

It is easy to thus conceit Edward Taylor, for we have only a skeletal outline of his life. From the biographical information at hand, Taylor may be left to look like one of the most rigid of the pure, ideologically narrow to the point of being a mere cardboard prop on the Puritan stage, a man who took himself seriously and was therefore a Puritan stereotype of a Puritan.

Yet we can still learn something about him from what he gave of himself to his poetry. From his works we can know him for the medieval man he was, for instance, if we are sensitive to his defensive tone, feel his crabbed style, and understand the roles he has discovered that his beliefs make him take. We can know him for the man of the Enlightenment he was when we recognize how he was a generalist rather than a specialist in a wide number of technical subjects, and a humanist who tempered his theology with the theanthropic assumption of God's manlikeness. We can know him, too, for the modern man he was if we are aware of the power of his illusions of alienation and hope and his uses of art to transcend anxiety.

But we may know Taylor *only* in such general terms, for, long and

full and influential as his life may have been, he left only a few traces
of it behind. In a sermon delivered in 1679 he tells us a little about his
childhood in England, and he intermittently kept a diary between
1668 and 1671 in which he describes his voyage from Wapping on
the Thames to Boston Harbor, his start at Harvard, and his winter
trip to serve the congregation in Westfield, Massachusetts, on the
frontier. There are a few letters from or about him that have survived.
And he kept several commonplace books, largely filled with theological and medical data and accounts of "special providences."
Beyond these there are only his sermons and his poems, in which he is
careful to conceal his daily life. Even in the records he kept of the
church at Westfield, he tells little of himself.

Still it has been possible to make sketches of his life and mind. His
grandson Ezra Stiles, president of Yale University from 1778 to 1795,
penned a biographical note about him as early as about 1767, re-
membering him mainly for his learning, his politics, and his piety
over the Sabbath. Stiles provided the leads for most of the approaches
to Taylor's life that were to follow. But he says nothing of him as a
poet.[1] A greatgrandson, Henry W. Taylor, Justice of the Supreme
Court of New York between 1850 and 1888, expanded Stiles' statement in 1857 with information of his own largely from within the
family but also from his own reading of Taylor's manuscripts. He
venerates his forebear mainly for his public life as settler, pastor,
and scholar. However, he apologizes, "Mr. Taylor cannot be said to
have possessed a poetic genius of a very high order, but he appears to
have had an abiding passion for writing poetry during his whole
life."[2] The one other sketch of Taylor written by a descendant is an
1892 family memoir by John Taylor Terry, who, even six generations
from Edward Taylor, writes of him with great pride. He is here
remembered for his religious example in community and family. But
again there is no favorable mention of his writing.[3]

It is primarily from the research of John H. Lockwood and Joseph
L. Sibley that we have as much of Taylor as we do. Lockwood
preached on Taylor's importance to New England history from the
pulpit in Westfield and then commented on him at length in his
two-volume history of Westfield.[4] To Lockwood, Taylor was a man
of heroic proportions; he saw him as pioneer, pilgrim, priest, and
zealot. "This Pilgrim Prophet" he calls him and "that grand personal-

ity which dominated the early life of Westfield for more than half a century."[5]

But Sibley, following the lead of Judge Taylor, was the first to find out that Taylor had been a writer of noteworthiness. Perhaps to please the audience of his biographies of Harvard graduates, Sibley saw Taylor's origins, interests, and goals as having been mainly intellectual ones. He saw his ministry and writing as extensions of his Harvard training and therefore as mainly an *intellectual* force for good in the Connecticut Valley. Though it is Sibley that we have to thank for bringing his poetry to light in our own century, he appears not to have read it with any special interest. He took Judge Taylor's word for it that Edward Taylor had throughout his life "a passion for writing poetry, . . . [even if it was] not of a very high order . . . ."[6]

Sibley's interest in Taylor's mind led to Thomas H. Johnson's in the 1930s.[7] In Johnson's eyes, as in Sibley's, Taylor was a man of substantial intellectual and creative ability.[8] The biographical notes since Johnson's—Norman S. Grabo's in 1961 and Donald E. Stanford's in 1953, 1960, 1963, and 1965—have focussed on those features of his life that made him a poet, especially on the Christian traditions that made literature out of his meditating and on the defense of orthodoxy that his poetry achieved.[9]

Taylor's life was one, nevertheless, that could not keep from expressing itself. What he wrote and the ways he wrote discover to us much of what was important to him about his life—its consistency, its material simplicity, its self-conscious participation in a divine pattern, its capacity for conflict between his stoicism and his desires, its devotion to matters of the mind over other kinds of activity. The hyperbolic nature of what he wrote describes his passion for a life devoted to his God, just as the deprecatory, scabrous, personalized, simplistic, tautological nature of his writings describes his consciousness of the insufficiency of all the acts of his life. His writings tell us that as the scale of historical biography goes, Taylor's was (as far as we can know it) an intense but largely uneventful life.

For our purposes there is something that is more important about his life: what we can know of how *he* conceived of his own life and how that conception convinces one that he was a man who felt in his bones a relationship between language and reality, between writing and living, between poetry and his own spirit. Language was for him, as it was to be for Jonathan Edwards a generation later, a correspondence of his earthly existence to a metaphysical reality. Language *was* a kind of life. And because that was his concept of his life, we have the gift of his poetry.

AS STUDENT

He was . . . every way a very Learned Man, . . . an incessant Student, but used no Spectacle Glasses to his Death.

Ezra Stiles, 1767

From the information at hand we come to know Taylor first as student and scholar. Ezra Stiles wrote of him: "He was an excellent Classic Scholar, being a Master of the three learned Languages: A great Historian and every way a very Learned Man."[10] The Puritan faith in the Mind appears to have been in his home from the outset, and after experiencing conversion as a very young man at the hands of earnest parents and an evangelical sister, Taylor's mind turned quite naturally to things of the mind. Under the Calvinist pressure to comprehend God and one's own fate, *knowing* the Word of God was the form his early spiritual experience must have taken.

We do not know much of the substance of Taylor's years, from his birth in 1642 until he was twenty, nor the years of his education, 1662–68, but we do know that Taylor was originally intended for the ministry by his parents. To this end he received an education, first under a nonconformist schoolmaster in Leicestershire, then probably at a dissenting academy like St. Andrew's or Coventry, and finally at Harvard College in the New World. When Taylor attended one of the dissenting academies, they were the last centers of the Puritan reform movement, turning out hundreds of ministers to go out and hold the English parishes for the long haul of the Calvinist Revolution. Education was, for the time being, the main form of Puritan subversion and reconstruction. The making of a pure Christianity was for many at the time an exciting obsession.[11] Taylor was educated to such a purpose at an academy. His training there gave him advanced standing when he arrived to study at Harvard in 1668.[12]

Taylor's education at the academy, as at Harvard, was an elitist one. He studied Hebrew, Greek, and Latin and the three "arts," logic, rhetoric, and ethics—all of them approaches to the theology intended to give him both competence and status in pulpit and study. The languages were to help him know the truth and the arts were to help him tell it. The arts structured his thinking, his expression, and his morality and perhaps encouraged the writing he would eventually do. But they were of less help in his eventual writing of poetry than was the reading in metallurgy, biology, medicine, and meditative psychology that he began in England and continued in the Bay Colony.

So strong was the influence on Taylor of the Puritan scholars and fellow Puritan students at the academy that thereafter his life was devoted to the business of learning, searching, discovering, knowing. Better than the lay Puritan, Taylor learned through his education that the structure of Calvinist theology was that of seeking to know. In a sermon delivered much later, in 1702, Taylor wrote of this article of his faith.

There is a naturall desire of Wisdom, as an Essentiall Property of the Rationall Nature. . . . And in greate desire after these Treasures of Wisdom betake yourselves to Christ to partake of them. Where should the Hongry man goe for good but to the Cooks shop? Where should the Thirsty go for water but to the Fountain? No man will let his bucket down into an empty Well if he be aware of it. No man will Seek Riches in beggers Cottage. He that would be Wealthy must trade in matters profitable. So if thou wouldst have Spirituall Treasures, trade with Christ. Wouldst have Heavenly Wisdom? Go to Christ for it.[13]

At the dissenting academy he attended, Taylor became qualified to keep a school at Bagworth, Leicestershire—a nonconformist school—and when removed from his post in the purge resulting from the Act of Uniformity in 1662, though well accepted by gentlemen and their families in that neighborhood, he set sail for the new *civitas dei*, Massachusetts, where pure believer and pure scholar could set an example to the unfaithful and the ignorant in word and deed.

He attended to his Greek studies on the ship voyage to America, and then upon landing he immediately made the acquaintance of Harvard President Charles Chauncy, who had been Professor of Greek at Cambridge University prior to his own exile. Taylor was admitted to Harvard on 23 July 1668 as a pupil of Thomas Graves, "senior fellow in a great and yet civill Classe," and of Joseph Browne, under both of whom Taylor studied for three and a half years. He joined in a protest when the reading was not sufficiently rigorous in one of his courses and he was chosen "Colledge Buttler," a position given to an undergraduate sober in his studies. Because of his ability with classical languages, he had advanced standing and his tenure was reduced accordingly. In his last year at Harvard he "was instituted . . . scholar of the house."[14] He pored over his books until held in high regard at the college. He then intended to stay on at the college as tutor and lecturer if at all possible.

Taylor's Harvard years were perhaps the happiest of his life. "So long as I remained in College," he wrote in his diary, "the Lord gave me the affections of all both in the Colledge and in the town, whose love was worth having."[15] He was graduated in 1671, and Chauncy encouraged him to stay on. It was very important to Taylor that Chauncy's "love was so much expressed that I could scarce leave him" and that Chauncy had told him in plain words "that he *Knew not how to part with mee*."[16] Yet Taylor decided to take a post quite some distance away, in Westfield—reluctantly and perhaps, he hoped, only temporarily—and he was to long constantly for the intellectual stimulus he had known at Harvard. He took almost all of his textbooks westward with him, and throughout his years in the frontier village, he remembered fondly—perhaps even enviously— the men he had known at school, as we see by the elegies he wrote on Chauncy, Zechariah Symmes, and John Allen (overseers of Harvard when Taylor was an undergraduate), and on Increase Mather (acting president from 1685 to 1701), and as we see by his correspondence over the years with such college associates as Increase Mather and Samuel Sewall. All of these became men of intellectual influence, while Taylor was conscious of the fact that he was an obscure minister and something of an aspiring writer out in the wilds. "It is not an extravagant claim to assert," writes John H. Lockwood, "that had he settled in Boston, instead of spending his life on the frontier, he would have been famous in the annals of colonial times."[17] In spirit Taylor no doubt often made his way back to the classes and books and conversations at Harvard, but in actuality only once, to receive his M.A., in 1720, when almost all of his learning and his writing were done.

Between those two highpoints, however, Taylor studied just the same. Though remote from an intellectual community, he remained "an incessant Student." It was what he enjoyed most and was to be remembered for in the area where he settled. Stephen Williams, a colleague in the pulpit at Longmeadow and a close friend, remembered about Taylor at the time of his death, for example, that "[He] was a man of worth, [of] good Grammer learning, and a very religious man of a regular life."[18] Taylor even went to neighboring villages in the valley over the course of several years to live in with other ministers in order to learn from them what he could.[19]

At first there were few books to be had on the frontier, and Taylor was too poor to buy them anyway. For many of his years on the frontier, he could not purchase "his necessary professional books" and so he took to the practice of borrowing from friends and transcribing their volumes by hand in order to get copies of his own.[20] By the time of his death in 1729 he had a library of 220 volumes, many of which were left behind in manuscript form, for he had copied them out by hand. It was a large library by anyone's standards of the time.[21] After his death his library was inventoried at £54 4s. 7d., more than a fourth of his total earthly worth.[22]

This anecdote shows his love of learning and his determination to continue studying in the wilderness. Perhaps only a John Berryman could pay proper homage to such a man, who, tired from his work in field and fort, weary from tending to the needs of hundreds of parishioners, and worn from seeing to his many children, could sit and copy out whole books by firelight—more than a hundred of them—so that he might feed his hungry intellect, and then write over forty thousand lines of verse besides.

This intellectual isolation in Westfield perhaps pained Taylor as much as anything in his life. In 1696 he wrote to his former Harvard roommate Samuel Sewall: "I am far off from the Muses Copses: & the Foggy damps assaulting my Lodgen in these remotest Swamps from the Heliconian quarters, where little save Clonian Rusticity is Al-a-Mote, will plead my apology: tho' mine Arrows are not feather'd with Silken Rhetoric nor filed with Academick Eloquence."[23] In Westfield he felt he did not have the time to study nor the stimulus to write as he desired.

But the foggy damps of the Connecticut Valley did not really keep the muses away. All his days Taylor remained a bookish man, a lover and promoter of learning, a scriptorian, and man of letters. We know from the inventory of his library and from mention he makes of his study that his reading was constant and fairly catholic. His library, though we do not know it completely, has some interesting features about it that reveal his intellectual range. For one thing, he must have been abreast of much of the thinking and writing in New England at the time, for his library was well stocked with the works of his contemporaries—twenty-nine of the works of Increase, Samuel, and Cotton Mather; a number of the works of Samuel Willard, John Norton, Nicholas Noyes, and John Wise, all ministers and versifiers; and there are works on matters of church and of state by writers of the period like Thomas Blowers, Samuel Cheever, William Cooper, John Danforth, and Joseph Sewall—some of which his friend Samuel Sewall sent to Taylor soon after their publication.

Taylor's interest in affairs of his own time is seen in the works he owned on the lives of various founders and leaders of the colony: the travel books of Sir Walter Raleigh, Nathaniel Crouch, and Louis le Comte (whose 335-page book on China Taylor copied out by hand); panegyrics on Oliver Cromwell and William of Orange; the summaries of recent church councils like William Barlow's and Thomas Vincent's; and books on laws and liberties on both sides of the Atlantic. From other books he had, he would have known some of the most controversial issues of New England, such as the Roger Williams case (from John Cotton's *Bloudy Tenant, Washed*), the New England witchcraft business (from Increase Mather's *Cases of Conscience Concerning Evil Spirits Personating Men*), the increasing Zionist political psychology of New England (from Nicholas Noyes' *New-England's Duty and Interest to be an Habitation of Justice*), and, to Taylor the most relevant and important, arguments in the anti-Stoddardean debate (from Increase Mather's *A Dissertation Wherein the Strange Doctrine . . . to Encourage Unsanctified Persons (while such) to Approach the Holy Table of the Lord, is Examined and Confuted*).

The ancient world of the Hebrews, Greeks, and Romans interested him, too. He owned Homer's *Iliad*, Theocritus' pastoral idylls, and Cato's maxims; books on Jewish history, Greek philosophy, and Roman law; and classical grammars and Scriptures. He should have known well the works of the early fathers of the church—Augustine, Origen, Chrysostom, Jerome, Dionysius, Clement, Justine Martyr, and Tertullian. As much as he hated things Roman Catholic, like Calvin he perhaps devoted a great deal of time to the works of Augustine in his library; it is unusual for a Puritan minister in New England to have had them.

As a typical Puritan, his library was well stocked with anti-Catholic works, such as Thomas Traherne's *Roman Forgeries,* Richard Baxter's *A Key for Catholicks,* Theophilus Higgons' *Mystical Babylon; or Papal Rome.* On the other hand, it seems natural that he would also have close to hand the writings of Calvin, John Foxe, John Owen, Richard Hooker, and William Ames. If his library is any indication, Taylor's needs in Protestant writings tended mostly toward the exegetical (such as William Greenhill, *Exposition of the Prophet Ezekiel* and Matthew Poole, *Synopsis Criticorum Aliorumque de Scripturae Interpretum*) and toward the apocalyptic (such as Cotton Mather, *Expectanda: or Things to be Looked For*; Edward Haughton, *The Rise, Growth and Fall of Antichrist*; and Thomas Brightman, *Apocalypsis Apocalypseos*).

To assist him in the practical matters of his ministry, Taylor had in his library Cotton Mather's instructions for evangelizing Indians and for teaching children the gospel, John Bulwer's on dealing with the deaf and dumb, Francis Fuller's and Thomas Doolittle's methods of calling sinners to repentance, and devotional guides like *The Whole Duty of Man* and Samuel Willard's *Some Brief Sacramental Meditations.* A few of these practical religious works tend toward the occult: Increase Mather on angels, on devils, and on comets; Nathaniel Stephens on satanism; Joseph Glanville on witchcraft; and Samuel Willard on the taboos of swearing.

Medical books, and a few on scientific phenomena, were important to Taylor. As a physician, he was greatly dependent on them for his training. "General and natural history," Henry W. Taylor writes of him, "was a favorite study."[24] In addition to general works on the natural world like Wendelin's *Contemplationem Physicarum . . . Naturalis* and general medical books like the popular Culpeper medical handbooks and John Woodall's *Surgion's Mate,* Taylor had technical books on chemistry, metallurgy, pharmaceutics, physiology, and public health. It was not merely "special providences" he was after in reading on such subjects, but practical information on drugs, diseases, and surgical methods. This is seen in the fact that Taylor copied off over 700 manuscript pages from these technical medical works so that he might have the material for reference.

More important for this discussion, however, is the fact that Taylor's reading included a number of poets. He had Homer and Seneca in his library, as well as collections of the verse of minor Greek and minor Roman poets, and he had the second edition of Anne Bradstreet's poems (though only perhaps because one of his closer friends was Simon Bradstreet, the poet's son). As we know from his own poetry, he also read George Herbert and Francis Quarles and the lesser verse of Robert Wild, Ralph Wallis, George Wither, and Michael Wigglesworth. He may have read a number of other poets of the seventeenth century but he is careful in his own poetry to conceal the fact.

Richard Hofstadter writes of intellectuals like Taylor in early New England:

> The Puritan clergy came as close to being an intellectual ruling class—or, more properly, a class of intellectuals intimately associated with a ruling power—as America has ever had. . . . It is doubtful that any community ever had more faith in the value of learning and intellect than Massachusetts Bay . . . . These Puritan emigrants, with their reliance upon the Book and their wealth of scholarly leadership, founded that intellectual and scholarly tradition which for three centuries enabled New England to lead the country in educational and scholarly achievement.[25]

Taylor was but one of these. His reading does not show that he was remarkable; he was simply "a learned man in an age of many learned men." Nor does Taylor's reading appear to have contributed substantially to the one remarkable thing about him—his writing of poetry. But his earnest studiousness and his appreciation for good scholarship trained him for the introspective poetry he wrote. The Puritan concern for depth of knowledge and depth of self-awareness was a single concern. The "naturall desire of Wisdom" in Taylor, in both bookish and meditative forms, was, as he put it, a matter of "betak[ing oneself] to Christ." In both study and poetry he no doubt thought that was where he was going.

Taylor's poetry is the poetry of an intellectual without being intellectual poetry. It does not require of the reader what his sermons do. This may be evidence for the argument of its essential privacy. The forms he uses for his poems are simple ones. The diction is sometimes archaic, but only occasionally technical. He makes considerable use of his knowledge of botany, physiology, medicine, chemistry, and theology, but without many burdensome terms from his reading.[26] There are, in fact, few specific references to his reading in his poetry. Probably the most difficult are the biblical ones. A Taylor glossary will never need to be a very large one, and that is because this is not a poetry in which he is trying to illustrate his feelings with references to a public world, but rather a poetry in which he is trying to come to terms with his feelings privately. The terrain inward did not need worldly wisdom so much as a joyous will and a proper goal in the salvation through Christ.

In his poetry itself Taylor is even scornful of his intellect: "Can my poore Eggeshell ever be an Hoard,/Of Excellence enough for thee? Nay: nay." (1.2) He finds it necessary to berate his intellectual abilities: "I . . . stand Blockish, Dull, and Dumb," he says of himself, "I faile thy Glory." (1.22) And he denies all his learning: "The Life of Reason . . . [is] but as painten Cloths" (2.81). But this is mere hyperbole necessary to his role of humility in the poetry. That his scholarliness is in reality a prime virtue in his thinking is seen in the fact that he elevates intelligence to the position of one of the greater glories of God: "Christ, where all Wisdom's Treasures hidden are, . . . how should he learn any learning more/ In whom all Learning's ever lodg'd before?" (2.41) And it is seen in the way he argues that man's power to reason, imagine, and become worldly wise "Runs parallell with blest infinity." (2.45) He betrays his intellectual disposition, too, by consistently defining both God and Man in terms of the functions of the mind. It is in fact at some transcendent point of supreme intelligence that God and man may (hereafter and in glory) meet. Knowing is a form that grace takes:

> If wisdom in the Socket of my heart
>   And Grace within its Cradle rockt do shine
> My head shall ware a frindg of Wisdoms art.
>   Thy grace shall guild this pilgrim life of mine.
>   Thy Wisdom's Treasure thus Conferrd on mee
>   Will have my glory all Conferrd on thee.
>
> (2.45)

Yet in almost all of his meditative writing, knowledge and illusion are in conflict in Taylor. The one gave his thought and life coherence and the other was fertile in him and originated solutions to his dilemmas as a knowledgeable man in a fallen world. The desire to know this world and his God led him to the desire to imagine his destiny, and so his poetry followed naturally from his study without being dominated by it. This was a productive tension, for his study and knowledge kept him in the world even as he cultivated in his verse the illusion of transcending it.

AS DISSENTER/DEFENDER

[He was] A Man of small stature but firm: of quick Passions—yet serious & grave. Exemplary in Piety, & for a very sacred Observance of the Lord's Day.

Ezra Stiles, 1757

Taylor's love of his God expressed itself in both passionately knowing and passionately defending his faith. His social and religious loyalties were the substance of his life and his writings. All his days he appears to have been a devoted subject in the spiritual warfare instituted by his piety. His ideal of church polity held him with the illusion of its possibility. In his dissent against world and worldliness and in his defense of the cause of covenant theology, he was one of the thousands who gave their lives in the course of the seventeenth century in the attempt to bring the reformation to a climactic moment of purity in polity and practice. He was, Henry W. Taylor writes, "an ardent republican in principle," whose writings breathe both "his aversion" to unbiblical politics and his "love of freedom" for the establishment of a City of God.[27]

There is no mention of this ardor in Taylor's account of his early years. But born in 1642, the year when civil war broke out in England to the temporary advantage of the Puritan cause, Taylor's fortunes were to be determined by the correspondence between his religious commitments and the shifts in political power in England. He grew up at a time when it was good to be a Puritan: Cromwell was the great hero of the Taylor family, the example of the prosperity of the Puritan colonies in New England showed the new possibilities of a

pure congregational Christianity, and the ministry was the best way
of serving in society the purposes of the spirit.

While he was at a dissenting academy studying, however, Puritan
fortunes changed: Cromwell died, Charles was brought to the
throne, and the Act of Uniformity of 1662 initiated the purge of
Puritans from government and church positions. Taylor was an
ardent antimonarchist by that time and had a strong aversion to the
laws of the existing authority.[28] Taylor's faithful nonconformity
became known, and as a result he lost a teaching position (probably
at the little village of Bagworth, near his hometown). At twenty, he
was by temperament a dissenter against Anglican pressures (he had
an "aversion to the aristocracy of England, alike in Church and
State," writes Henry W. Taylor[29]), though he seems to have kept fairly
quiet about it for about six years, until 1668, when he finally made
his decision to leave England for the Bay Colony. With the restoration of Charles in 1660, the troubles endured by all the nonconformist clergy left Taylor with no alternative but self-exile. John Bunyan
went to jail and Andrew Marvell accommodated himself quietly to
Restoration politics, but for a number of years Edward Taylor considered making the trip to the Western continent as the only solution
for him. Like John Winthrop before him, however, he no doubt felt
divided loyalties about going—loyalty to both the English cause that
he was deserting and to the American example in which he hoped to
play a part.

Taylor's earliest poetry was written in bitter protest against the Act
of Uniformity:

An Act there came, from whence I cannot tell,
Some call't an Embryo from th'Pit of [Hell].
.   .   .   .
In the thrice glorious Church it proov'd a fire,
Melting our Gold, and leaving nought but Drosse:
T'will cost us Time, and Teares to summe our losse.
This sad Dilemma, that new Law did bring
Displease your God, or else displease your King.
And men of Conscience need not long to muse
What in this case to leave, and what to choose.[30]

The poem shows that at twenty Taylor was already very much
involved in the causes of the Puritan clergy. He recognizes in the

poem that to be a Puritan was thought to be something of a "Foolish Fanatick, silly Scismatick,/Round-headed Fury, Crack-brain'd Lunatick" but finds his excess of piety preferable to the "thin-soul'd Priests . . . stuffed with straw . . . Their lives being lively Comments of their Preaching" that he finds on the side of the opposition. The Act, as the poem shows, hardened his Puritan defensiveness more than any other fact in his life. The issue of uniformity made him a nonconformist. Conscience transcended the State.

Taylor the dissenter was in his small way an archetype, combining reactionary loyalties and visionary idealism. America was soon to be filled with such dissenter/defenders. In the name of purity they were to challenge tradition and seek a greening America for more than 300 years. In leaving England, Taylor was dissenting from the old and seeking his spiritual fortune on a new frontier. No utopian, he nonetheless saw a future for his God in America.

In his political principles on both sides of the Atlantic, however, Taylor was not entirely the "ardent republican" that Henry W. Taylor makes him out to be. To be sure, he greatly detested James II and his colonial tax collectors, Sir Edmund Andros and Edward Randolph. He rejoiced in what William of Orange and the Revolution of 1668 represented for the Puritan cause. During Queen Anne's reign his sympathies went out to the dissenters. And he considered the establishment of the House of Hanover in England a triumph for religious liberty. He was, in addition, a congregationalist who opposed all facets of presbyterian church government. But these positions suggest less of a love of the principles of republicanism than they do a pious loyalty to the Puritan cause: Taylor was watchful of any shift of power from the crown to the clergy, jealous of the need to preserve religious purity in the Bay Colony, and anxious to establish the freedom of the minister to dictate his will to his community. This means that his politics were Calvinist in their exclusivist and oligarchical demands. His writings look backward to Geneva rather than forward to New World democracy. The Puritan elect were to him a natural/spiritual aristocracy.

Taylor spent much of his life writing to this end: to secure for himself (or to assure himself about) a position in that aristocracy. Ezra Stiles maintained that Taylor "concerned himself little with domestic secular affairs." And yet he appears to have attended to the issues of state in the provinces and Parliament consistently. He kept up a steady correspondence with Samuel Sewall, Increase Mather, and others, who communicated to him the major events of the Assembly and the colonies.[31] More important, his sermons and poems have a decided secular and politically domestic side to them: the maintaining of the New England Way. This interest corresponded with the dominant issue in his religious piety: the concern for the establishment of an elect nation.

For all of his nonconformity to the dominant church and political authority in England and his religious class-consciousness in New England, however, it is difficult to think of Taylor as any kind of rebel. To be sure, in England his conscience dictated a higher morality to him than that of civil authority and his dissent took a sincere form, the hardship of voluntary exile. Yet in America those same positions made him defensive, piously protective, exclusivistic, institutional. He could refuse to sign an oath of loyalty in England in 1662 and yet be the first citizen to sign an oath of allegiance to Charles II in Westfield in 1678! The libertarian in England became the reactionary in New England.

Yet there is a consistency in his dissent/defense: he did not become a different man on new soil. In the controversies into which he entered, early and late, he held to one position, the desire for the restoration of a pure Christianity to the lives of men. The initiation of a superior society and the maintaining of a status quo were to him one work. He could not think of the restoration in which he was involved in terms of innovation but in terms of the triumph of the ancient, the pristine, the pure, over a corrupt modernity. That is why in his particular social context Taylor must be characterized as an active conservative harking back to such things of the past as: Christ's organization for a Church, a Hebraic oligarchy for the model of a heterogeneous society, a morality operating on the principles of Ramist logic, a world saturated with the divine providences of medieval science, an outmoded baroque style of poetry for expressing oneself. In his independence of spirit he was fairly rigid. Going on to a better religion, a new world, and the wilderness frontier was therefore not inconsistent with a reactionary defensiveness, piety, and repression. Taylor was America in the making.

In 1671 when Taylor took up his work as minister in the frontier town of Westfield, he began his duties under the assumption that a congregation could be formed out of those who met the requirements of the Half-Way Covenant. The Covenant since Calvin had meant that conversion to Protestant Christianity would precede the sacraments of membership, and since the Synod of 1662 it had meant that congregations would be made up of only the sanctified and their children. This became a spiritual law of the land in most New England communities for a number of decades, and it meant that a purity of faith would be maintained by the select in the New World. To defend the Covenant, as Taylor, the Mathers, and many others did assiduously, was to defend the whole of the New England experiment. Though such covenanting elitism may have been of concern only secondarily as the early settlement of New England was carried out, it soon became a way of linking the adventure and the optimism in the New World with the need to sustain the church of the Old. It became, as it had not in England or on the continent, a way of justifying the journey to the colony, a way of linking church and state in one's conscience, a form of loyalty oath, a faith-proof of one's patriotism, a means of maintaining law and order in church and state. The discussions in defense of maintaining the Covenant therefore took on epic proportions in the course of Taylor's lifetime. To the clergy, if not entirely to the laity, the future of America lay in the balance.[32]

Public confession and private preparation for the Sacrament of the Lord's Supper were to Taylor, as to most of the defenders of the faith in the period in New England, the central factors in maintaining the Covenant. Only those of proven conversion were permitted to participate. This distinguished between the patriots of the cause of the New Canaan and the indifferent and alien. ("The Holy Ghost . . . styles all such as are not visible saints dogs," Taylor wrote.[33]) The sacrament encouraged a conformity to the cause of both nation and church among those aspiring to knowledge of their election, and it gave pride to those so committed. It served as a monthly reminder of the settling of the nation, the goodness of God, the duties of service to the church. It was a renewing of the Covenant. For these reasons, the work of an articulate minister like Taylor was to argue the sanctity of the Lord's Supper as being a pledge of allegiance to the religious ideals of the founders.

In his 1679 sermon on the organizing of the church in Westfield, Taylor reveals how ecclesiastical matters (and particularly a sacrament like the Lord's Supper) are to him political matters: "If this is

not Gods habitation thro' the spirit, then God hath no Politicall
Visible Ecclesiasticall Habitation on Earth."[34] Preparing oneself to
live in the ideal church-state was of primary importance to Taylor:

> Consider you are never fit for this Habitation till you are pre-
> pared matter. The New Jerusalem that came down out of
> Heaven was prepared as a Bride adorned for her Husband. This
> new Jerusalem is the Church: this Husband is that Glorious one
> her Lord that dwells in this Habitation. Therefore this Habita-
> tion is build not of Rubbish Stone, but of Wrought Stones. Oh!
> therefore prepare.[35]

In this light Taylor's writings on the subject of preparing oneself for
the Lord's Supper, whether in the form of thornily legalistic sermons
or meditative poems, are *social* documents of historical note—
documents that are integral with his role of dissenter/defender.

At the time that the church in Westfield could finally be organized
(in 1679), Taylor set an example of commitment to the Covenant by
giving his testimony of the truth of his conversion and faith. This was
the beginning of a defense of the covenant that was to occupy him
until old age overtook his powers of mind. His defense, more than
anything else in his life, turned him into a writer.

When in 1677 the energetic and successful young minister at
Northampton, Solomon Stoddard, began liberalizing the requirements for baptism and the Lord's Supper by admitting any consent-
ing adult, both Increase Mather and Edward Taylor came to the
defense of the faith—Mather in a sermon in 1677 ("A Discourse
Concerning the Danger of Apostasy"), in which he angrily branded
the practice heretical, and Taylor in a sermon in Westfield in 1679
called "A Particular Church is Gods House."[36] Taylor's attack on the
liberalization was based on what he deeply felt to be the need for a
public profession of faith and repentance prior to gaining the status
of the chosen. Self-examination was to him the only "Sufficient
preparation for the Lord's Supper." Without it the whole cause of the
church—and ultimately of the Puritan social experiment in New
England—was lost.

Taylor was never to enter into contentious debate with Stoddard as
others were to do in the course of the next three decades. His defense
was simply to make sure that his own congregation and his own life
represented a light to others, preparing himself and them to be the

elect of the nation in fulfillment of the New England dream. He was
never to yield to the liberalization personally, and the Westfield
church was one of the last in New England in holding out against the
change, later eliciting Jonathan Edwards' complaint (his only reference to Taylor):

> About the same time, Mr. [Nehemiah] Bull of Westfield [said]
> that there began to be a great alteration there, and that there had
> been more done in one week before that time that I spoke with
> him than had been done in seven years before. The people of
> Westfield have till now above all other places, made a scoff and
> derision of this concern at Northampton.[37]

He might have felt as Samuel Mather did on this issue, writing in a
letter to Taylor: " I pray god to guide us in all things, and to help us in
this backsliding time, but I have the comfort, truth will live when I
am dead."[38]

Taylor wrote to Stoddard on 13 February 1688, warning him of
the pernicious effect his influence could have in undercutting the
ideals for which the church in New England was being established. " I
dissenting from your motions entreate you . . . whether the thing be
warrantable." Taylor's concern in his letter is as much a political one
as it is religious. He feared that the liberalization "will greatly reflect
upon those that led this people into the Wilderness" and "will be
grievous in the Ears of Gods people in other parts of the World" who
look to New England's "Apostacy in Mr. Stoddards Motions, in
which Deus Prohibeat."[39]

In a letter in reply four months later, Stoddard said that he felt
what he was doing was "necessary for the Country, that we might not
go on further to forsake God."[40] The concern of both, it appears, was
for the social/political implications that the change in definition of
regeneration might have for the Abrahamic destiny that the new
colony had been seeking to achieve for over a half-century. "The Will
of God" concerning "the Land" is a central issue. In this jockeying for
positions both Taylor and Stoddard were calling into question the
other's loyalty to the dream. Several writers who were also concerned
for religion in the life of the nation, among them Increase and Cotton
Mather, jumped into the debate heatedly;[41] but Taylor's major
works on the subject, the sermons of his *Treatise Concerning the
Lord's Supper* along with three others on church discipline, were not
published at the time. They make up the earliest and most articulate

rebuttal of a position which Taylor prophesied could change the psychology of the nation.

Taylor's ultimate defense on the issue was the Westfield sermons Stoddard never heard and the meditative poems he was never given the opportunity to read. That Taylor's participation in the debate took these forms shows that he preferred being exemplary rather than contentious. In the poems, Taylor, from 1682 on to the end of his life, went through the exercise of preparatory meditation, and in the sermons he constructed arguments sustaining the principles of the Half-Way Covenant, and in particular the exclusiveness of the Lord's Supper, thereby making himself and his congregation a small fortress against the assault of modernization. Stoddard complained of Taylor and the others who remained conservative on the issue: "Many Persons do make an idol of the Lords Supper; crying it up above all Ordinances both of the Old and New Testament, as if it were as peculiar to Saints as heavenly glory."[42] Taylor's reply was to simply go on quietly advocating and practicing preparationism as a form of loyalty to God and country.[43]

In early 1694 Taylor wrote a series of essays against the spreading influence of Stoddard, delivered them as sermons to his congregation, and prepared them for publication. He argued at length from both Scripture and New England tradition. "All societies are constituted by covenanting: a covenant is the formal cause of all societies," Taylor reminded his fellow settlers. "Now this covenant must be made with God and the society. You must not attend it in a slighty way, but in the integrity of your soul, that the awe of God may be upon you."[44] The sacramental controversy was one of the principal tests of God's people:

Among the Protestants it is of like import in respect unto church proceedings, that it is one of the main things on the account of which the old and new Nonconformists have deserted Episcopal government, and suffered persecution, loss of their public ministry, poverty, imprisonment, and to avoid such mixt administrations of the Lord's Supper, and to enjoy an holy administrating of it to the visibly worthy was that that brought this people from all things near and dear to them in their native country to encounter with the sorrows and difficulties of the wilderness. . . .[45]

As ten of his poems written during 1711 and 1712 suggest, Taylor preached at length on the subject of the Stoddardean heresy again later. And in 1713, at a time when Stoddard was having great success converting ministers in the colony to his "easier" democratic Christianity, Taylor lectured his own congregation on their laxity of faith and refused to administer the Lord's Supper to them until they submitted to his stern will in the matter.[46] None of his works got into print and he did not preach very widely (only in Springfield, Boston, and perhaps Hartford, as far as we know), so he was not much of an influence for maintaining the ideals of the settling of New England.

His poetry was the most significant form this defense took. For over forty years he worked at it as a way of keeping himself faithful to the ideal of a New Jerusalem. Perhaps one reason behind the poetry was to keep himself from slipping into the position that Stoddard had fallen into, and as a result to remain a righteous and humble example to his congregation—and the congregation an example to the valley and the colony.

In this sense most of Taylor's meditative poems are social documents. Such a "political" reading of them helps to account for the legalistic language and certain kinds of imagery. Christ takes on government titles like King, Judge, Magistrate. Taylor assumes the role of subject, vassal, servant, guest, court entertainer. And the Lord's Supper is consistently a *royal* feast. Of special interest is the fact that Taylor often calls the location for the feast of subject and lord New Jerusalem, New Zion, a Promised Land.

None of Taylor's poems have this social function as much as the group of ten that he wrote while preaching on the Lord's Supper from June 1711 to December 1712. (2.101–11) Throughout this group, references to "Grace's Splendor" are combined with references to "shining Institutions" in order to suggest Taylor's social preoccupations during his sacramental preparations. To him the exclusiveness of the Lord's Supper made the New England social contract and the Biblical law one covenant:

> The Basis of thy gracious functions stands
>> Ensocketted in thy Essentiall Grace
> As its foundation, Rock (not loose loose Sands)
>> Bearing the Splendor of this shining face
>> Th' New Covenant, Whose Articles Divine
>> Do far surmount lines wrote in Gold for Shine.

And as the King of Zion thou putst out
    Thy Institutions, Zions Statutes, th' Laws
Of thy New Covenant, which all through out
    Thy bright Prophetick trumpet sounds, its Cause.
    To this New Covenant, thou sets thy hand
    And the Royall Seale eternally to stand.

A Counterpane indented right with this
    Thou giv'st indeed a Deed of Gift to all
That Give to thee their Hearts, a Deed for bliss.
    Which with their hands and Seales they sign too shall.
    One seale they at the Articling embrace:
    The other oft must be renew'd, through grace.

Unto the Articles of this Contract
    Our Lord did institute even at the Grave
Of the Last Passover, when off its packt.
    This Seale for our attendance oft to have.
    This Seal made of New Cov'nant was, red di 'de,
    In Cov'nant blood, by faith to be appli'de.

Oh! this Broad Seale, of Grace's Covenant
    Bears, Lord, thy Flesh set in its rim aright.
All Crucifide and blood, (Grace hath no want)
    As shed for us, and on us us to White.
    Let's not neglect this gracious law nor breake
    But on this Flesh and blood doth drinke and Eate.

                           (2.102)

It was natural for Taylor to use political metaphors in such a context, for to him "New Covenant worship" was New England worship. They show how Taylor equated the Lord's Supper with what he thought of as the American Dream.

Though Taylor could have had no premonition of it, the substance of his defense of the New England sacramental Way (but not its quiet form) was mythic. In his lifetime he lost out to the innovators, but as it turned out, the seed had already been sown—by Taylor and many others in that first century—that would flower as an American nationalism.

AS MINISTER

You will say of your little old wife the Congregation of
Westfield—
　"Conjux crede mihi, si te quoque collis habebit, Te sequar
ascendens, et me quoque collis habebit."
　　　　　　Samuel Sewall to Edward Taylor, 16 Feb. 1720

Taylor was not licensed to preach—either in dissent against or in
defense of anything—when he left England for the Bay Colony in
1668. Perhaps he originally intended to teach school only and not to
attempt the ministry. But his schooling at Harvard College and his
association with excellent educator/ministers while there became a
kind of ministerial call to him. He would have stayed at the college as
"scholar of the house" but it was not difficult to persuade him to take
the first congregation offered him. It was the work he was made for.
And though at first Taylor felt unfulfilled in his position as frontier
pastor (he was 29 at the time), he became increasingly devoted to his
work. It is not necessary to be hyperbolic about the single most
important fact of his life—that "he had served God & his generation
faithfully for many years," as his tombstone inscription put it.

　In his diary, Taylor tells fairly specifically how he came to that
service—except for his voyage to the New World, the only event in his
life that he documented with daily notes. On 17 November 1671, the
day after Taylor had been asked to remain at Harvard, Goodman
Thomas Dewey, a messenger from the tiny settlement of Westfield on
the Connecticut River, came to Boston to inquire about getting a
minister. The area that was developing into the community of
Westfield had been settled since the early 1660s and had had two
ministers before 1671 but now had no one to preach there. Dewey
was hoping to get the Reverend Mr. William Adams, pastor at
Dedham, to move to Westfield, but he was "not as yet movable." So
he turned for advice to Increase Mather, who promptly recommended that he go and see the bright and mature student Edward
Taylor at the College.[47] Taylor talked with Dewey but put him off by
sending him to President Chauncy and several of his instructors—
"Reserving liberty," Taylor called it, "to advise with friends." In this
Taylor could put the faculty to a test regarding their view of his
prospects: did they regard him highly and sincerely enough as scho-

lar? or did they think that he would do better as a minister? Chauncy was, as Taylor reported his impression, "altogether against it at this time." Both Samuel Danforth, a young tutor, and Urian Oakes, a Fellow, advised Taylor to take the position, though they did so reluctantly, knowing his value to the school.[48]

This advice left Taylor undecided. So he went over to Boston the next day to speak with Mather, and he spoke with Peter Thacher, also a scholar of the house. Their opinion was that he should go. Mather had a sincere interest in the establishment of the church in the Connecticut Valley, for his brother Eleazar had been the first minister in Northampton until his death in 1669. But Taylor was still undecided for the next two days. On the twentieth he talked with Dewey once again, trying to communicate his indecisiveness to him; yet he somehow left him with the impression that he would indeed go with him to Westfield, if only temporarily. Goodman Dewey was determined to return to Westfield with a minister, and his expectations were raised by Taylor's prayerful "preparation" on the matter. On the twenty-sixth, even though it was snowing very heavily, Dewey came for Taylor to go with him and the three others from Westfield. Taylor spent his last evening with President Chauncy, proceeding in the matter, he felt, "by Prayer and cou[n]sell."

> Wherefore tarrying till then, I not knowing how to cast down Goodman Dewy's expectation[s] after I had raised them, set forward, not without much apprehension of a tedious & hazzardous journey, the Snow being about Mid-leg deepe, the way unbeaten, or the track filled up againe, and over rocks and mountains, and the journey being about an 100 miles; and Mr. Cooke of Cambridge told us it was the desperatest journey that ever Connecticut men undertooke.[49]

Taylor interpreted the safe passage through the wilderness all the way over the hundred-mile track to the banks of the Connecticut River as God's approval of his decision to go to Westfield.

The reception of the new minister in Westfield, "the place of our desire," seven days later was extremely cordial. Taylor first stopped at the home of the Cook family, "who entertained us with great joy and gladness, giving me many thanks for coming"; then, in spite of a sudden storm, he went to the Whitings, where the men of the town came to welcome him, and finally to the Ashlys, where he was to stay until the Whitings could take him in comfortably. It was a great event to have a minister from Cambridge come to live at the outpost.

Taylor lost no time beginning the work they wanted him to do. On the next day, Wednesday, 3 December, he preached to the nine approved members of the church and their families a first sermon, with others listening. So far as we know, it was the first sermon he had ever preached. Its text was Matthew 3:2: "Repent ye, for the kingdom of heaven is at hand."[50]

For eight years, Taylor was a faithful minister to the needs of his wilderness saints, though he was not ordained their pastor and had no formally organized church until 1679. In those intervening years, the farmers of the settlement built him a log parsonage (1672) and a meeting house fortified against Indian attacks (1673). He was in the town only a year before it was voted that "the town render their earnest desire of Mr. Taylor's continuance with us in the ministry and are willing to give him land house & maintenance as is formerly recorded."[51]

Why his own ordination and the formal organization of the church at Westfield were delayed until 1679 is a matter for conjecture: perhaps the settlement was for a long time simply too small; Taylor's own discouragement may have kept him from proceeding; the Indian wars could have preoccupied him; his indecisiveness about settling in the valley permanently hounded him; and the insecurity of the settlement itself was always immanent. Inside his first two years, Taylor became acquainted with everyone in and around the settlement, built a church, and met with others to organize the settlement. "When I had served some two years here," Taylor wrote in 1673, "we set up conference meeting at which I went over all the Heads of Divinity unto the means of the application of Redemption before we did enter the church state."[52] But there were difficulties. He asked Solomon Stoddard at Northampton for the assistance of one David Wilton in his work of organizing the church, and Taylor almost refused to proceed "without further encouragement from Northampton."[53] In addition, several of the members became disheartened from the difficulties of the settlement and moved away to other towns. Therefore, according to the church record that Taylor kept, "A sore temptation was thrust in upon us by the Adversary that seemed to threaten the overthrow of all proceedings into a ch[urc]h state by those by whom that interest was before most apparently devolved." Taylor hoped in 1674 that God would at last "open a door to let us into a ch[urch]h state," but the door opened instead into King Philip's War. His handful of people was sorely pressed by the terror of Indian attacks and all concern for major church matters was postponed.[54] In Taylor's eyes the devil was succeeding in destroying the settlement. Taylor persisted nonetheless:

But God, whose designs shall never fall to the ground, hath not only showed himself gratious in this one respect, but also in the others & therefore after he had stilled the noise of War, hath in some measure restrained the Adversary of the Gospel & hath recollected that little strength that he hath preserved . . . we came to determine on entrance into a church state. . . .[55]

All of this shows that after a couple of years among the settlers, their interests became his, and he gradually recognized that they needed his energy, his talent, and his foresight to conduct the business of the community. He would stay. Taylor wrote of his role of minister in Westfield the following:

See What ground of joy, & praise towns have, when Christ comes to erect himselfe a Church amongst them. Then he Comes to dwell there by his Spirit: & this is matter of joy & praise. If towns rejoyce when Noble Persons come to dwell in them, because of their Nobility, & Generosity: & because of the Good Deeds expected of them. What ground of joy then have towns when God comes & sets up house among them? makes himselfe an Inhabitant, nay an Householder among them? How dothe he by the Spreading of his Wings over them, Spartle his nobility & Scatter his Generousity upon them? How doth he in the Sprindging of his bounty over them, Relieves, & feed their very Souls? Protect, & Save them from the Powers of Darkness? & takes them, & theirs for his own for ever? Oh! what ground of joy, & Shouting?[56]

In the spring of 1679 it at last seemed right to proceed to organize the church. At that time there were about nine accepted members in the settlement. "Our work came on apace," Taylor wrote, "for temptations having attended our work one time after time before, I for my part was unheartened until now to prepare . . . ."[57] Governor Leverett had written Taylor the summer before, allowing Westfield "to enter church state and commend[ing] them to the Lord's gracious blessing."[58] Taylor and the whole town fasted together on the Thursday before "the day of assemblage," and Taylor preached on the text "The Lord our God be with us as he was with our fathers."

About fifteen elders and ministers from neighboring communities arrived the next Wednesday to write the articles of faith for the covenanting members and to give Taylor instructions for the procedure of the meeting the following day. On Thursday, Taylor preached at great length "a formal commission to the christian people of Westfield" in the form of a sermon, "A Particular Church is Gods House," in which he proclaimed the organization of the church "a State of Peace, & Goodwill among the Saints . . . under a Politicall Confederation." And then seven of the members, including Taylor, related their conversion experiences and their testimonies of the truth of their faith, telling the enormity of their sins and the security of their spiritual experiences. The articles of the covenant were then agreed upon by all, and a moderator pronounced them "a church of Christ orderly gathered according to the rules of Christ in the Gospell."[59]

The moment Taylor had waited for for almost fourteen years then arrived. The members of the church were asked, in traditional Congregational fashion, whom they might choose for their officer. "Whereupon," Taylor wrote in the Church Record, "the brethren of the church laid my unworthy self under a call unto the office of Pastor unto them."[60] Four men laid their hands on his head and in prayer ordained him. Solomon Stoddard sealed the ordination with a blessing and a prayer of his own, and Taylor was at last working under the impressed will of God and of those he must serve.

In the years that followed, the town appears to have done everything respectful toward their minister. They protected him in the various Indian threats on the settlement ("It was unanimously voted that all persons shall work themselves and their teams at repairing of the Fort a boute Mr. Taylors house forthwith. . . .") and helped him with his crops when needed ("It was voted . . . to take care about Mr. Taylors hay & corn in hay time & harvest for the gathering of it in and the town are to spin Mrs. Taylor a days work apiece in haytime & harvest. . . .")[61] They taxed themselves and paid him generously, between £50 and £80, to care for the Taylors' needs. They ordained him no other officers until 1692; he carried the responsibility of the church alone for thirteen years. In all, he held town and church

together for fifty-five years and preached in neighboring towns and in
Boston a number of times as well.

In his last years, he had help in the pulpit from two sons-in-law,
Benjamin Lord of Norwich and Isaac Stiles. In 1722, when ill health
drew on, two members of his congregation tried without success to
convince Taylor to accept a colleague to help him. He appears to have
been angry when finally replaced in his pulpit in 1726 by Nehemiah
Bull. He preached only once after that, a kind of funeral sermon for
himself from Zechariah 1:5: "Your fathers, where are they? And the
prophets, do they live for ever?" Yet his mind was not gone at that
point, as some have suggested, for his strong sense of his mission to
establish the tradition of preparatory Puritanism firmly in Connecticut Valley soil was still very much with him.

In this settlement of farmers and trappers, Taylor the minister
leaves the impression of having been tedious, pedantic, and remote.
He was well enough loved as figurehead, as agent of divine help, as
inspirer of hope and endurance, and yet at the same time lofty,
separate, supernumerary. His rhetoric and his logic-splitting were
reassuring to those conscious of the spiritual status of the community
and anxious about the continuance of tradition but largely irrelevant
to many of the needs of their lives. And so would his poetry have
been, had it become known. At first he no doubt felt out of place,
with his loyalties not so much to the individuals themselves but to
some *ideal* of a church.

The major work of the minister in that frontier town was not
preaching and praying, but as Taylor's own Church Record shows,
consoling families, settling disputes, administering confessions and
punishments, saving lives, maintaining civic rights. More than anyone else, he held the town together.

As his 1713 sermons on church discipline show, he spent much of
his time in the pulpit calling local sinning saints to repentance:

Have a care that thou do not Sin. Go away & Sin not, Watch
against Sin. Sin is the Costliest thing in the world: & its intoller-
able in Church members. Gods churches tho' there are many
Sinners in them, they are not to beare with Sinners. . . . Alas!
alas! what a pitty is this? Shall a church member thus stand out
without fear in his Sin? Shall a visible professed member of
Christ, thus appeare a member of the Divell? & so constrain the
church to deliver him up to Satan as an impenitent hardned

Sinner? Oh! then let every church member have a Care of themselves that they Sin not.[62]

Yet ironically his exhortations are the weakest parts of his sermons, which are not programs for living so much as outlines of standards for thinking. Study went into his preaching and provided a high example to follow; his other kinds of experiences by and large did not.

There is something of a caricature in Taylor the minister: inevitably dogmatic, even on the dangerously practical frontier; exclusive, even amid greatly increased daily opportunities; all too sure of himself, abusive, rhetorical; and anxious before the fact that new life on the frontier might demand new beliefs as well. His learning and his defense of Puritan rites were not enough for the lives on the frontier.

His concern in his extant sermons was with man in the cosmos; they do not reveal that he looked very long at the world or at man struggling. The style of his preaching was geared to only one radical possibility for man: preparation for a savior's rescue. It was bound to be a style at odds with the worldly needs of any frontier life. Surely there was a disparity between the hell and heaven that he preached and the abundance of the world his churchmembers occupied, between the special providences he loved to point out and the daily providence afforded by the frontier itself, between life as a frozen ideal and *living*. In his preaching—and this is true of the pulpit everywhere in seventeenth-century New England—he failed to link the spiritual breakthrough that the settling of New England represented with the psychological breakthrough to another stage of human development that was also going on on the American frontier.

The ideas that went into Taylor's preaching may be more important to intellectual history than they were to his audience in his own place and time. Taylor's success as a minister lay elsewhere than in the dogma he served. If his poetry is any indication, from his own personality came something else into his preaching that his frontier brethren needed: the service of tragedy—that is, getting them to accept the hard terms of their spiritual condition with stoicism and with some measure of hope as being the form that God's grace takes. He was no doubt much more at one with his people in this Christian service than he was while involved in the conventional work of sustaining the superstructure of the faith in their midst.

Yet that superstructure was something very dear to him. He wrote a long series of poems, *Gods Determinations*, in justification of the work of the ministry and the institution of the church. In it the soul of man is described as moving gradually toward the joy of church fellowship. The metaphors he uses to describe the organization of the church are predominantly ones of sweetness. They catch his ministerial devotion to the institution of the church.

> Christ's Spirit showers
> Down in his Word, and Sacraments
> Upon these Flowers
> The Clouds of Grace Divine Contents.
> Such things of Wealthy Blessings on them fall
> As make them sweetly thrive.

It is understandable that Taylor would conceive of his ministerial role as being like that of an artist/artisan:

> Now the Instruments that God makes use in framing this building are his Word, the Ministry of his Word, & his Ministers thereof. These are the golden Pipes convaying the Holy Oyle into the Vessells of Honour, from the Fountain of Grace, & Life. These are the Tooles & Artists which God imploys in building himselfe an House.[63]

As a tool of God, Taylor sees himself in this statement as nonetheless creative, indeed needed by God to raise the building artfully. Therefore, the better he makes his music, the better he is of service in making a place for "the Vessels of honour," the elect. Significantly, it is not far from this "golden piping" of his preaching to the art of his poetry. Both were means of sustaining faith—the one publicly, the other privately.

We cannot be sure, however, that the extant sermons are representative of Taylor's art of preaching. The eight sermons of his *Treatise*, the fourteen of his *Christographia*, and the three against Stoddard were written for special occasions and are perhaps in a form close to that needed for publication. His other sermons may not have been thus serialized and may in fact have been prepared for more freely expressive delivery. Samuel Sewall, for one, was impressed with Taylor's extemporaneous preaching in Boston: "I have heard him preach a sermon at the Old South upon short warning, which, as the phrase in England is, might have been preached at Paul's Cross."[64] It is likely that much of his preaching to his local flock was in the same form. Taylor would never have yielded to informality in the pulpit and yet may have preached in more practical manner than the extant sermons suggest.[65]

Whatever form they took, we know his sermons to have been of considerable importance to some of his poetry. Some of his meditative poems he wrote hot upon the composition of his sermons, distilling the main points upon which he was preaching and then applying them to himself. Meditations 2.42–56, for example, are reductions of the *Christographia* sermons and extend the programmatic ending of each sermon personally as "the expression of stirred affections."[66] Others he wrote as he was preparing himself to write his sermons. "My tongue Wants Words to tell my thoughts, my Minde/Wants thoughts to Comprehend thy Worth, alas!" (1.34) The predominance of rhetorical imagery in the poems, and particularly his persistent pleas for ability to express himself,[67] suggest that they were indeed "preparatory" to his sermons; that is, they humbled him as in prayer as he prepared to think out and write down his sermons. Still others have little or no connection with any preaching he did but grew out of unknowable needs for expression.[68]

Though connected significantly to his work as a minister and to his conscientiousness in that role, his meditative poetry has, however, an additional relationship to his life and beliefs than that of an appetizer or dessert with the dutifully prepared main courses of his sermons. His concentration on the religious and social significance of the sacrament of the Lord's Supper and his preaching on the sacrament day would naturally make him claim that "this rich banquet makes me thus a Poet," yet the poetry also has a life of its own apart from all that: it *created* a life within, where the sermons merely reported or pointed to one.

In this light, his role as minister and his role as poet are separate lives. Poem and sermon often led to each other, to be sure, yet in the private exercise of the one he could be, by virtue of his uses of the language, an extension of his sermonizing self that was both out farther and in deeper than he needed otherwise to be. Poetry must have come as quite a surprise to him—and come fairly late in his life—as a means of going beyond mundane Westfield and its ministerial needs.

AS FAMILY MAN

What a rich blessing God sent us in him, almost fifty-eight years
experience has taught us. . . . He was eminently holy in his life
and very painful and laborious in his work, till the infirmities of
great old age disabled him.
  Taylor obituary, *Boston News-Letter*, 7–14 August 1729

Apart from his meditating, Taylor's personal life figures only minimally in his poetry. And yet there are a few features of it that were
models for his meditating and therefore of importance to what he
wrote.

We know of no interest that Taylor had in women, love, marriage,
or "the flesh" until his last year at Harvard. He was then about 29. So
long as he remained at the college, as Taylor tells in his diary, "the
Lord gave me the affections of all, both in the Colledge and in the
town."[69] In the town there was a married woman by the name of
Elizabeth Steadman, for whom Taylor appears to have had a highly
spiritualized infatuation. In his diary he writes of going to pay for his
winter wood and meeting her:

> Elizabeth, lying at that time under trouble of Spirit, though she
> has not revealed it, complained with griefe of my strangeness,
> saying that they [my friends at the college] were not good
> enough for my company, and withall, said, with teares in her
> eyes, that she was persuaded that if I knew her condition, how it
> was with her, I would come oftener to their house; which when
> I perceived that she was a woman of a troubled spirit, I went
> oftener, and was, though an unworthy creature, an instrument
> of some use unto her for her comfort and support; who after-
> ward proved a great and good nurse to me whensoever I was in
> any kinde of affliction.

Taylor's relation with her caused a small stir at the college, however,
and threatened his graduation.

> Some there were that added afflictions to me by their whisper-
> ing, back-bitting tongues, which made me much desirous to go
> from Cambridge, judging it to be some who spoke me fair to my
> face, but grudge me my Charitable and well grounded Esteem of
> goodwife Steadman, the object of their envy. When on this

account I purposed to lay down my a [sic] place at our Commencment, the President, by his incessant request and desires, prevailed with me to tarry in it as yet.

Rumors persisted nonetheless and Taylor found it necessary to attempt to find lodging with the family of a Mr. Flint. He was there only a few days when the call to go and serve as minister in Westfield came. The "affair" may have been one of the factors in Taylor's willingness to leave Cambridge and the college at that time, even though his future as a scholar there looked promising.[70]

Taylor had been in Westfield almost three years before he met, courted, and married Elizabeth Fitch, the daughter of a ministerial colleague, James Fitch of Norwich, Connecticut. Fitch had spent seven years under the instruction of Thomas Hooker, and it is perhaps through his study with Fitch that Taylor became acquainted with Hooker's doctrines on preparatory meditation. Along with her father, Elizabeth had the reputation of being "highly educated & accomplished."[71] Some years after her death, Samuel Sewall recorded a conversation he had with Taylor on the subject of the courting:

> July 15, 1698. Mr. Edward Taylor comes to our house from Westfield. Monday July 18. I walk'd with Mr. Edward Taylor upon Cotton Hill, thence to Becon Hill, the Pasture, along the Stone-wall: As came back we sat down on the great Rock, and Mr. Taylor told me his courting his first wife, and Mr. Fitch his story of Mr. Dod's prayer to God to bring his Affection to close with a person pious, but hard-favoured. Has God answered me in finding out one Godly and fit for me, and shall I part for fancy?[72]

Taylor felt he had God's word for it that Elizabeth was "Godly and fit" enough for him to marry.

A love letter that Taylor wrote Elizabeth in September of 1674 shows his great affection for her. In it, as in his poems, he bemoans his inability to express his love adequately, passionate as it is:

> Look not (I entreat you) on it as one of Love's hyperboles. If I borrow the beams of Some Sparkling Metaphor to illustrate my respects unto thyself by, for you having made my breast the cabinet of your affections (as I yours mine), I know not how to

offer a fitter Comparison to Set out my Love by, than to Compare it to a Golden Ball of pure Fire rolling up and down my Breast, from which there flies now and then a Spark like a Glorious Beam from the Body of the Flaming Sun.

And he ends up, as he does in his poetry, justifying his personal desires in theological terms:

My Dear Love, lest my Letter Should be judged the Layish Language of a lover's pen, I shall endeavor to Show that Conjugal Love ought to exceed all other love. . . . But yet, though Conjugal Love must exceed all other, yet it must be kept within bounds too. For it must be Subordinate to God's Glory. The wish that mine may be so, it having got you into my heart, doth offer my heart with you in it as a more rich Sacrifice unto God through Christ. . . .[73]

The love verses that Taylor included with his letter, a designed acrostic, tell in stumbling conceits of the "highest Steams of Love" and the "True-Loves-Knot" he felt for his "Dove." The "ring of love" that represents his affection for Elizabeth is, of course, included in a design of the trinity. Similarly, in lines penned to her in October of that same year, he proposes marriage to her; and he speaks of "That long'd for Web of new Relation, gay,/That must be wove upon our Wedden Day." In November, Taylor married Elizabeth and took her to his rough-hewn house in Westfield. Samuel Sewall noted in his diary on this occasion: "Thorsday, Nov. 5, Mr. Edward Taylor, of Westfield is married (as he gave out.)"[74]

The home life that Taylor had with Elizabeth and their eight children was quite different from the one that Taylor had known in the small midland village of Sketchley, Leicestershire, England. His father, William Taylor (who appears to have pronounced the family name *Tealor*) was a semiliterate yeoman farmer of fairly comfortable circumstances. His mother died when Edward was still in his teens; she had given birth to a family of five sons and one daughter.[75]

In the Connecticut Valley, Taylor and his wife raised their family in considerably humbler, harder conditions. In the fifteen years of their marriage, Elizabeth gave birth to eight children, a number of them only a year apart—Samuel in 1675, Elizabeth in 1676, James in 1678, Abigail in 1681, Bathshua in 1684, a second Elizabeth in 1685, Mary in 1686, and Hezekiah in 1688. Five of the children died in their first year. Taylor appears to have had a strong determination to have a substantial family. Yet only three—Samuel, James, and Bathshua—lived to maturity.

After the death of his first two daughters in 1677 and 1682, Taylor wrote an elegy, "Upon Wedlock, and Death of Children," that is full of love for his family and faith in his God. Writing in 1682 at the time of the death of his second daughter, Taylor describes his first four children in the elaborate metaphor of "slips here planted, [that] gay and glorious grow:/Unless an Hellish breath do sindge their Plumes." He is happy for his sons Samuel ("a manly flower") and James ("another manly flower, and gay") but very sad at the loss of his little daughter Elizabeth ("a glorious hand . . . soon did Crop this flowre") and most recently the loss of his baby daughter Abigail, whom he has watched dying of "tortures, Vomit, screechings, groans,/And six weeks Fever [that] would pierce hearts like stones." At the death of the first baby girl he experienced an "unlookt for, Dolesome, darksome houre," and at the death of the second he can only exclaim stoically, "Griefe o're doth flow." He consoles himself finally with a piece of wit created by his hope: his children were a gift of God to him and with their death he can return the grace:

> That as I said, I say, take, Lord, they're thine.
> I piecemeale pass to Glory bright in them.
> I joy, may I sweet Flowers for Glory breed,
> Whether thou getst them green, or lets them seed.

Taylor's second son, James, left home at thirteen to take an apprenticeship in Ipswich. When he died of a fever while selling horses in Barbados in 1701, Taylor wrote in sorrow, still failing to understand and accept his death:

> Under thy Rod, my God, thy smarting Rod,
>   That hath off broke my James, that Primrose, Why?

He will not "quarrel at the Stroke, Thy Will be done," he says, and accepts the loss as a trial of his faith, a further sanctification.

Shortly after the birth and death of their eighth child, Taylor's wife died. That was in 1689, when she was only 39. In his "Funerall Poem Upon the Death of my ever Endeared, and Tender Wife," Taylor tells how much he loved her:

Some deem Death doth the True Love Knot unty:
But I do finde it harder tide thereby.
My heart is in't and will be squeez'd therefore
To pieces if thou draw the Ends much more.
.   .   .   .
Five Babes thou tookst from me before this Stroake.
Thine arrows then into my bowells broake,
But now they pierce into my bosom smart,
Do strike and stob me in the very heart.

He feels it his duty to write his grief out of his system by penning lines of verse about her but finds that his sorrow is too great. The best he can do, he says, is catalog her virtues ("I in Hyperboles her praises dress"). He cannot find enough good to say about her. With extravagant conceits Taylor turns her into a domestic angel to fix her joyfully in his memory. After her death he was not to write any more verse of so personal a nature. No one else in his life moved him to write as she had.

In still another elegy on his wife written a few months later (1.34), Taylor seems to have reconciled himself to her death much better. His mourning is finished and he feels assured that under the hand of the King of Glory, "Cruell Death lies Dead." He has reconciled himself to his loss of his first love.

It was three years before Taylor married again. Alone he cared for the three remaining children in the house, ages 5, 11, and 14. Then in 1692, when he was fifty (and about eighteen years her senior), Taylor married Ruth Wyllys of Hartford. Through the Wyllyses, Taylor identified himself even more closely with Connecticut Valley traditions. Ruth's maternal grandfather, John Haynes, had been Governor of the Bay Colony in 1635 but had gone with Thomas Hooker to found Hartford and had become the first Governor of the Connecticut colony. Her paternal grandfather, George Wyllys, had also been Governor in Connecticut. Her father was in the Connecticut legislature for 36 years. The Wyllyses were for over 140 years the most prominent family in Connecticut government and one of the wealthiest. When Ruth married the Reverend Mr. Taylor from the settlement up the river, she sacrificed that status for her love of him.[76]

Upon their marriage, it was a different life that Taylor took Ruth home to. She took care of the two remaining Taylor children, but in the next few years they had six children of their own—Ruth in 1693, Naomi in 1695, Anne in 1697, Mehitable in 1699, Keziah in 1702, and Eldad in 1708 (when Taylor was 66 years old)—along with the job of raising a grandaughter Elizabeth, the orphaned daughter of his oldest son Samuel.[77]

That all of Taylor's children were impressed by their father's station and devotion in the ministry is seen in the facts that each one of his six daughters (even the adopted one) married a minister (all of them from Connecticut) and that one of his two surviving sons became a minister in North Haven. Among his grandchildren there were seven clergymen as well. From Taylor also came a tradition of large families (14 in the case of his son Eldad, 15 in the case of one granddaughter), a tradition of involvement in civic affairs (there were several governors, several secretaries of state, and a host of legislators and justices from him in the three generations following), and an intellectual tradition (among his descendants in the century after his death there were four presidents of Yale, one of Williams, and one of Columbia). There are no poets among his descendants.[78]

The inventory of the domestic items in Taylor's possession at his death, like the domestic imagery in his poems, reveals little about his home life, except that it was fairly humble. Perhaps much of the private nature of Taylor's poetry derives from its domesticity. His home life is most certainly invoked by many of his poems. For the most part, in fact, their setting is not church nor outdoors but home. It makes a difference to realize that many of his poems are written from the point of view of the meditator in the privacy of his home; otherwise one may miss the sense of the enclosed, personal, humble nature of the preparatory meditation that Taylor feels.

It seems perfectly natural for Taylor to play the role of house-servant in his poems ("My Noble Lord, thy Nothing Servant I/Am") or hired hand ("I'le Waggon Loads of Love, and Glory bring") or child entertainer ("I . . . shall sing forth thy praise over this meate"). It seems natural, too, for him to invoke his Savior from the kitchen ("What Grace is this knead in this Loafe?"), from the dining room ("Lord, make thy Butlar draw, and fill with speed/My Beaker full"), from the bedroom ("make thou mee thine that so/I may be bed wherein thy Love shall ly"), and from the work room ("Make me, O Lord, thy Spining Wheele compleate"). These are to Taylor among the best characterizations of a man's earthly life; and because they are the means for sustaining life, they are the best characterizations of the appearance of the divine in the world. Home in Taylor's poems is a place where trouble and grace are inextricably intertwined and therefore an appropriate symbol of the world as a whole. The anxieties that Taylor voices in his poems make them cold; their warmth comes from Taylor's identification of his home life with things divine.

Yet family life plays no significant part in what Taylor wrote. His poetry is farther inward than the plane of domestic relations. Except for his three elegies, one could not explicitly know from his poetry that he had ever loved or that he had a wife and family and cared for them deeply; his is a poetry of spiritual duty, of lonely pilgrimage, of individual exercise of soul. In it he must leave his Christiana behind and make his way alone to the Celestial City. He betrays none of the devotion to mate and home that Anne Bradstreet does in her poems. Everything is the love of God. This does not mean that Taylor, even in marriage, was merely contemplative, for the conjugal language used in his Christ poems is authentic language from an authentic life— again suggesting the warmth of his home life but also its ultimate irrelevance to the business of his personal salvation.

Formally—that is, in the pulpit mainly—Taylor was reserved about sexual matters as well. Through sex (which Taylor calls "the spermatic principle"), original sin is carried from generation to generation and is therefore foul:

> There is in the Spermatick Principalls, the originall of all Indisposition unto, and opposition against, all Sanctity, and Righteousness, and a Consequent of the loss of Gods Image in Holiness, by Sin: and the Springhead of all Vice, and Naughtiness, as the proper effect of Sinfull [desdement] by the fall. Which when the Rationall Soule is infused making it perfect Humane Nature then this Originall of these things is indeed Original Sin inherent: and this is found in all Conceptions made in an Ordinary way.[79]

It is thus through sex, as Taylor says in his poem "Upon a Spider Catching a Fly," that Satan has access to man:

> Hells Spider gets
> His intrails spun to whip Cords thus
> And wove to nets
> And sets

> To tangle Adams race
>   In's stratigems
> To their Destructions, spoil'd, made base
>   By venom things
>   Damn'd Sins.

It is the male that communicates this sinfulness, the chain of which is broken only with a virgin birth like Christ's:

> The Seed and Posterity of the Male kinde would have been all reprobates, and the Elect Should not have been the offspring of the Man, but onely of Virgins, and so the Ordnance of Marriage should have been wholy to have brought into the World a generation onely of Persons to go to hell.[80]

It is simply in the nature of man, Taylor believed, to be "brutified by Sensuality" and "infatuated by Carnality." The "Prolifick Matter" of man is something to be purified; there is no place for uncleanness in the Kingdom. Taylor is his angriest on the subject of aberrant sexuality:

> Neither fornicators, nor Idolators, nor adulterers, nor effeminate, nor Sodamites, nor theeves nor Covetous, nor drunkerds, nor revilers, nor extortioners shall inherit the Kingdom of God. But the fearfull and Unbelievers, the abominable, and murderers, and Whoremongers and Sorcerers, and Idolaters, and all Lyars shall have their portion in the lake that burns with fire and brimstone. . . . O! methinks this Should indeed make thy Stony heart to fly apieces, and to Sinke within thee.[81]

For all of his theological reservations about sex, Taylor was a virile man. It is not easy to forget that he sired fourteen children and was 66 years old when the last one was born. Then too, for forty years, as long as he wrote poetry, the erotic became the major metaphor for his spiritual desires. There is most certainly something sexual, in addition, in his dwelling on the sacrament of the Lord's Supper as a wedding for the eight sermons of his *Treatise* and on Christ as a spiritual version of the physical man in the fourteen sermons of his *Christographia*, but even more so in the passionate metaphors of physical attractiveness, sex play, and mating in his poems. At 71 he started a long series of erotic Meditations (2.115–65, his most sustained series):

Thou all o're Lovely art, Most lovely Thou:
　　Thy Spouse, the best of Loving Ones: Her Love,
The Best of Love: and this she doth avow
　　Thyselfe. And thus she doth thyself approve.
　　That object robs thee of thy due that wares
　　Thy Spouses Love. With thee none in it shares.

(2.115)

It was still occupying him when he finally laid down his pen in 1725:

Heart sick my Lord heart sick of Love to thee!
　　　　　　　　　　pain'd in Love oh see
Its parchments ready to crack, it was so free.

(2.165)

He was 83 at the time.

AS FRONTIERSMAN

*Edward Taylor . . . lived and died in Westfield 17–, the first
minister that ever preached in Westfield, who fled from England in
the time of the persecution, who landed in this then howling
wilderness, among the savages of the wilderness.*
　　　　Eldad Taylor, inscribed in Taylor's copy of Origen.

Because Taylor's interests appear to our time to have been mainly
otherworldly and literary and because his poetry itself gives few clues
to his world, it is easy to overlook the fact that his was a frontier life.
He had grown up in a rural setting—his family in Leicestershire
farmed and kept livestock, he knew the work on the land that went
into a rural industry like the weaving trade, and he had always had a
keen eye for divine providences in natural phenomena—but the
American wilds demanded an entirely different life. In 1671 when
Taylor went west with Goodman Dewey and the other men from
Westfield—making his way, as he tells it in his diary, from Malbury to
Waterfield and to Springfield through over a hundred miles of "Snow
& woods . . . by the markt trees . . . having neither house nor
Wigwam in o[u]r way," and then across the frozen Connecticut River
to the settlement of Westfield—he entered a new world that his

spiritual determination would help him meet. This frontier was a world that would help create and shape the poetry he was to write there.

The years of Taylor's long life on the frontier were hard ones. He lived in a rough-hewn, four-room hut that the farmers and trappers of the area had built for their minister, living first alone, then with his wife Elizabeth and a first family of eight children, and then with his second wife Ruth and six other children. He sustained their lives with a small farm and a few cows, pigs, horses, and hives of bees and with handwoven clothes, handmade household goods, and homemade ale. As the inventory of his belongings at his death shows, he lived fairly modestly. Though he had an income from the taxes of the town, he had to work in field and house all the time as well. Disease and death worried his household always; only one of his fourteen children survived him.

These were also dangerous years. From the time Taylor went to the Valley until he died, the settlement was not free from the threat of Indian attacks and colonial wars. In 1675 and 1676, King Philip's War threatened all of the Connecticut Valley towns. Several communities near Westfield were burned out, and Westfield was afraid of its exposed position; a trapper's settlement in the Berkshire foothills, it was a hundred miles from any settlement to the west and, except for Northampton, two hundred to the north. Taylor led the fearful community through the dangerous summer and fall of 1675 and into the spring of 1676, when Hadley and Westfield were the only towns in the county to go unharmed by the Indians. While other settlements were being destroyed, Taylor made the decision for the townspeople that they should see it through in Westfield rather than move to Springfield. Officials of the Bay Colony insisted that they leave, but when Taylor and others threatened to renounce their loyalty to the Bay Colony government and move to Connecticut to join the settlers at Hartford, they relented. The decision had an influence on the outcome of the war. Had they left the settlement, other communities would have become discouraged and the upper valley eventually deserted.

In his record of the town for those years, Taylor reported the war mainly in terms of an "Adversary of the Gospel" abroad upon the land and wrote of the fears of the people as "temptations" to give in to the dictates of that adversary. More specifically, he wrote of the horrors of the summer of 1675 in terms of danger to individual lives:

> But summer coming opened a door unto that desolating war
> began by Philip, Sachem of the Pakonoket Indians, by which
> this handful was sorely pressed, yet sovereignly preserved, but
> yet not so as that we should be wholly exempted from the fury of
> war, for our soil was moistened by the blood of three Springfield
> men, young Goodman Dumbleton, who came to our mill, and
> two sons of Goodman Brooks, who came here to look after the
> iron ore on the land he had lately bought of Mr. John Pynchon,
> Esq. who being persuaded by Springfield folk, went to accom-
> pany them, but fell in the way by the first assault of the enemy
> upon us, at which time they burnt Mr. Cornish's house to ashes
> and also John Sacket's with his barn and what was in it, being
> the first snowy day of winter; they also at this time lodged a
> bullet in George Granger's leg, which was, the next morning
> taken out by Mr. Bulkley, and the wound soon healed. It was
> judged that the enemy did receive some loss at this time, because
> in the ashes of Mr. Cornish's house were found pieces of the
> bones of a man lying about the length of a man in the ashes.[82]

And of the attack on the town in the winter of 1676, Taylor wrote:

> Also in winter some sculking Rascals upon a Lord's day in the
> time of our afternoon worship fired Ambrose Fowler's house
> and in the week after Walter Lee's barn, but in the latter end &
> giving up of Winter on the last snowy day thereof, discovering
> an end of Indians, did send out to make a full discovery of the
> same designing only three or four to go out with orders that they
> should not assault them, but to our woe and smart, there going
> 10 or 12 not as scouts but as assalants, rid furiously upon the
> Enemie from whom they received a furious charge whereby
> Moses Cook an inhabitant & Clemence Bates a soldier lost their
> lives, Clemence in the place & Moses at night; besides which,
> we lost no other of the town, only at the Falls fight at Deerfield,
> there going from our town 9 men, three garrison soldiers fell,
> thus though we lay in the very rode of the Enemie were wee
> preserved, only the war had so impoverished us that many times
> some were ready to leave the place & many did, yea many of
> those that were in full Communion went to other places.[83]

Amid such events Taylor tried to keep the settlers together. He assisted them in building and rebuilding fortifications, and he worked to house soldiers from other settlements who had come to defend the town. After the war was over Taylor wrote that "in obedience to the call from Providence," his "poor wilderness people" had exercised a "special duty of self denial" and had successfully worked to withstand the Indian threats.[84]

Yet there is no explicit reference to these events in either his poetry or his extant sermons, nor, for that matter, to his other work as the wilderness saints' lawyer and doctor. The events of the world around made one kind of record and the events of the world within, another. In his *Treatise* he bemoans the claims of the work of the community on his time:

> Where I have one thought of spiritual concerns, I have twenty laid out upon the things of the world. Truly this is the condition of God's children here in this life. While we have these bodies of clay to look after, and are betrusted with the concerns of families, towns, and public duties in our hands, they necessitate our thoughts; so that we lay out a great deal of our contemplative substance all the day long upon them, and are constrained to put off spiritual concerns with some transient ejaculatory thoughts. . . . I doubt not but it is thus with many a thousand of the choicest of God's children that are singled out by Him to eminent service for Him that the managing of the concerns of their particular callings are so circumstanced with difficulties and attendants, which with the circumstances of their personal refreshment summon, maybe, out from them a thousand thoughts for one bestowed upon spiritual things, save in a transient way.[85]

In this regard Taylor's Church Record tells what his poetry cannot: that he had a very strong sense of community. As a theocrat, he felt called to keep his eye on and hand in the affairs of both congregation and community so that no one would be allowed to be godless. In his service to community Taylor was no latitudinarian, no egalitarian, certainly no democrat. He was a man of doctrine and he demanded uniformity of belief. He would have made the picture of a self-righteous autocrat. His major participation in public values was to maintain the sacrament of the Lord's Supper as a check against the emergence of any detestable democracy. He probably did not know how his participation in the gradual localization of authority would strengthen a democratic trend that would undercut the effect of that ritual.

In the dispersion of settlements, the American wilderness was creating an independence that went against the grain of all theocrats. At Westfield Taylor was hired to serve the community, not lead it. The townfolk exerted their will against his on a number of issues. And by 1691 when the colonial franchise was no longer limited to church members, Taylor lost the power he had to determine an elect citizenry by manipulating admission to the Lord's Supper. When he died in 1729, the town had moved considerably, as the entire colony had, toward republicanism.

The meditative poetry he wrote between 1682 and 1725, coming as it does from the period of such changes, might be read as a reaction to this irrevocable democratization of Zion. He wrote it when the picture was quite clear: the Bible Commonwealth was losing out to the adversary. The privacy of Taylor's poetic meditations was the world he staked out against the new claims of a new world. With it he was sealed off from the world and alone with his God. This poetry was the extreme Taylor went to to exclude the world.

The contemplative approach in a world of action like that of the frontier in the seventeenth century was a paradox. The meditative preparationism promoted by ministers in the valley, under the influence of Thomas Hooker at Hartford (of which Taylor's meditative poetry was a product), was, for one thing, increasingly at odds with the life of the open road—and would eventually lose out to it. Taylor's poetry itself did not participate much in the business of living on the earth, except as personal corrective of the claims of the world, as complement to the action, as a form of play with heavenly matters over against the enjoyment of the good things and endurance of the difficult things in this life.

That is not to say, however, that his American experience, and in particular the frontier, does not appear in the language of his poetry.[86] Of his Atlantic crossing, for instance, Taylor was able to make attractive analogies:

Accept me, Lord, and give my Sailes thine Aire,
    That I may swiftly sayle unto thyselfe.
Be thou my Refuge and thy Blood my faire.
    Disgrace my Guilt, and grace me with thy Wealth.
                            (2.28)

Though the experience of his Harvard schooling was entirely lost to the language of his verse, other types of experience were not. There are quite a number of references to the fighting of wars ("All Wisdoms Troops do quarter in thy Tents," 1.13) and to artifacts of war such as arsenals, troops, camps, garrisons, battlements, and arms. There are references, too, to the conventional business of a community ("Thou freely givst what I buy Cheape of thee," 2.79), especially in his use of the language of income, prices, debts, accounts, purchases, leases, property rights, wills, suits, statutes, and courts of justice. There are also quite a few references to being a community's minister. In his poem "The Joy of Church Fellowship rightly attended," for example, he stands at his pulpit watching his congregation singing gloriously, glorying himself in their faith, repentance, and exclusiveness. When these images are viewed in groups (some 43, 68, 193, and 348 references to these respective interests of his in the *Preparatory Meditations* alone),[87] one can easily become convinced that most of them are a direct result of Taylor's life in the New World.

Furthermore, the imagery coming from Taylor's work as village lawyer, doctor, and farmer provided his poetry with its roots in this world more than any other of the language of his imagery. And while such imagery outlines little of his daily life, it reveals the correspondence Taylor felt between the success of his work among his wilderness saints and the worth of his own soul. Just as he, as Christ's minister to the community, had in real life played judge and advocate to the town's plaintiffs, physician to the town's sick, and agronomist to the town's farmers, so he turns his Lord into the law-maker/ -defender/-enforcer that he himself was:

> My Case is bad. Lord, be my Advocate.
>   My sin is red: I'me under Gods Arrest.
> Thou hast the Hint of Pleading; plead my State
>   Although it's bad thy Plea will make it best.
>   If thou wilt plead my Case before the King:
>   I'le Waggon Loads of Love, and Glory bring.
>
>   (1.38)

and on other occasions turns Him into a village doctor like himself:

> thou . . . are Physician who
> Healst all Diseased Souls both small and greate.
> None dy of any Spirituall Sores that to thee goe.
>
> (2.160)

and on still other occasions a farmer like himself:

> Make me thy Branch to bare thy Grapes, Lord, feed
> Mee with thy bunch of Raisins of the Sun.
> Mee stay with apples; let me eate indeed
> Fruits of the tree of Life: its richly hung.   (1.37)

In these examples, Taylor has God playing the roles that he as a man had had to fill in order to effect, through poetry, an identification of his life with that of his Lord, and thereby simulate his salvation in verse. To be sure, such language could have come easily enough from Taylor's reading or his imagination rather than from his experience. It is more likely, though, that the range of references in his poems corresponds roughly with the range of his own experience.

Because of the concreteness of the language of his imagery, one can probably sense some few features of his daily world. One could probably piece together, for instance, a partial picture of a household scene from his references to such things as spinning wheels, washing tubs, winepresses, and baking of bread. And one could probably imagine a real barnyard setting from his mention of such things as dunghill cocks, geese, chickens, bats, worms, and spiders. Maybe the Westfield setting itself also moved him to catalogs of forests, fields of grain, storms, and pastures full of livestock. The wilderness around him might have moved him just as easily to his many references to flora and fauna. All of these show that in its celebration of the abundance of the Creation, Taylor's poetry is very much in the tradition of Christian nature poetry. His life on the American frontier might have been as much an impetus to a poetry of abundance in his hands as his belief in a benevolent God.[88]

Yet all of these details of a frontier life are curiously artificial in Taylor's hands, for he holds them as little in themselves. Nature is important for analogy only. Grapes become spiritual grapes, grain becomes the bread of life, a rose is not a rose but someone risen, even the sun becomes the Son, the light of God. Little is loved for itself but only in its analogical reference to something transcending man's world. This artificiality does not mean that Taylor did not know how to live in the world, but means instead that he was sensitive to the artificial nature of art, especially of the poems he wrote himself, as opposed to the genuineness of nature. The earth to him had a life apart from the life of fallen man. Fallen man's salvation could not come through nature but through faith—and in esthetic terms, that meant through imagination. In his poems Taylor projects an artificial world born of his faith; in it he comes in conjunction with his God, or hopes to. To put things of nature in his poems, the work of the mind of a fallen creature, man, would degrade the Creation. They therefore have value in that artificial medium only as symbol, emblem, comparison, something that is not itself. In that form, they remain untarnished by the corrupting mind of man. There is not a touch of the pantheist in Taylor; nature to him does not need the *addition* of the divine. That Taylor uses so little of his real world, so little of the American landscape on the frontier in his poetry, says that he believed it did not need the transforming, regenerative power of his faith/imagination, whereas to him man does.

The frontier actually appears in fairly specific, if only brief and artificial, form in Taylor's poems. He refers several times to "this pilgrim life of mine" (1.4, 2.45) and to his work of having to "Chase all thine Enemies out of my land" (1.4) and converting "the Wilderness to the promised land" (2.162). Taylor mentions cabins, rattlesnakes, stocks, and Indians. Indian life, especially, is used in ingenious ways: the Lord becomes a tribal chief (1.25) and an Indian scout (2.42); the will of God Taylor sees coming like "barbed arrows" (2.36, 92, 135) and the temptations of Satan like "fiery darts" (2.67b, 112); man's body is a "Leanetoe tent" (2.22) or a "Mudwall tent" (2.75); the salvation of man is like "Prisoners sent out . . . Padling in their Canooes" along the bloodstream of the crucified Christ (2.78); the sacramental bread becomes venison (2.71) and the sacramental wine is served in "Earthen Pitchers" (2.94); and to make it a humble feast, the sacrament of the Lord's Supper is made out to be

> like th'indian broths of Garbag'd deer
> With which the Netop entertain his guests
> When almost starv'd, yea Welcome Sir, its our Mess.
>
> (2.159)

Taylor's meditative poems are perhaps authentic frontier writings,

however, in a larger sense. For one thing, their very appearance in
rough-shod form—a form different from that of the verse he wrote in
England, at Harvard, and for educated audiences on special
occasions—suggests that they were organic to their environment in
the Connecticut Valley, indeed perfectly natural to his personal
experience on the frontier. For all of their formal features, his poems
are rough hewn. The rhythms of his lines stumble; the rhymes are
often off; the syntax is collapsed; the mechanics of punctuation,
spelling, and capitalization are erratic and fairly arbitrary; images are
introduced, changed through punning or conceiting, and often lost in
the handling; ideas are thin and repeated doggedly. Yet this rough-
hewn quality of Taylor's poetry does not betray lack of poetic ability
so much as it suggests, for all of the formalism present, a folk quality,
a ruggedness and rawness of expression, a primitivism. In contrast,
in its correctness and polish, the form of Michael Wigglesworth's
poetry has little of the frontier life about it; it fits versification
formulae too neatly, whereas Taylor's is, if not consciously experimental, at least free, relaxed, awkward, more natural. Over against
other New England poetic products of the time, Taylor's poetry is cut
from native wood roughly; it has to it some of the grain and fiber of
the source of its life.

Similarly, the hyperbole and exaggerated humor of his imagery
smacks of a quality demanded by the expansiveness and grotesque-
ness of the frontier of the sort we find in writers like Nathaniel Ward
and Cotton Mather. Taylor's humor is neither so broad nor so black.
But yet the difference of his amplified language from that of any poets
he might be compared with in seventeenth-century England suggests
a local influence, an encouragement to overstate, an experienced
expansiveness of spirit. It seems natural to Taylor to have wanted to
extend conventions, stretch bounds, exploit abundance. It is likely
that it was the openness and opportunities of Connecticut Valley
frontier life that encouraged this in him.

At the same time, Taylor's is perhaps more important as a frontier
poetry in its reactionary privacy. The frontier is a paradigm of the
fallen world and Taylor meditating is a paradigm of the human
condition: not that Taylor saw it this way, but that he writes under
such an assumption encouraged by his faith. Over against the
dynamic, Taylor also needed repose. This is what Thorton Wilder
calls "the loneliness of America" that is created by (and in opposition

to) the frontier activity. Matters of the soul and matters of the world did not cohabit easily in Taylor. The one was too healthy; the other, like pain, increased his spiritual consciousness. This other state of mind, distinct in its methods from those above ground, was such in him that it conceived of nothing outside itself and periodically confirmed his humility. In his meditating he could know that he existed. In the pain he simulates in his poetry he felt he gained consciousness of himself and his God. Active life in the wilderness could not promise such awareness. So then again, the frontier is fairly irrelevant to his poetry, except as a flagrant unreality to be countered by matters of the spirit.

In Meditation 1:4 Taylor tells about having to choose between "The gawdy World" and "The Rose of Sharon" and how the "Pilgrims life" in New England made choosing the rose/Christ possible and necessary:

My Silver Chest a Sparke of Love up locks:
    And out will let it when I can't well Use.
The gawdy World me Courts t'unlock the Box,
    A motion makes, where Love may pick and choose.
    Her Downy Bosom opes, that pedlars Stall,
    Of Wealth, Sports, Honours, Beauty, slickt up all.

Love pausing on't, these Clayey Faces she
    Disdains to Court; but Pilgrims life designs,
And Walkes in Gilliads Land, and there doth see
    The Rose of Sharon which with Beauty shines.
    Her Chest Unlocks; the Sparke of Love out breaths
    To Court this Rose; and lodgeth in its leaves.

AS DOCTOR/SCIENTIST

He was . . . Very curious in Botany, Minerals & nat. History.
                        Ezra Stiles, 1767

Where Taylor's interest in the Science, pseudo-science, and the occult that dominate his poetry came from is difficult to know. There would have been little in Taylor's study at the dissenting academy he attended or at Harvard to stir such an interest in natural phenomena and make the major preoccupation that he eventually had.[89] He was no doubt self-taught in such serious sciences of the time as alchemy, astrology, simpling, and pathology.

Throughout his years in the Connecticut Valley, Taylor collected several commonplace books full of stories of natural phenomena from his own daily experiences or from occurrences he heard or read about—phenomena that to him amounted to miracles, monstrosities, and remarkable providences. They show him hunting constantly for evidence of the divine in the phenomenal, bizarre, and exotic.

The scientifically sensitive eye of Taylor is seen in a letter he wrote to Increase Mather in 1683 regarding various phenomena Mather had inquired about for his study *Illustrious Providences*:

26th 5m 1682, the Haile Storm was; of which I have nothing down in my diary of any lightning, & therefore with us it was not terrible in that respect. Here it was of no long continuance, & the Hail stones were most like musket bullets & wallnuts; yet many there were like hen's eggs, 3 or 4 inches about, gasht with hallows. . . .

16th 6m 1681: About 2 hours after twilight Mr. Younglove & Sergᵗ Norton of Stony-Brook (alias Suffield,) saw arise under the North Star, a light in the sky like the broad streamer of the Blazing Star, but paler, which passing southward, had its fore end verging something westward, & a hook at it turning East-ward, making it appear just like a sithe, onely the hook had not a proportionable length to the stock or sneath; which they judged to compass a third of the Horizon, & in about 3 quarters of an hour pass over their heads into the South, till the tops of the trees hid it out of their sight. . . .

16th 5m 1681. At Mattatuck, about 16 miles s. w. from ffarmington about 10 a clock at night, there was seen by about 6 or 7 men, a black streake in the Skie like a Rainbow, passing from s. w.: to n. e., & continued about three hours, & then disappear'd. This I had, at pᵣ a second, (yet credible) hand. About this time it was credibly reported with vs that the Quakers vpon Long-Iland were on the Lord's day to have an horse race, & being met together, & the Riders mounted for the Race, were dismounted again by the All Righteous, of an angry, offended Justice, striking them with torturing pains, whereof they both dyed, the one the next day, the other 3 or 4 days after. . . .[90]

Taylor also collected cures—from the alchemical cures of Riverius and John Webster to the herb and mineral cures of Nicholas Culpeper and William Salmon, along with extracts from other popular medical books of the time. He left a large number of folios transcribed by hand from the scientific works loaned to him by Samuel Sewall and Cotton Mather. These show Taylor's fascination with the fall of man as made evident in man's pathology.

These two scientific obsessions, the sublime and the depraved, the phenomenal and the pathological, were the extremes in almost everything Taylor wrote. The one turned him into something of an occultist and other into something of a village doctor. They represent expressions of the two sides of his theology, his devotion to his God and his interest in his fellow man.

In 1681 Increase Mather called on the clergy to gather examples of the evidence of the divine exhibited in the natural world. He was asking for a quasiscientific approach to the theology. Edward Taylor probably knew of this request, for he sent accounts of a number of special providences to Mather in the years following. His *Metrical History* might even have been written in response to such a call.

The special providences in which Taylor took such an interest were natural phenomena seen as miracles. Scientific cause was seen as an act of God. The rationalist faith of the Puritan made it easy to reconcile the religious and the scientific. Natural occurrences had natural causes yet also fulfilled the word of the Lord. The physical world was thereby made didactic.

This is seen in several things that Taylor wrote. In August of 1683, for example, when the Connecticut and Woronoco rivers overflowed and caused destruction to homes and farms, Taylor saw this rather conventionally as a revelation of God's displeasure with man's sinfulness. The result was his poem "Upon the Sweeping Flood." Taylor wrote several poems of this sort, one of which is a 191-line polemic arguing that the London fire of 1666 was a foretaste of eternal fire for heretics.[91]

Sometime during the two decades before the turn of the century, Taylor was busying himself with a much longer poem of a similar nature, his *Metrical History of Christianity*, in which he is concerned with the grand and awful phenomena of the past through which God may have revealed himself. The result is an elaborate catalog of sublunar horrors—fire storms and earthquakes that punish the wicked, wars and plagues that are the mercy of God at work, diseases and deformities that show forth His will and power. To Taylor, God appears in the form, as he put it, of "things that hap not ordinarily." In such terrors of the globe and contortions of human history, Taylor could believe that science and theology became one.

Taylor's eye for special providences is his most noticeable response to the new science of the period. His interest shows the way in which New England theologians were overhauling their doctrines in an adjustment to the new age. For a minister like Taylor the accommodation was helpful in arousing his congregation, but it was also of service to his own faith, convincing him that a free agent oversees the world. He therefore dwelt fondly with the autonomous naturalism that special providences implied, for they were proof of a superior intelligence and a divine finger at work. To this extent Taylor became a poet of oddities.

Most peculiar of all of Taylor's semiscientific writings is his long poem on the mammoth bones that Indians dug up at Claverack, New York in 1705. Taylor read in the *Boston News-Letter* for 30 July 1705 of the finding of "one of the far great Teeth of a man" that was "lookt upon here as a mighty wonder" and immediately wrote a poem on the subject. The discovery was taken by many as proof of the existence of antediluvian giants in prehistoric America. Taylor's poem expresses his gratitude for living in a land chosen for God's revelation of himself through such phenomena. Government officials investigating the find considered it such, as did Cotton Mather writing to the Royal Society in 1714 ("[this] confirms the Opinion of there having been, in the *Antediluvian* World, Men of very large and prodigious Statures"),[92] and Edward Taylor in a report he wrote in 1706 after seeing some of the teeth and bones for himself ("a monstrous person," he called it). In his poem on the bones, Taylor describes the mammoth as one of the marvels of God:

Oh! Glorious One! Who would not thee adore,
Who made didst natures Kirnell ripe before
And plantdst the Tree of Nature to mentain
The glorious acts of Nature in the Same?

.   .   .   .

> We do conclude that by such Stories
> Something there did appeare of Natures glory
> In those large instances, and have just ground
> From th'Gyants bones at Clavorack lately found.

He prays that the Lord might "Open . . . our sight" to see how "Nature exceeds itselfe" with such phenomena, for then one might see the remarkable assertion of God into the events of the world.[93] Taylor's scientist grandson, Ezra Stiles, was sufficiently impressed with Taylor's observations, it must be mentioned, to report his grandfather's interest in the bones to Thomas Jefferson and Thomas Hutchinson in letters in 1784 and 1785.[94]

None of this versifying of his interest in natural phenomena should suggest, however, that Taylor was any outstanding observer or disciplined experimenter. Though his scientific interests were wide and varied, Taylor was too dependent on intermediary sources of information, too skeptical of the authority of his own senses, to be thought of seriously as a scientist. Ezra Stiles remembered him as being "Very curious in Botany, Minerals & nat. History," but we cannot call him a scientist in any serious sense, the way one could Cotton Mather, William Brattle, or John Bartram. There is nothing of the inductive in his thinking. Taylor made no attempt to reconcile revelation with the new science as Cotton Mather did in his *Biblia Americana*. He probably did not feel the need to do so, since it was to him merely one body of knowledge available to him. He did not allow the empirical to change his faith, except to strengthen it.

As his poems on special providences show, he observes and records only for the purpose of providing evidence for his religious assumptions. He felt secure in believing the world was subject to immutable natural laws, but it was the divine *purpose* of those laws and not the facts that he was curious about. He was a scientist of the workings of God, which is to say that he was merely a theologian. He could not believe with John Cotton that though "To study the nature and cause, and use of all Gods works, is a duty imposed by God upon all sorts of men, . . . [yet] the study of these natural things, is not available to the attainment of true happiness,"[95] but he also could not let his curiosity go so far as to believe with Jonathan Edwards that to determine the will of God one need merely "judge of tendencies in the natural world."[96]

It is curious that Taylor's searching for special providences does not enter into his meditative poetry at all. Obviously his scientific observations did not mix well with the meditative process. It could take him *beyond* himself too far, perhaps, for his own introspective good. On the other hand, Taylor's medical/pathological interests sit well with his meditative poetry and become an important part of it. That is because the medical was to him a concern with one's fallen nature just as his meditative poetry was. Had he wanted, the sublimity of his special providences could have been used for imagery of salvation at the point in his poems where Christ comes to rescue man. But Taylor appears to have ignored that possibility in favor of the more esthetic, sensuous metaphors of sweetness and loveliness. His experience with medicine was of use in dramatizing his scheme of salvation, however, for it was pathological like his concept of poetry.

It is not unusual that Taylor should have become a village physician. It was a practice anyone could pick up and Taylor had the need. Anyone with an antimonial cup and a copy of Culpeper's *English Physician* became a doctor. No real distinction was possible between those who were generally viewed as physicians and others who cared to practice medicine. The ministers who followed a sort of pastoral practice were often better informed than the "doctors," even though their medical advice was incidental to pastoral care. Taylor did not acquire a really professional knowledge of medicine as Cotton Mather did; the people of the colony were nonetheless sufficiently used to the incursion of clergymen into medicine that they welcomed his double ministry.

Because he was, as Ezra Stiles tells us, "Physician for the town all his life," Taylor found it easy in his poems to conceive of fallen human nature in terms of pathology and salvation in terms of cures.

Halfe Dead: and rotten at the Coare: my Lord!
    I am Consumptive: and my Wasted lungs
Scarce draw a Breath of aire: my silver Coard
    Is loose. My buckles almost have no tongues.
    My Heart is Fistulate: I am a Shell.
    In Guilt and Filth I wallow, Sent and Smell.

(2.14)

His pathological view of man of necessity gave a coherence to his roles as minister and doctor, as did his view of Christ (and of course himself, Christ's minister) as salver/savior:

Shall not that Wisdom horded up in thee

.   .   .   .

Provide a Cure for all this griefe in mee
    And in the Court of Justice save from Stripes,
    And purge away all Filth and Guilt, and bring
    A Cure to my Consumption as a King?

(2.14)

The language of pathology was also the language of his theology, and, when he wrote his meditative poetry, being a physician aided him in characterizing the sorry state his meditating taught him he was in. It is not coincidental that the language of disease and the language of health are integral with Taylor's concept of the sacrament of the Lord's Supper (for example, one eats the Bread of Life and drinks the purgative wine to move from sickness to health), for Taylor conceived of the sacrament as a uniter of physician with patient, and minister with penitent. Medicine thus encouraged his meditating and his meditative poetry.[97]

Believing as he probably did in disease as proceeding from original sin, Taylor found it necessary in his sermons to first convince his parishioners/patients of their innate depravity. Anxiety was part of the cure, since he utilized sickness to promote religion: a minister could serve the souls of Westfield the better for having also tended their bodies. There is some indication in his meditative poems that Taylor, like Cotton Mather, sought to establish an emotional state in his parishioner/patients that was conducive to their recovery. He perhaps had some concept of psychosomatic medicine (though less intense than that which made Cotton Mather notorious): the purpose of a number of his poems and sermons was to convince that Christ is a cure.[98]

Taylor's medicine was backward even by standards of his own time. Most of the medical books he relied on were discredited ones.[99] Taylor thought more in terms of a generalized pathology after the medieval manner than of particular diseases after the modern. Often, general states of debility concerned him rather than particular diseases, though Paracelsus was teaching him a concept of distinct diseases, each with its own causes and cures. Only in part did he learn to identify specific diseases diagnosed in individuals and seek to find specific causes and remedies. He was not a taxonomist. Over against a serious student of science like Cotton Mather—who worked with smallpox inoculation, ornithological nidification, plant hybridization, psychiatry, and theories of disease—Taylor was little more than a conventional religious consoler, bloodletter, and herb-healer.[100] He did not have the open and encyclopedic mind of Mather; he was neither erudite nor original.

The medical references in his poems and sermons suggest that his cures were a combination of faith and sympathetic chemistry. In his poems he refers to giving sweatbaths, purges, and plasters, and to washing boils and "drain[ing] ill Humours," but in his practice he appears to have relied mainly on simpling, the use of herbs for medicine. In Meditation 2.27 is an example of his practice:

The slain Dove's buri'de: In whose Blood (in water)
    The Living Turtle, Ceder, Scarlet twine,
And Hysop dipted are (as an allator)
    Sprinkling the Leper with it Seven times
    That typify Christs Blood by Grace applide
    To Sinners vile, and then they're purifide.

Early in his first decade on the frontier, Taylor began his practice by collecting a fat manuscript volume (which he called his Dispensatory and derived largely from the pharmacopiae of Nicholas Culpeper and William Salmon) in which he listed over four hundred plants, roots, barks, and oils, and their curative powers. Taylor's practice leaned to the iatrochemical rather than the iatrophysical. He emphasized chemical drugs much more than Mather, though his botanical and biological remedies were not used in any eclectic fashion. Though Taylor was little interested in astrological botany, he followed his Culpeper closely and naively, believing that medicinal herbs, spices, and minerals were stamped by nature with the clear indication of their curative powers.[101]

Taylor's belief in such a doctrine of signatures helped him carry out the work of a physician after a religious manner. The many references to herbs for medicine in his poems suggest that he may have kept a "psychic garden" and that he used herbs from it for cures according to the signature of the divine on them, that is, according to names, appearances, or some other quality indicating the medical will of God. Taylor felt with many in his time that plant life was a platonic counterpart to the universe, as microcosm to macrocosm, and as such was stamped by God with an indication of its uses. Flowers or roots shaped like insects, for instance, cured insect bites. Ferns were for baldness, white pomegranate seeds for toothache, adders tongue for snakebite, heart treyfoyle for heart ailments, walnut shells for skull wounds and walnuts for headaches. This doctrine came to Culpeper, and then to Taylor, from Paracelsus (the Swiss physician Theophrastus von Hohenheim, 1493–1541), who wrote of it:

> I have oft-times declared, how by the outward shapes and qualities of things we may know their inward Vertues, which God hath put in them for the good of man. So in St. Johns wort, we may take notice of the form of the leaves and flowers, the porosity of the leaves, the Veins. 1. The porosite or holes in the leaves, signifie to us, that this herb helps both inward and outward holes or cuts in the skin. . . . 2. The flowers of Saint Johns wort, when they are purified, they are like blood, which teacheth us, that this herb is good for wounds, to close them and fill them up.[102]

Taylor echoes this when he writes:

These all as meate, and med'cine, emblems choice
  Of Spirituall Food, and Physike are which sport
Up in Christs Garden.

(2.63)

My food will Food and Med'cine to mee bee
Which Grace itselfe cooks up aright for mee.

(2.161b)

The fairest Flower in all Gods Paradise!

Stept in, and in its Glory 'Counters all.

.   .   .   .

  Heart-aching Griefes, Pains plowing to the boanes,
Soul piercing Plagues. . . .

(1.18)

ye Flowers in Graces Garden shall
Leap into bliss to garnish Glory's Hall.

.   .   .   .

Sure it is, Graces flowers do ly
Yonder in glorys Knot most sparkling ly.

("Elegy on Francis Willoughby")

No special observation or experimentation was necessary to be a
doctor with faith and herbs, only an eye for the esthetic qualities of
plants and a mind fixed on the glory of God.[103] Taylor was trained by
Culpeper in this, but was trained for it by his theology and poetic
sense as well.

Taylor's subject in his poems is religious, however, and not
medical/botanical, and yet because of his belief in the correspondences between the natural and the supernatural, he finds it appropriate to use medical-botanical language as he dramatizes the
ministerial/personal subject of preparatory meditation. In many
ways this was merely a word game, but one that was enough to turn a
minister-physician into a poet. The existence of certain words for
certain things (Herbs of Grace, St. John wort, Palma Christi, Plas-
trum Gratiae Dei, etc.) kept his faith intact, for in their double
meanings Taylor's belief in the divine and his hold on the physical
were brought together and unified. Language, as used in the pathology and botany of the time, gave Taylor much of his faith. Yet it is odd
in the final analysis to have a scientist in early America for whom
etymology, synecdoche, and puns should serve to hold up the
heavens, as they do in the poetry of Taylor.

AS POET

*Here all the Fulness, and Excellency of Grace is yours. Hence
ariseth unspeakable delight. The Church having been
demonstrating the glory of God, and of his majesty in Zion, and
his Temple, doth reflect all upon God: and in a triumphant
Epiphonema winds up her tune With this heart transport of joy.
This God is our God, forever, and ever. Why So may the
Consideration of the Fulness, and Flourish of all glorious Grace
in Christ, introduce Such a Rapture into the Soule of Such, as are*

Savingly implanted in him, as may increase their inwarde
melody of this String, so much till its Cadency end in the like
heart ravishment of Sweetest Consolation thus.

                                                    Christographia

Although many roles in Taylor's life had an influence on his poetry
and appear in it, there was not much in his personality that actually
led him very naturally to the writing of it. Taylor was a poet mainly of
special occasions, most of them sectarian and personal. He was not a
natural but a dutiful poet, not consistently a poet. His poems came
quite naturally from how he thought and how he lived, but for the
most part he resorted to poetic expression by and large as specific,
rather formal events, dictated. By and large his is a poetry written not
out of any thoroughly conscious and well-developed esthetic sense,
but out of necessity, out of duty.

     duty raps upon her dore for Verse.
That makes her bleed a poem through her searce.

                                                    (2.30)

Poety was special, not normal, with him.

In England as a young man, Taylor wrote rather conventional
verse for conventional occasions—a political injustice, a letter to a
friend, a death, a doctrinal argument. None of it suggests he *intended*
to be a poet apart from such occasions. He wrote his first verse when
he was twenty, a poem protesting the ousting of dissenting clergy
under the Act of Uniformity of 1662, called "The Lay-mans Lamentation upon the Civill Death of the Late Labour[ers] in the Lords
vinyard." It is a mock elegy demanded by a special event: "Heare
lieth (as't weare) interrd our good news bringers/(O saddest news)
our Israels sweetest singers." It mixes satire of church and state
(Anglican prelates are men "stuffed with straw") with pleas for
justice for the Puritans ("how shall wee be puzled/For Spirituall
Corn? o[u]r Oxen being muzled"). This shows that Taylor had
considerable acquaintance with satiric verse of the period—and
perhaps some practice before the writing of this poem, though no
earlier verse survives. Significant about the poem is the fact that at
this early point in his life, he should have chosen verse as his means of
expression, his protest, his defense. It suggests that he conceived of

poetry in terms of an attack on enemies and a defense or refuge for his faith on special occasions.[104]

The other few poems that Taylor wrote while still in England are also occasional poems. They give some indication of his later poetry in the way they mix piety and playful language and in the crude contentiousness. His "Letter sent to his Brother Joseph Taylor and his wife after a visit" (ca. 1668) is an acrostic poem in doggerel-couplets which attempts a pious conceit or two.[105] In his lines "An other answer wherein as recited everie verse of the Pamphlet and answered particularly, by E. T." (1666), Taylor is scabrous and crude. He was using his pen to fight the menace of the Roman church in England ("Your Holy Mother is a whore . . . it sents of Satans spawn . . . the Devil in you's a foole") as he was to do in later poems, "Pope Joan" and *A Metrical History*. It too resulted from an occasion, the publication of a popish pamphlet.[106] These poems show that Taylor had little serious use for poetry in his life apart from special occasions. He did not initially know himself for a poet in any other sense.

There is also nothing in the diary of his college or early frontier years nor in the comments of others who knew him to show that Taylor had any unusual interest in writing. Samuel Sewall, who lived with him at Harvard, did not know he wrote any more than consolatory verse. The only poems that we have from his college period are several funeral elegies and a public declamation delivered shortly before his graduation—poems he was moved to writing by his new self-confidence as student and scholar in his last year at Harvard. They are topical poems dictated by specific events and have their significance in teaching one that it may be necessary to read almost all of Taylor's poems as topical. They should all be dated, even the Meditations, as resulting from specific duties. They document the order and orderliness of much of his life.

The funeral poems of 1671–72 are of interest also for the self-consciousness with which Taylor appears to have been moved to writing by topical events. All of his poems of this period grew out of his attachment to Harvard. In his elegies on John Allen and Charles Chauncy, Taylor writes that he was moved to write verse by the deaths of Harvard's founders and leaders in order "to tell's the Quondam Glory/Of this Plantation."[107]

Taylor did not write any verse again until the occasion of the courting of Elizabeth Fitch in the fall of 1674. On that occasion, Taylor complains (again in superficially inflated and wittily sophomoric language) that he is not well practiced in the art of "Spin[ning] out a Phansy fine," but is worked up to the writing of his "Coarse Iambick" by his engagement and prospective marriage.[108] Similarly, Taylor was moved to writing special verses by the most important events in his life in the years that followed—such events as births, deaths, ecclesiastical matters in Westfield, natural catastrophes, and personal crises. Taylor's title for his meditative poems, *Preparatory Meditations before my Approach to the Lord's Supper*, tells even *their* attachment to events located at particular times.

As Taylor explains in his *Treatise*, he was moved again to the writing of poetry (that was in 1682, when the settlement was calm and his ministry going well) by his concentration on the need to defend the sacrament of the Lord's Supper as a special occasion. From 1682 until 1725 he wrote poems growing out of the special observance of those sacramental occasions. "This rich banquet makes me thus a Poet," he wrote of its effect. The occasion of the sacrament resulted in his "singing," his writing of poetry:

> This is a frame [of] mind suitable unto the wedden feast, which is eucharistical and matter of spiritual thanksgiving, and praise to God. . . . When therefore the soul is put into such a frame whereby he groundedly praiseth God, and renders Him thanks for spiritual things, . . . Oh! the joy that spreads itself then over the soul. Oh! how it then is filled with singing.[109]

Dutifully for many six-week periods for 43 years Taylor responded to such occasions with short meditative poems in which his singing became his way of soaring above and involvement in his fallen condition. But as always, they were dutiful responses to specific occasions and not poems that he was naturally moved to by his own emotions or ideas. Though, as he put it, his "too little Skill" often frustrated his "will to honour [God]," Taylor recognized the need for self-discipline and duty. He was driven to writing his poems not by desire so much as by discipline. He did not write out of an inner compulsion but out of a disciplined response to an order exterior and superior to himself. He did not make the mistake of responding to his own enthusiasm. Instead, occasions determined by the divine (the sacrament, in the case of the Meditations) dictated when and what and how he would write. Though his writing was sometimes frustrated by his fallenness ("my Power's down born,/Its impotency"), Necessity to him was the author of his poems.[110]

The individual poems that resulted were not only made by specific occasions but were themselves special occasions—in fact, examples of taking advantage of his spiritual highpoints. To lift those special meditative moments in simulation of his spiritual aspirations, Taylor used a style which he called "Hyperbolicall." He was moved to writing hyperbolically only when his emotions were inflated by his attachment to special occasions. It was his purpose, he said, "T'run on Heroick golden feet, and raise/Heart Ravishing Tunes, Curld with Celestiall praise." (1.21) Taylor did not let his emotions appear in this serious verse of his, but substituted for it an inflated language taken from the dregs of the baroque tradition in poetry in England. His best verse therefore abounds in puns and conceits. The topical motives for writing were themselves responsible for the hyperbolic style. It is because he wrote so seldom that Taylor wrote so extravagantly. Because of this he was indeed a Puritan metaphysical poet.

In his poem on the Claverack bones, Taylor describes this method of using language to raise something from the realm of nature in the world to a simulation of the spiritual:

> We finde
> Stories unkinde to us, and them, because
> They fog them with their metaphorick laws
> That by Rhetorick steps such Strides oft take
> That oft a Molehill do a mountain make.
> But yet we do conclude that by such Stories
> Something there did appeare of Natures glory
> In those large instances. . . .

These poetic/spiritual occasions that his inflated language created ("those large instances") were none the less real to him for being momentary and illusory. Each time he wrote he entered into them as fully as his skill with language would allow. For this, he was not a mystic, but a simulator, a dissimulator, a poet.

The Meditations that Taylor wrote all those years now read differently when collected together than when read at intervals corresponding with the occasions that inspired them. Together, they show a man others could not have known in real life, or had only passing glimpses of. The poetry, for all of its overlapping, is improved by the accumulation, though one must forgive the resulting repetitiousness and redundancy, the excesses of language, the lack of freshness and variety that then appears: these cannot be attributed to the man himself.

Read alone, each Meditation shows his dependence on language for personal liveliness, his hope-inspiring, self-conscious image-making, his wit-filled fascination with the hellish, and the self-motivating sweetness of his relation with God. But the Taylor we know from the *collected* poems is bound to approach the hyperbolic—and perhaps mythic. Maybe this is what he wanted: the creation of a Self above oneself. This would in part account for the disparities between his prose and historic/argumentative poetry and the Meditations and between his life in Westfield and his being a poet, while still accounting for the coherence of his poetry with his theology.

The mythic Taylor is something Taylor was not: a poet. In his poems he created himself singing. The persona of his Meditations is not himself but the Taylor of his desires: a man actively engaged in a relationship with God. In that role, that illusion, Taylor could make a meeting with the divine forbidden by his theology. He would make that journey in his poems and afterwards deprecate the means by which he made it. He therefore worries constantly about the adequacy of the poetic means of transportation to that illusory realm, for, if his poetic workmanship is good, he believed, then he could rest assured that God, through that skill, had chosen him, moved him, saved him, and if the work is poor, then he is without spiritual assurances.

The mythic Edward-Taylor-the-Poet is related to the real nonpoet Edward Taylor as Ideality is to Fallen Reality. He is imagined, honored, and imitated, even envied, for as a persona in the poems, he sings, he creates a spiritual life for himself, he has freedom to aspire, he has duration, he delights, he approaches his God. In reality, Edward Taylor of Westfield, Mass.—that cantankerous, self-righteous, didactic man—could not do any of those things. In Reality, he had to live according to his nature. And that was fallen. In his poems he was something else again—something of himself, to be sure, but something *else* as well. Poetry made it possible for him to be mythic, if only occasionally and only briefly. He would have been lost without it.

This self-mythologizing process began in 1682. The majority of his poems thereafter became different from the earlier ones as a result of it. Before that time preparatory meditation after the model provided by Richard Baxter and Thomas Hooker had no serious hold on his mind.[111] His emphasis at that time was on public confession more than private meditation. Not until 1682 does Taylor appear to have discovered that intensely masochistic poetic process which provided him with a medium for his illusions. Then, in the first poem of his *Preparatory Meditations*, he turned inward, calling himself "a Crumb of Dust" that must, in spite of the inherent contradiction, "write aright." He holds his heart on the rack, tracking the abominations of his life, as Hooker recommended, and then pleads for help from God. It was a process that he was later to describe as one in which "My Mental Eye . . . Did double back its Beams to light my Sphere/Making an inward Search, for what springs there." (2.27)

Throughout 1682 and 1683 Taylor had considerable success in using his poetry as the medium of his active introspection. He found out how it lowered him into the hell of himself ("oh! my Dross and Lets . . . If off as Offal I be put") and raised him to full sight of the love of God ("Oh, Matchless Love! filling Heaven to the brim!"). The transport experienced on those first sacramental occasions encouraged him to try to recapture the experience while writing more poetry:

Oh! that I always breath'd in such an aire,
    As I suckt in, feeding on sweet Content!
Disht up unto my Soul ev'n in that pray're
    Pour'de out to God over last Sacrament.
    What Beam of Light wrapt up my sight to finde
    Me neerer God than ere Came in my minde?
                              ("The Experience")

At the outset he tried several forms for his simulations: short, ecstatic poems built on a series of inflating, self-transporting exclamations (1.1, 7); long, rambling poems built on the full explication of a single image, involving himself intimately with his subject by means of the length (1.4); poems that used conceits as riddles, exploring man's relation to God ("The Experience," "The Return," "The Reflexion"); and poems of medium length in which he moves from the confession of his worthlessness to the expression of his desire for grace (1.8). He settled on the last of these as best representing both his personal spiritual needs and the form he felt Christianity had given man in the cosmos.

Between 1684 and 1692 Taylor wrote most of his First Series on that model. To suggest the hoped-for perfection of his poems, he stopped at Meditation 49.[112] In most of these Meditations his worry about the quality of his writing became the main metaphor for his concern over his acceptability in the eyes of God:

> How shall I praise thee then? My blottings Jar
>   And wrack my Rhymes to pieces in thy praise.
> Thou breath'st thy Vean still in my Pottinger
>   To lay my thirst, and fainting spirits raise.
> Thou makest Glory's Chiefest Grape to bleed
> Into my cup: And this is Drink-Indeed.
>
> (1.10)

The series begins with fairly doctrinal poems (1.10–17) but ends with an emphasis on personal joy (1.42–49), suggesting that Taylor may have begun by seeing his verse close to the subjects of his sermons but gradually found the exercise of writing his poems itself liberating.

In 1693 when he began his Second Series, Taylor had a different purpose in mind. He decided to explore the subject of Christian typology in an elaborate sequence of poems. (2.1–30) This occupied him until 1699, when he began a series of sequences—in 1699 and 1700 on the subject of God's love (2.31–35), in 1700 on the Christian concept of order (2.36–38), in 1700 and 1701 on the body of Christ (2.39–41), from 1701 to 1703 on his Christology (2.42–56), from 1704 until 1710 on texts from John and Canticles (2.60a–98), and from 1713 until 1725 almost entirely on Canticles alone (2.115–53, 156–57b, 160–65). Many of these were probably connected with sequences of sermons like those of the *Treatise* and *Christographia*, but many were also composed *as sequences of poems*.

Taylor wrote other poems in these same years—long Biblical paraphrases, his *Metrical History of Christianity*, and "Verses on Pope Joan"—for which we cannot know either the occasion or the motive. They are unlike anything else he wrote. They would have served neither the doctrinal nor preparatory purposes that his other poems did. It is also difficult to determine the date and motive behind his long collection of poems, *Gods Determinations*, except to recognize that it was written in reaction to the failure of half-way members to complete their work of conversion. The motive behind *Gods Determinations* was less that of preparatory meditation, however, than the need Taylor felt to dramatize in verse the journey of the elect toward their Celestial City. This was not a subject he could deal with in the form he chose for his private Meditations. Though as a whole *Gods Determinations* has the form of an extended Meditation, in its parts it is clearly more didactic and explanatory. It is institutional verse, written to outline the relation of the individual to the faith. Though a number of attempts have been made to name the form of *Gods Determinations*, it is best considered as an anthology of Taylor's more public poems, perhaps even as a collection that he prepared for publication.

Though there was a falling off of the number of poems he wrote in his last years (only three in 1722, four in 1723, none in 1724, and one in 1725, along with three "valedictory" poems written during Taylor's long illness, 1720–1724),[113] there was no diminishing of Taylor's poetic interests. At the end of his Second Series of Meditations, just as at the end of the First, he was his most joyous:

> Sweet Lord, all sweet from top to bottom all
> > From Heart to hide, sweet, mostly sweet.
> Sweet Manhood and sweet Godhead and ere shall.
> > Thou art and best of Sweeting. And so keep.
> > Thou art made up of best of sweetness brast.
> > Thy Fruit is ever sweet unto my tast.
>
> > > > > (2.163)

Even in his last years, between 1721 and 1729 when he was severely ill much of the time, the tone of Taylor's poetry is that of sweet praise:

> Accept, my Lord, the praises that I bring
> Tho' very mean, till I am entred in
> Thy dining Chamber Whose rich Happiness
> Will raise my Tunes to blessful thankfulness.[114]

While some of Taylor's scurrilousness and hyperbole remains in the lines of his last poems, the dominant tone is simple hope:

> I hope to take a flight up ere 't be long
> > Into a purer Air by far than thine
> That never touched any bawdy Song

Nor tooke the sent of Sinfull lungs like mine.
A Coach most pure of Heavenly Musick joyes
Enravishing with sweetest Melodies.[115]

There is less self-deprecation and much more love-longing in the poems of the last years before he laid down his pen. This fact may be autobiographical: as he faced old age and the immanence of death, he conceived of himself going beyond this world more than he had done before. There are several indications at the end of this series, as at the end of the other, that Taylor wrote as much as he did and in the way that he did in the attempt to become one with the mythic persona of his Meditations. Like Whitman, he projected a personality in his poems which he then strove to become like. In his last Meditation (2.165), written when he was 83, he says, "Heart sick my Lord heart sick of Love to thee! . . . It so affects true love." As Taylor believed all along, the illusion of a loving relationship with his God would in time become a reality.

For Taylor this was a fully legitimate use for the writing of poetry. It was not for the communication of himself and his beliefs so much as the discovery of himself and his faith; not so much for moving others as moving himself, if only momentarily and illusorily; not out of desire but out of need. For that reason, before he died, as a Taylor family tradition held, Taylor requested that his poems be destroyed. They had served their purpose.

The gravestone of Edward Taylor, Westfield Cemetery, Westfield, Massachusetts. Photograph by Donald E. Stanford.

Eldad Taylor, son of Edward Taylor. Courtesy the Westfield
Athenaeum.

Ezra Stiles, grandson of Edward Taylor. The Bettmann Archive.

Samuel Sewall. The Bettmann Archive.

Increase Mather. Engraved for the New England Historical and
General Register. The Bettmann Archive.

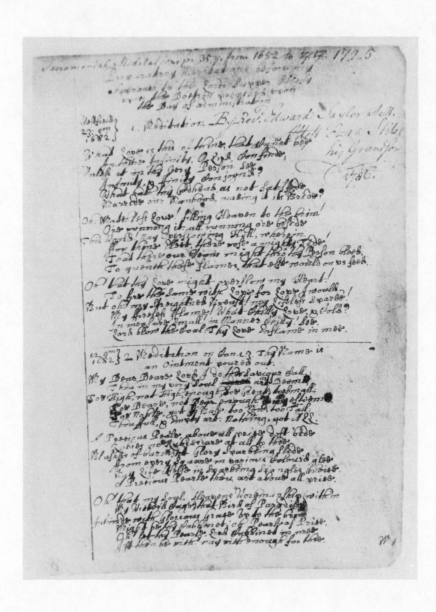

Manuscript page of Meditations 1 and 2 (First Series) from *Poetical Works*, Yale University Library.

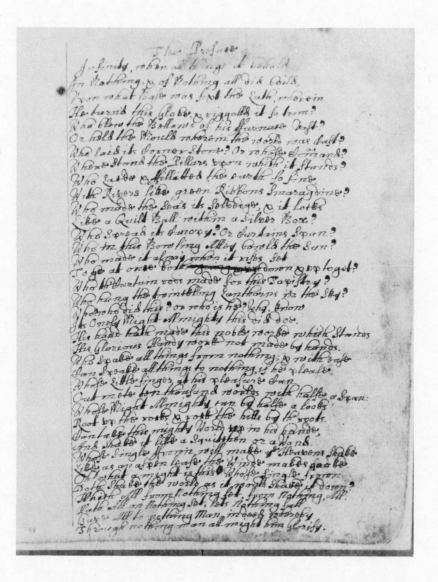

Manuscript page of the Preface to *Gods Determinations* from *Poetical Works,* Yale University Library.

Chapter 3

The Emergence of
an American Poet

I'l sing this Song, when I these Drops Embrace.
My Vessell now's a Vessell of thy Grace.

(1.28)

The neglect and the discovery of Edward Taylor's poetry have been made more interesting by the desire to believe the Taylor family's story about his injunction against publication. Having willed himself into anonymity, Taylor's unexpected emergence in the twentieth century has been almost as interesting as the poetry itself and the gap that it fills in American literary history. The phenomenon of finding Taylor at that point in American literary history where we were sure so good a poet could not appear has become integral to the poetry itself. The find romanticizes him for us; the wooden preacher takes on a little color thereby.

Shortly before his death in 1729, so the family story goes, Taylor "enjoined it upon his heirs never to publish any of his writings."[1] Though the existence of his poetry was to be reported a number of times,[2] it was lost to us for over two centuries. The unpublished manuscripts fell first into the hands of Taylor's grandson Ezra Stiles through Taylor's son-in-law Isaac Stiles, then into the hands of his great-grandson Henry W. Taylor and others in the Taylor family, and finally to Yale University, the Westfield and Redwood Athenaeums, and other libraries, whence it has been recovered and now published. It has taken over 35 years to locate, transcribe, and publish his poetical work—and some poems and much of his prose remain unpublished. None of this was intended; we invade his privacy as we read him today.

Yet publication *was* on Taylor's mind. He was an incessant student and an industrious writer, producing in the course of 67 years works totalling about 3,100 manuscript pages. As far as his descendants knew, he had "an abiding passion for writing poetry during his whole life."[3]

A number of these writings he apparently intended for the public in one form or another. He wrote a 485-page *Commentary on the Four Gospels*, for example, which was so well thought of that Cotton Mather wrote to Dr. John Woodward and other wealthy persons in the Royal Society of London trying to induce them to publish it.[4] The *Christographia* sermons were circulated separately and then later gathered and revised for publication; too complex for the ear, they were to have been printed and read. Eight other sermons, now titled *Treatise Concerning the Lord's Supper*, were his contribution to the public debate over the Stoddardean heresy. There is also supposed to have been a quarto volume containing many short occasional poems prepared for publication,[5] and quite a number of Taylor's funeral elegies, acrostic love verses, and poems for special occasions were read by the bereaved, the beloved, and interested audiences from Westfield to Boston. Even the poems of *Gods Determinations* and his *Metrical History of Christianity* smack of widely read genre pieces of the period used for soteriological and educational purposes; they show that Taylor did not write in a social vacuum but had a sense of audience, a sense of what was happening in the religious experience of declining New England.

All of this should show that for the archetype of a private poet in our literary history, Taylor had intents and purposes that were noticeably public. Only the *Preparatory Meditations*, a few of the more meditative sections of *Gods Determinations*, and several of his miscellaneous poems seem to have been composed for purely private rather than public ends. Though Taylor copied out a few of them for slight revision,[6] the form in which they have come down to us suggests intermediacy and private satisfaction rather than finality and publication. Where the more public poems are didactic, even dogmatic, the meditative poems are dramatic. The one type is for the most part in drier, more constrictive decasyllabic couplets, the other in the freer, more dramatic sestet of Robert Southwell, George Herbert, and Christopher Harvey (a stanza form which Taylor called "A brisk Tetrastich, with a Distich sweet"). Most of his poems turn outward and are descriptive, narrative, stilted, and technical, but the private poems turn inward, their substance lost in their inward action. Even the full title of Taylor's *Meditations* suggests a privacy about them: "Preparatory Meditations before *My* Approach to the Lord's Supper. . . ." He spoke publicly, but his private poetry made it another world with a language of its own. It would appear that in not making these poems public, Taylor may have been asking, as Emily Dickinson was later to do, How do you publish a piece of your soul?

To account for the privacy of such poetry, it has been a temptation to turn to Taylor's personality and find there a modesty and humility that would have prevented publication.[7] Items from his biography encourage this for a reason: his choice for his ministerial labors of the humbler, remote Westfield over Boston, the publishing center, or Cambridge, the intellectual center; his notoriously rigid piety and reputation for sweetness, personability, and selfless service; his emphasis on the psychological and occult side of Puritanism. Though we know his life poorly, it appears to have been self-sufficient, defensive, insignificant, inward, and thereby one for which a public was not needed. He simply seems to have lacked the vanity of desiring fame, especially at the end of his life when he was no longer interested in writing.

Yet he was at the same time a thorny, proud, contentious personality, a man of quick passions, a man who kept an interest in the public affairs of the area and the colony and who maintained an association and correspondence with the leading public figures of the period. He was a vigorous advocate of unpopular causes, a curious, constant, powerful man, a man abreast of the issues of his time and sure that God had raised him up in hard times to defend the faith. No one who knew him or knew of him thinks to attribute to him the qualities of modesty and humility of the sort that would have prevented him from baring his soul publicly. So it is unconvincing to presume in him an indifference to his writing, a life too lofty to communicate, an exclusiveness with no responsibility to the world. Because of the Puritan suspicion of the incomprehensible and uncommunicative, to find a modesty and humility behind his injunction against publication is to see his spirituality as schizophrenic, even heterodox.[8]

And though Taylor's orthodoxy is unassailable, at least as he revealed it to congregation and community, in his private life, the inward life which his meditative poetry parallels, he may have been something else—noncovenanting Calvinist, vulgarizer of the faith, secret antinomian, arminian enthusiast, esthetically an Anglican or even Catholic, liberal neoplatonist or humanist, sensualist and mystic, even pagan.[9] For such positions (take your choice), he might have had to hide his private thoughts and passions from soberer eyes, and so withheld his poetry from publication. He knew an incompatibility between his style and his belief.

But in a way, the discovery of Taylor's writings did not so much find a skunk in the garden as point up the carelessness of much of the gardening; we were, perhaps, not well prepared for the sensuously meditative, the joyously logical, the humanistically knowledgeable, and the appropriately personable in high Puritanism, and Taylor has in part forced the adjustment. In view of a life devoted to the hard labor of justifying the status quo, a mind sharpened in a very narrow theological groove, and esthetics that could not possibly be distinguished from dogma, it seems clear that if Taylor would not publish his poems, it would have to have been because of his *devotion* to Calvinist principles, not because he was afraid of them.

That his devotion to dogma overwhelmed and limited his skill with his art—and that he knew it—might be seen as a more convincing reason for his not publishing. A man of wide reading and esthetic sensitivity, he might have seen how flawed his verse was by comparison and therefore suppressed it. His meiotic sensibility, as well as his sensitivity to criticism, would have discouraged him. His lack of polish may have embarrassed him, his verses' complexity and obscurity may have warned him, his lack of confidence in his own theory and practice may have humbled him. He may have been simply still another example of a writer conscious of having written something inferior and anxious to forget the fact.

But if Taylor could sense all of this about the unacceptability of his poetry, then he would also have had a sense that the American Puritans would have found his poetry exciting and instructive. He would have known that his work was superior to *The Tenth Muse Lately Sprung Up in America* or *The Day of Doom* or *New England's Crisis*, collections of verse that the first century of Puritans had taken pride in. If he were simply stoical about his lack of ability to write well, he would not have been the meticulous craftsman that he often attempted to be—conscious of technique, working hard to achieve different effects, reworking his lines until they were as dramatic as he could make them—only to do little or nothing to prevent their loss.

It is also possible that Taylor knew he was artistically and intellec-
tually always a little out of touch with his times. His fervor, his style
of thought, and his form of verse were all fairly dated. He wrote and
thought in 1725 the same as he had written and thought in 1682, as if
literary history had been suspended; he was, oddly, a contemporary
of Dryden and Swift. The baroque mode that he loved was old
fashioned by at least fifty years; his use of it is a relic. By the
eighteenth century the meditative tradition had few apologists and
few literary uses, even on the Massachusetts frontier. The year 1700
is too late for a morality-play-cum-versified-theological-sermon like
Gods Determinations. His *Christographia* sermons are imitative of
Increase Mather's sermons *The Mystery of Christ Opened and
Applied* (1686) and behind them by two decades; his *Metrical
History* is imitative of Matthias Flacius' *Magdeburg Centuries*
(1516) and John Foxe's *Actes and Monuments* (1563) and behind
them well over a century. And all of the verse and prose that Taylor
wrote in the Stoddardean controversy was written in defense of a
cause that was unpopular, untenable, and already pretty well lost.

But, though almost everything about him fits an earlier world
better, there is nothing to convince one that Taylor had any concern
whatever for literary fashion or fashionability of thought—or in fact
any reason to concern himself. His call was to the defense of the New
England Way and he fulfilled that call with whatever verbal skills he
had. That his defense was a strong and almost lone one would hardly
be reason for not publishing.

It now seems that these are all reasons without much foundation,
reasons that look to Taylor's personality and temperament or to an
external world that did not touch his, rather than to his esthetics or to
the lasting qualities of his poetry. Self-effacing, alarmingly personal,
botched, and archaic as his poetry is, there is yet something about the
nature of Taylor's approach to poetry that justifies its privateness.

In its privateness Taylor's poetry was bound to take on some of the
personality of a life lived in the New World, and so a related issue is
how his poetry belongs to an *American* tradition of letters rather than
simply to a Puritan tradition. Louis L. Martz answers to this in the
negative: "Is there anything in Taylor's poetry that could be called
distinctively American?" How to justify Taylor at the head of American poetry, and not merely as a transitional figure, a link with the

heritage, a bridge to what evolved, is a question of historical interest.

To be sure, Taylor was a man of two cultures. He was educated at both an English academy and Harvard. He both taught at Bagworth, Leicestershire, and preached at Westfield on the American frontier. The books he read, the hymns he sang, and the sermons he heard were produced in both London and Boston, and the writers he learned from were British and American. Also, in his loyalism he saw English and New England polity as one, and the confessions of faith on the American frontier were to him no different from those in Puritan England. He appears to have transplanted himself without disturbing his roots, to have become a colonial without dislocation.

The very fact of his writing his more meditative poetry out of personal experience—with that personal experience having its referents, its color, its issues and forms from these shores—could superficially show him to be a provincial. And the earnestness with which he sees his person, his personality, his personal experience as the proper subject for his best poetry perhaps sets him squarely in a tradition of American letters with Walt Whitman and Emily Dickinson. From one point of view, his poetry may indeed be seen as a personal diary which has its symbolism from an involvement in a New Zion (a symbolism that was to inform a tradition from Edwards to Faulkner); a diary with its extravagances of metaphor bringing heaven down to New England *huswifery* and husbandry (a realistic, vernacular metaphoric mode that from Emerson to Frost was to become an American way of poetry); a diary of a self-conscious and lonely poet in the wilderness whose poetry is the fruit of isolation (a recurrent motif in American letters from Anne Bradstreet and Philip Freneau through Hawthorne and Emily Dickinson).

Yet these are mere surface connections with what was to be an identifiable American culture. From his poems one could not, I think, really reconstruct his personal life in Westfield, nor the daily Puritan life, nor an attitude toward time and place. Was his verse rugged and raw because he moved to Massachusetts? his metaphors hyperbolic and humor exaggerated because he lived on the frontier? his language excited and engaging because he wrote alone? Was it the environment that made him more than one expects from a devout man of the time who used his imagination and biblical lore and ordinary skill in rhyme to concentrate his attention on the aweful ideas suggested by his faith? Simply because he was here does not mean that the spirit of his work was.

His language too has been overrated for its Americanness. It might be thought possible to turn to Taylor's earthy diction, his homely images, his natural speech, his neologisms, and see there the qualities of an American vernacular. Or one might see in his privateness a freedom to invent and play with the provincial words of his native country. But while Taylor's idiolect is highly nonstandard, it is in a number of ways fossilized speech. Much of Taylor's usage is of course difficult to the modern reader though common in his time, but a part of Taylor's diction was obsolete at use (words like *attent*, *flurr*, *pillard*, *pistick*, *dub*, *tittle-tattle*), another part was made up of archaic survivals in America not current in standard British English but entrenched in regional English dialects (*jags*, *lugg*, *frob*, *grudgens*, *nit*, *frim*, *womble-crops*, *fuddling*, *ding*, *clagd*, *bibble*), and still another part was made up of highly specialized, technical terms derived from Taylor's reading but not in general use (*anakims*, *mictams*, *calamus*, *catholicons*, *catochee*, *surdity*, *syncopee*, *barlybreaks*, *noddy*, *ruff-and-trumpt*). Charles W. Mignon has identified in Taylor's usage diction from several English and Welsh dialects which fossilized in the colonies but which has become obsolete, and in all of Taylor's writings he has found only three Americanisms (*Cordilera*, *dozde*, *Netop*).[10] All of which, instead of substantiating the local character of his speech, makes Taylor obscure and relatively much more remote than any other colonial writer. He relies as heavily on the unfamiliar as on that which would communicate with others in his own time and place, and what has often passed for fresh, coined, homely, realistic in him is in large part, it would appear, verbal obscurity and intended for his eyes alone. Instead of speaking New Englandly, Taylor wrote in a personal idiom that was in many ways uncommunicative. Taylor's language was unique but not because he was on these shores.

More than in his personal experience and his language, it may be that Taylor's real importance as an *American* poet is in his defense of the New England Way of theology. Since that way required him to link his piety with community polity and his introspectiveness with citizenship in the New Israel in America, it might follow that the extent to which Taylor was an ardent defender of New England covenant theology is the extent to which he was an American poet. Taylor's life and writings may indeed be seen as having their main motivation in the idea of the self prepared for grace as a test of visible sainthood, for to Taylor the meditative preparationism required by the Half-Way Covenant justified the whole purpose of the emigration to America, safeguarded the purity of gathered churches, and helped to fulfill God's unique covenant with New England. Therefore, in almost everything he wrote—sermons arguing against Stoddardean liberalism, historical verses tracing the evolution of religion toward New England purity, poetry dramatizing the personal value of preparing oneself for membership in church and community—he was, it would appear, a kind of nationalist. His meditative poetry may be almost completely dominated by the peculiarities of the New England situation. On no other shores would he have had to be so passionately patriotic in his piety.

But like the usual reasons for his injunction against publication, these reasons for his relevance to American culture seem imposed with hindsight on the poetry and not derived from any sight that Taylor himself had. While demonstrating something of a New England life, a New England tongue, a New England mind, his poetry still remains apart and aloof from any relationship with the external world. So instead of looking to Taylor's personality—his self-consciousness, his naturalness, his reactionariness—we need to look to his works. In his works themselves lies a more convincing reason, a reason that at one and the same time establishes Taylor as an important private poet and an important American poet.

When it comes to both issues of publication and nationality, it is important to emphasize that Taylor was concerned not so much with poems as products as he was with the production of poems; that is, not so much with the product as with the process, not so much with Meditations as with meditating. He was, as Roy Harvey Pearce has noted, a man "in action," and a Taylor poem is "the act of a man whose imagination is *now* engaged in *creating* something."[11]

For the most part, Taylor deprecates his poems *as products*:

I fain would praise thee, but want words to do't:
    And searching ore the realm of thoughts finde none
Significant enough and therefore vote
    For a new set of Words and thoughts hereon
    And leap beyond the line such words to gain
    In other Realms, to praise thee: but in vain.

                            (2.106)

As finished products his poems seem to him mere "blottings," "wordiness," a "sylabicated jumble," "ragged Nonsense," "Languague welded with Emphatick reech."

> What shall I say, my Deare Deare Lord? most Deare
>   Of thee! My choisest words when spoke are then
> Articulated Breath, soon disappeare.
>   If wrote are but the Drivle of my pen
> Beblackt with my inke, soon torn worn out. . . .
>
> (2.142)

It appears as if in their "steaming reechs," Taylor's poems correspond with and even symbolize to him the insufficiency of his own self. Like him, they are products of a fallen world cast off by God and existing passively for recognition and acceptance.

> Whether I speake, or speechless stand, I spy,
> I faile thy Glory.
>
> (1.22)

> Mine Eyes, Lord, shed no Tears but inke.
> My handy Works, are Words, and Wordiness.
>
> (1.24)

Almost everything that he produces, no matter how well intended as praise to God, is poor: his faculties are "ragged," his pen "jar[s]," he "lisps," his voice is "rough" and his tongue "blunt" or "tied," his style is "homely," his rhymes are "wracked to pieces," his attempts to write are "laughable," his finished poems are "poore Eggeshell[s]" —all of which, of course, are Taylor's complaints about the sorry features of his own inadequate life.

> My tatter'd Fancy; and my Ragged Rymes
>   Teeme leaden Metaphors: which yet might serve
> To hum a little touching terrene Shines.
>   But Spirituall Life doth better fare deserve.
>   This thought on, sets my heart upon the Rack.
>   I fain would have this Life but han't its knack.
>
> (2.82)

Taylor's view of created things is so dim that when it comes to evaluating the products of his pen—even though his desires have been intent, his hope sincere, his effort devoted, and his devices polished—what he has written seems to him worthless. As products his poems are "dirty thing[s]."

> My Deare Deare Lord what shall I render thee?
> >   Words spoken are but breesing boxed Winde.
> If written onely inked paper bee.
>
> >   >   >   >   >   >   >   (2.158)

Yet in spite of the impossibility of producing anything of worth, Taylor sees importance in the process of using language as a means of meditating on meaning. In fact, he is obsessed with the need to write. Though the purposelessness of a poem itself ought to inhibit the act of composition, it doesn't, for Taylor finds joy in the duty of going through the process. He seems even to accept from the outset the futility of his efforts, but he nonetheless longs to express himself:

> I am this Crumb of Dust which is design'd
> >   To make my Pen unto thy Praise alone,
> And my dull Phancy I would gladly grinde
> >   Unto an Edge on Zions Pretious Stone.
> >   And Write in Liquid Gold upon thy Name
> >   My Letters till thy glory forth doth flame.
>
> >   >   >   >   >   >   ("Prologue")

This insistence on the value of the process of singing/writing makes Taylor's poems very repetitive. Most of the *Preparatory Meditations* have a recurring tripartite structure, beginning with a comment about the desire to write ("Fain I would sing thy Praise"), continuing with a complaint about the inability to write ("I cannot sing, my tongue is tide"), and concluding with an affirmation of the process of writing and the hope that God will make it possible ("Accept this Lisp till I am glorifide."), though leaving the poem open at the end to invite God's poetic closure of this on-going process. (1.43) So intense was his interest in the process of writing that on most subjects in his poems he is not finished until he has made some comment about the difficulty of producing a product from the process, often shifting, contorting, mixing his metaphors to get back to his theme: process vs. product. The musical imagery throughout these poems betrays his love of singing—even though it is singing, as Taylor himself knows, which results in only sour songs. As John

Cotton advised in his *Singing of Psalmes a Gospel-Ordinance* (1650), a private Christian "who hath a gift to frame a spirituall Song may both frame it, and sing it privately for his own private comfort." In fine, such poems must be seen as constant complaints about the inability to write amid the need/duty to write.

This is not to say that glory eludes Taylor, for he has glory *as* he sings rather than *in* his song. The opportunity of carrying out his duty to sing praise to God is for him enough; and the result of his singing, his poems, is largely irrelevant. If he is moved to write, he knows that by some divine favor his life has been made dynamic, and it is that spiritual momentum which is important. Without such a process, the product (his life, his poem) is worthless.

> Thy Praise shall be my Glory sung in state.
>
> (2.53)

> Ile tune thy Prayses while this Crown doth come.
> Thy Glory Bring I tuckt up in my Songe.
>
> (1.44)

> Thy Speech the Liquour in thy Vessell stands,
>   Well ting'd with Grace a blessed Tincture, Loe,
> Thy Words distilld, Grace in thy Lips pourd, and,
>   Give Graces Tinctur in them where they go.
>   Thy words in graces tincture stilld, Lord, may
>   The Tincture of thy Grace in me Convay.
>
> (1.7)

Such an act as writing was to Taylor a quest for signs of an assured salvation, so to him the process was a matter of spiritual life or death.

Taylor's orthodoxy itself demanded a concern with process rather than product. The condition of the Fall is static and man has mobility only as he works to discover his predetermined spiritual status. His life becomes dynamic as he engages in this process of self-discovery. Nature is in flux and by concentrating on *process*, the Puritan participates, if only through his imagination, in the nature of things as they lie beyond the condition of the Fall. Through thinking of his writing as a process, Taylor, like many of Reformed persuasion, could reenact the process of salvation and live in the illusion of a spiritual development of oneself.

Through introspective meditation the Puritan engaged in a process of transferring truth from the memory and intellect to the affections and the heart and will. In Taylor's predestinarian cosmology, this process was the only thing in which a Puritan could willfully engage in the whole act of salvation: he moved through a series of interior stages of contrition and humiliation, affection and repentance, examining himself mercilessly, arousing in himself a longing desire for help, and thereby predisposing himself for the possibility of saving grace. Without this process, he could not experience the transformation determined for him or even anticipate it, nor would his consciousness be involved in it. But because of the process, he could discover the determined direction of his life. In this there is a careful distinction between the movement and the thing moved, between God in action in a man's life and the man himself, between the process and the product.[12]

This intensely personal process of anticipating salvation dominates the esthetics of Taylor and lies behind his injunction against publication as well as his relevance to American culture. As a poet, language helped Taylor to achieve the condition of "preparedness" he desired. Meditation was for Taylor, as for many Puritans, a *verbal* art. Concentration on the means (language) of arriving at meaning (salvation), he finds his life becoming meaningful (the purpose of praise that he finds himself created for). To be sure, to concentrate on such devices of language as sound, syntax, and imagery is to end up with a poem, a product, but it is the process of working at one's praise that is most important to him, not the result.

Taylor's private poems are themselves for the most part accounts of the process that Taylor went through in preparing himself to be disposed for saving grace. They are not poems *about* the process, but poems showing Taylor *in the process* of preparation. They are miniature dramas in which Taylor is reenacting over and over again that which was to him the most meaningful process of man's life. In fact, the form of a number of the Meditations is so close to the experience dramatized that it can legitimately be called imitative. The form of his poems is fully organic to the ideas in them.

And because he was concerned mainly about the process of writing his poetry, I think that Taylor would have considered as largely irrelevant the modern charges against him of bungling ingenuity, lapses of taste, and awkward performance. It was a perfect preparation that he was after, not a perfect poem. The writing of poems no doubt helped Taylor get to that point of self-realization desired, and after that objective had been achieved, they were no longer needed. There would have been no reason whatever to publish them. They were useful as devices, as part of the process, of preparing to preach upon and partake the sacrament of the Lord's Supper.

For that reason, a dominant subject in Taylor's poems is Taylor's poems. He is obsessed with writing about writing. He is the Puritan poet's poet, for the poet's worth becomes to him an important metaphor for talking about the business of salvation. Just as he must deprecate himself as a fallen creature of a fallen world, so he depreciates his poems as products. But in addition, just as he accepts the necessity of his existence, so he values the process of writing poetry. Most of the Meditations, and some of the sections of *Gods Determinations*, show Taylor involved dutifully in this process, cursing the results and yet relishing his spiritual activity and hoping for acceptance of his disposition.

A proper preparationist fixes his mind on an object in his meditation, and language was the most natural object for Taylor to use:

> My tongue Wants Words to tell my thoughts, my Minde
>   Wants thoughts to Comprehend thy Worth, alas!
>
> (1.34)

The work of adjusting sound to sense (for example, the agony of the despairing soul in the cramped rhythm of "My Sin! my Sin, My God, these Cursed Dregs,/Green, Yellow, Blew streakt Poyson hellish, ranck" [1.39]), the dramatizing with syntax ("And pick me headlong hells dread Whirle Poole in" [1.39]), the structuring of one's illusory movement from despair to hope, and the concentrated involvement of intellect in the leaps from image to image (in "The Reflexion," the smells of the food at a banquet become the smell of a rose, the rose suggests a garden of mud, the mud suggests the fallen condition of man, the rose blooms in the mud when there is sunlight, and the light of the Son comes through the church windows and falls on the sacrament, which is the banquet that shows how the Lord rose)—the work with such formal devices of verse-making helped to make Taylor aware of both his human dilemma and the shape of his own personality within that dilemma. The projection of himself into the many minute formal devices of a poem is ultimately a process of self-discovery. Sound, syntax, image, and structure are features of himself in action, and a poem is therefore his body, his mind, his life in all the static worthlessness of his fallen state and in all the active intensity of his spiritual desire.

The process appears to give Taylor the opportunity to make intense these spiritual desires, so intense in fact that with sensuous language he was able to come as close as a Puritan dared come to the point of mystical union without crossing the line over into sensuality, pride, antinomianism. In the process of writing, Taylor discovers something of the divine; he discovers the divine in the process. I do not want to suggest by this that language was for Taylor therapeutic or theoleptic, but that it was a means of making meaning. In fact, language served both to exalt Taylor (dramatizing his desires) and to keep him properly earthbound (the limitations of human speech as a reminder of his human impediments, his fallen condition). Thus, making his hope articulate was both a reaching upward for meaning and a confession of meaninglessness.

Ultimately Taylor's poems do not *mean* very much. They instead show a man watching himself in his worthlessness desiring worth. The meaning of his life therefore lies not in his self nor in his desires (nor even in the object of his desires, God and salvation), but in *the act of desiring*. If he can continually convince himself of the ability to act out his desires, then he can continually reassure himself that God, in His activating love of man, is drawing him to Him. The meditation on one's worthlessness thereby becomes in Taylor's poems the meditation on the process of God's love. In this way the masochistic process of Hookeresque meditation becomes a positive program of conviction of divine love—a moving through the dark self to the realization of light, of worth. This is a reenactment in miniature of the human condition, giving a spatial condition (the Fall) a time dimension (eternal salvation). In being self-destructive, the process of Puritan meditation, at least as Taylor performs it in his *Meditations*, is therefore life-giving. When Taylor's writing stops, his faith also lags, and when his faith is weak his writing stops. The process of one is the process of the other.

What I am trying to suggest is that because he was interested in the process of writing rather than in his writings themselves, Taylor's private poetry makes one more example of what John A. Kouwenhoven calls "the national preoccupation with process."[13] Kouwenhoven finds this fascination to be a central quality which those artifacts that are peculiar to American culture have in common. The American skyscraper, with its effect of transactive upward motion, arbitrary cutoff, and repeatable upward thrust; the American gridiron town plan, with its unfinished completeness, its infinitely repeatable units; jazz, with its freedom of innovation within a rhythmic pattern, its bounds-ignoring momentum, its unresolved harmony; the Constitution, as an infinitely extendable framework; Mark Twain's fiction, with its irreverence for proportion and symmetry, its river-like momentum, and its characters who are, as was Huck Finn, ready to "light out" again; Whitman's *Leaves of Grass*, with its restless, sweeping movement on long lines, its openness at the end; comic strips and soap operas, with their lack of ultimate climax, their emphasis on the continued facing of problems without resolution; assembly-line production, with its timed operations, repetitive work, intermediacy, unfinishedness; chewing gum, with its nonconsumability, its value for action but valuelessness as commodity—all such things unique to American culture have, when judged esthetically, the central quality of *process*. To Kouwenhoven, "America is process." This quality involves mobility, everchanging unity, mutability, development, and other facets which militate against the idea of man's (and society's) permanence and perfection and pitches him instead into a condition where change, progress, impermanence, and unfulfilled desire have almost moral value.

Indigenous too to Taylor's esthetics is this principle of process. He has a rigid pattern, a cage or skeleton, within which he works (for the most part, the decasyllabic line, the six-line stanza, the fear-hope-desire pattern or the certainty-despair pattern for a structure, and these repeated over and over again as a process of consecutive occurrences without climax, without conclusion, without concern for time, without finish, without resolution), but he finds a way of moving, of being moved, within the frame. Through imaginative use of language, he has freedom within fate, freedom of movement within the determined framework of covenant theology. This redramatizing of his search for signs of salvation suggests vitality within unity, movement in conflict with stasis, desire vs. the human condition. And to do this in preparation of oneself for finding an acceptable place in the pattern of the sacrament of the Lord's supper suggests how poetry served Taylor as illusion: as he wrote he was imagining himself undergoing change in a predetermined universe.

It may be a temptation to think that Taylor's purpose was to try to produce poems that would be so finely wrought, so carefully formed, so fully representative of his mind and spirit that they might serve as signs to Taylor of his election, proving over and over again to himself, like a Puritan merchant realizing proof of his election through his business success, how success with poetic devices is a sign of his justification. But this view must be modified by Taylor's rejection of the products of his pen and the joy he takes in the process alone.

To think of Taylor as conceiving of his poems as great poetry (an assumption that debunkers of Taylor begin with) is the same as saying he lacked critical ability or esthetic sensitivity or knowledge of poetry. He knew how bad his poems were, just as he knew how insufficient he himself was. But to think of Taylor as thinking primarily of the value of the process he was going through each time he wrote a Meditation is to admit significance in him (to be sure, a different kind of significance) as a poet.

In this light, one begins to see purpose even in the "flaws" of his poetry—purpose in his choice of old-fashioned baroque for his metaphors; purpose in his annoying insistence on anaphora, anacoluthon, ploce, polyptoton, and other disruptive scholiastic rhetorical devices; purpose in his corny borrowings from Ramist logic, Biblical typology, and the poetry of Herbert and Quarles; purpose in the erratic mechanics of his punctuation, rhymes, syntax; even purpose in his boring repetitiveness, his awkward unevenness, his outmoded fervor, his banality and bathos. They all must have appeared to Taylor effective devices for moving himself to that depth of soul that he desired, and therefore artistically justified, even esthetically functional.[14] Because he was writing for himself alone and not for others, Taylor was free to write of his soul and his God in the language he wanted. How these devices look and sound to us is not as important as how they moved Taylor.

In these ways, Taylor is the exemplary private poet. That he should so greatly enjoy the process of meditating by means of the language of poetry is evidence of its centrality to his esthetics. And being central, it works to include him centrally in American culture as, I feel, no other feature of his thought or style does. Ironically though, his humble love of the poetic process as he knew it almost lost his writings for us. How many other poets were there in early New England who, in being American in the same way, are, as Taylor once was, lost, neglected, undiscovered?

Whether Taylor intended his poetry to provide an example for others to follow we may never know. But by seeing how the process of writing was important to Taylor where the products of his pen were not, I think it is possible to justify his injunction against publication and at the same time make him relevant to the American tradition in literature.

Chapter 4

Art's Cramping Task

Grace gilds this shade with brightsom shines
  Godward
And manward doth bring —— a blest reward.

                                        (2.162)

THE POETRY

Any defense of Puritan poetry is doomed to come off like a bad war—great effort for little ground. One would not defend a culture to save it. The object seldom seems worth the pain. It is not enough for one to have been able to document the facts of the Puritan poets' lives and works or to have made the discovery of an esthetic philosophy in gestation among them, for the poetic production is thin and easily transcended by their metaphysics and their history. Over against the drama of time and place and the heavy requirements of the soul among them, the poetry of early America is for the most part merely "a little recreation." In the vast expanse of the New World and the dark abyss of the Puritan soul, it by and large takes up only the little space of the few pages it is written on. It is easily lost to mind.

To make things worse, the contribution that Puritan poetry has made to American culture is almost entirely insignificant. Though one may feel grateful for any document of the period that gives us the feelings of a man, his mind and his times, the poetry of the period is often made to sit in a gap better filled by the prose. It is a way into the ideas and life-style of early Americans that is inferior to the sermons and histories and journals. Over against the Puritans' art of oratory and the handcrafts, the poetry is by and large an artistic embarrassment. Most of the exclamations about it in modern critical exercises are of necessity apologies about it.

Sorriest of all, to know Puritan poetry well is to become acquainted with the worst about the Puritan mind. You learn that in place of a delicate sensibility, the Puritan had a gross and busy stoicism. You find that he was not easily shocked by dissonance or inclined to pleasure. You discover that he would not employ long periods of leisure in free revery or in harmoniously arranging forms, colors, and sounds for the purpose of enjoyment. You come to understand how his beliefs stiffened him as a man, fettered his writing, and left of an artist only a being who was the slave of his watchwords. You are made aware why he had little or no independence of spirit, no wide curiosity, no comprehensive education. Through studying his poetry you become convinced that he was emasculated by his sectarianism. If you are sensitive to it you will endure with a condescending smile the low key of his verse with its superficial uses of form, its short imaginative reach, its bad doctrinal air, its pretensions to spiritual exercise. And this can become an attitude toward his whole life. In the main, to make a case for Puritan poetry is to champion dullness and sterility. Ideal Puritan poetry is a dull poetry. Through it the Puritan becomes a dead stereotype.

This cold, hard state of Puritan poetry is, to be sure, a comment on that which is cold and hard in the faith. The conformity to conventional poetic forms itself betrays a lack of interest in beauty. To read the poetry is not to become acquainted with why Puritans wrote but why they wrote so little verse. In its suspicion of the pleasures of the senses, man's creative efforts, and the world as a whole, it is evidence against the value of its own existence. It was written under the severest of limitations: the conviction that it would not be any good. Only seldom—and Edward Taylor is one instance—did it rise above these conditions.

But it is not so much that Taylor is a cut above the other New England versifiers and poetasters that one should consider him. It is that the scale for measuring them is no scale for him. He must be looked at with a very different eye. By and large he will not meet their criteria. For the most part, they read (misread?) the esthetic implications of the theology as having implications for the theology—that is, their poetry was an expression of tenets. On the other hand, Taylor read (misread?) the theology *as* esthetics. They therefore became dull apologists and he became a real poet.

His is, simply, a Puritan poetry with a difference. Whereas the handful of other poets in New England are, to a man, public in their

poetic intentions, for instance, Taylor's best poetry is wholly private
and meditative. Where they sought to communicate—communicate
their beliefs, their history, their lives—Taylor sought merely to express himself, and to no one, except perhaps to his God, a far more
critical audience. Where the bulk of their poetry is mere artifice—that
is, the glossing of self-aggrandizement, the pretending to epiphanies,
the defining of the inscrutable, the selling of the products of
piety—Taylor was a man moved by specific occasions to the writing
of poetry fairly easily, even of necessity. Whereas most of their works
are admittedly unneeded polishings of God's altar, Taylor was able to
turn his words themselves into a sacrament upon the altar: the
Word-made-flesh, the words-made-bread-and-wine, language-as-
holy-communion.

Taylor's life of spiritual intensity led to poetry. The Christian virus
of intensity, of flagellation tormented him more than it appears to
have affected others who put their hand to poetry in the period.
Poetry was his way of refining his excruciations and his hopes. He
thereby became very conscious of himself.

> Astonisht stand, my Soule; why dost not start
>   At this surprizing Sight shewn here below?
> Oh! let the twitch made by my bouncing Heart
>   Gust from my breast this Enterjection, Oh!
> A Sight so Horrid, sure its Mercies Wonder
> Rocks rend not at't, nor Heavens split asunder.
>
> (1.18)

His verse perpetuated such extravagances of his faith, its macerations
and will to suffer, its tragic desires and illusions. Taylor would have
been a different man without it.

This jubilant despair of his poetry was, above all, Taylor's way of
escaping passivity and dullness of spirit. It engaged his mind, it kept
his faculties alive.[1] His aspiration to communion with the absolute
was expressed in the activity of his writing. He therefore had a strong
will to write: "I want a power, not will to honour thee." (2.38) With
his activity, his struggle, Taylor kept his attention focused on time,
on, that is, the business of being and becoming. It was not his nature
to seek deliverance through the activity of poetry; he cannot locate
himself *above* the actions of his little life. His poetry was instead the
activity of a beggar: he has nothing, he is only himself, and he

endures. Working at it, he discovered what he knew: that he is doomed to corrupt wisdom, that he is a victim of time, that his weaknesses both appall him and appeal to him. His poetry therefore gave his life a tension that created vexingly personal ties between him and his God, and so he pursued it to the end of his days. "Lord help me," was his persistent theme, "so/That I may pay in glory what I owe." (1.41)

Taylor's beliefs led him to this tension as it led no other poet of early New England. Perhaps that was because he knew the esthetics of the theology better. Or because those aspects of it that interested him the most were tension-producing, poetry-producing aspects. Or maybe because in his role as minister he came easily to a career of words. However it was, poetry was the form that Taylor's appeal to God took: a poetry that was eagerly sought after and ultimately rejected by him; a poetry as full of hell as of the simulations of salvation; a poetry aggravated in the form of its hope, light in its saintliness, obscene in its personal revelation; in short, a poetry of considerable interest.

Taylor's poetry might suggest that all was reasonably well with him in Westfield—the contest between purists and impure in England is remote; the bitter exegetical debates at Harvard and in Boston are for the most part out of earshot; the church in the Connecticut Valley, except for the heresiarch Solomon Stoddard, is coming along. And because of the peace and progress, poetry was Taylor's way of reinstating himself in hell. With it he could be reinvigorated by his sufferings. In it he could relive the resources of his misery and his dreams of glory. By means of it he could know often the stimulus of his anxieties.

Taylor's poetry is confessional and therefore an aberration from normal Puritan poetry. He relies on his life, pretending to believe in it and having little respect for the secrets he discovers in it. The paradox of this poetic self-consciousness that his poetry makes possible is that he knows a great deal about himself but is on the other hand *nothing*. Taylor's ostensible reason for this poetry is to get outside himself, to make himself conscious of something beyond himself, to praise (even perhaps contact) his God. Only in doing so can he hope to have anything of the divine come into his poor life. But his method in this is to turn inward to probe the grounds of his own life, of evil, of Being itself. And there he gets stuck. He seems aware that his poetic method foils his efforts in this way. But it is all he knows to do. His psychological sense turns him into a spectator of himself—a hellish preoccupation. As he celebrates his Lord and Savior, his subject is Himself Fallen, or Man Since The Fall. And in this he counterfeits hell and the desire for heaven.

With his poetry Taylor torments his conscience to get himself a few sensations. Perhaps he was, after all, a sensualist enlivened by humility, sin, and hellfire. His poetry feasts on his tortures. It helps him get drunk on his vices and virtues. His pain gives him pleasure.

What is important in this method, however, is not the pathology but the style. With poetic form Taylor can manipulate his anxieties in order to convert absence into mystery, into substance. For subject there is no person of worth present in his poems: "What am I, poor Mite, all mightless thing!" (2.48) But his individual tone restores his voice to our ears, his eccentricities of rhythm and metaphor give us the gestures of his limbs and eyes, his ejaculations and resolutions give us his emotions, reveal his subjective state. Through style he becomes a man again: "New mould, new make me thus, me new Create . . . New Heart, New thoughts, New Words." (1.30) In addition, the form of his expression keeps him close to the earth and away from metaphysical and mystical flights. His words bind him to things, keep him in servitude to the fallen creation. With them he has ground to stand on. While his words do not give him the otherness he desired, they at least give him a surer sense of self.

An expressive style is the only original experience that he makes himself out to be even minimally capable of: "I'le sing thy glory out/Untill thou welcome me." And though obsessed with expressiveness, he does not allow his style to become something autonomous, something that gives him power. In many religious writers individual style is heresy, for it disapproves of accepted expression and the submission to consecrated style. But Taylor avoids such heresy by making style subordinate to thought. Or rather, he works to make style and thought one thing. I do not think he succeeds very often, yet he works hard at the fusion: "My Quill makes thine Almightiness a String/Of Pearls to grace the tune my Mite doth sing." When he succeeds, however, one can see the relation between Taylor's temporal universe (the cosmology that gave his self-consciousness the shape it had) and his style. A formal analysis of his poems shows just how self-conscious a craftsman he could be at times, how much a poet.

A poem like Meditation 1.39 makes a good case for the adequacy of Taylor's abilities:

My Sin! my Sin, My God, these Cursed Dregs,
    Green, Yellow, Blew streakt Poyson hellish, ranck,
Bubs hatcht in natures nest on Serpents Eggs,
    Yelp, Cherp and Cry; they set my Soule a Cramp.
    I frown, Chide, strik and fight them, mourn and Cry
    To Conquour them, but cannot them destroy.

I cannot kill nor Coop them up: my Curb
    'S less than a Snaffle in their mouth: my Rains
They as a twine thrid, snap: by hell they're spurd:
    And load my Soule with swagging loads of pains.
    Black Imps, young Divells, snap, bite, drag to bring
    And pick mee headlong hells dread Whirle Poole in.

Lord, hold thy hand: for handle mee thou may'st
    In Wrath: but, oh, a twinckling Ray of hope
Methinks I spie thou graciously display'st.
    There is an Advocate: a doore is ope.
    Sin's poyson swell my heart would till it burst,
    Did not a hope hence creep in't thus, and nurse't.

Joy, joy, Gods Son's the Sinners Advocate
    Doth plead the Sinner guiltless, and a Saint.
But yet Atturnies pleas spring from the State
    The Case is in: if bad its bad in plaint.
    My Papers do contain no pleas that do
    Secure mee from, but knock me down to, woe.

I have no plea mine Advocate to give:
    What now? He'l anvill Arguments greate Store
Out of his Flesh and Blood to make thee live.
    O Deare bought Arguments: Good pleas therefore.
    Nails made of heavenly Steel, more Choice than gold
    Drove home, Well Clencht, eternally will hold.

Oh! Dear bought Plea, Deare Lord, what buy't so deare?
    What with thy blood purchase thy plea for me?

Take Argument out of thy Grave t'appeare
    And plead my Case with, me from Guilt to free.
These maule both Sins, and Divells, and amaze
Both Saints, and Angells; Wreath their mouths with praise.

What shall I doe, my Lord? what do, that I
    May have thee plead my Case? I fee thee will
With Faith, Repentance, and obediently
    Thy Service gainst Satanick Sins fulfill.
    I'l fight thy fields while Live I do, although
    I should be hackt in pieces by thy foe.

Make me thy Friend, Lord, by my Surety: I
    Will be thy Client, be my Advocate:
My Sins make thine, thy Pleas make mine hereby.
    Thou wilt mee save, I will thee Celebrate.
    Thou'lt kill my Sins that cut my heart within:
    And my rough Feet shall thy smooth praises sing.

This poem is a meditation on the metaphor of Christ as defense attorney from I John 2:

If any man sin, we have an Advocate with the Father, Jesus Christ the righteous: and he is the propitiation for our sins: and not for ours only, but also for the sins of the world.

Just prior to this text, John warns that "If we confess our sins, [God] is faithful and just to forgive us our sins, and to cleanse us from all unrighteousness." Taylor's poem is a confession for the express purpose of being cleansed from the filthiness he feels, from the burden of self that he carries.

The contrasts in this text give the poem its structure. It moves from the meiotic ("My Sin! my sin") to the amplified ("Deare Lord"), with the announcement of Christ the advocate as pivot. The imagery at the outset suggests life under a curse: the excremental, the diseased, the evil, the uncontrolled, the painful, the trapped, the hellish—making up life's burden, a burden which Taylor feels could "drag" him down to damnation. At the end of the poem, however, the imagery is that of hope: the loved, the cured, the beatified, the joyous, the freed, the heavenly. And to Taylor the only factor that can work the miracle of turning the curse into such a blessing is the figure of the magical Savior, who plays simultaneous roles of liberating lawyer, comforting lover, source of light, host in a new home, nurse to the sick, skilled smithy/carpenter, wealthy buyer of goods, and loving fighter—all in one. This plenitude of grace in Christ is in contrast to man's helplessness.

The sound is carefully manipulated in the poem to assist these contrasts. Such uses may have come instinctively with Taylor's intense verbalizing of his meditative experience. In the first stanza the rhythm is abrupt and thrusting. The many junctures and extra stresses show that at the point in his remoteness from grace his "Soule [is] a Cramp," as he says. The words of this section are cacophonous with stops and affricates that grate against each other crudely. The words are mainly monosyllabic to demonstrate the excruciating reality of damnation. The syntax is inverted and collapsed. The rhymes are impure. The vowels moan and cry. From the sound of his lines ("my rough Feet"), Taylor is indeed experiencing hell—or great fear of same.

As soon as a savior is introduced, however, the plosives give way to softer fricatives and semivowels ("Lord, hold thy hand; for handle mee thou may'st/ In Wrath") to suggest the "Ray of hope" he has discovered. The rhythm has become a regular iambic meter and the rhymes are pure. The painful ejaculations have become joyful exclamations and one line moves more gracefully now into another. There is at last some light in the dark pit of himself where he has been trapped.

At that point where he lapses into fear of unworthiness, admission of guilt, and doubt of the efficacy of Christ's atonement, the rhythm, syntax, and sound again jar and mock. His anxiety emerges in questions and short, determined phrases. There is at this point a confusion of the direction of the poem's argument. Only when Taylor experiences the "Surety" that the Lord will be his "Friend" is the syntax relaxed, the rhythm calm, and the sound smooth. Through faith his "rough Feet" have then become "smooth praises."

Taylor has in the imagery and the form moved from sinning to singing. This means that he has not only moved from fear of the worst fate to hope of a regenerate state but also that he has moved from obsession with self (itself a means of regeneration but also a sin) to devotion to God: "I'l fight thy fields while Live I do . . . I will thee Celebrate." Through singing a song that moves from roughness to smoothness, from complaint to praise, from fear to hope, he has started to escape, he believes, the trap of himself. Or rather, he has done what a poet (and an effective preacher) can do: he has used language to *simulate* escape, transcendence, salvation.

At several points in the poem Taylor uses elements of form even more cleverly to simulate the experience he is putting himself through. Wrestling with the devil in his soul, his rhythm and syntax catch his fear of being thrown into hell: "Black Imps, young Divells, snap, bite, drag to bring/And pick mee headlong hells dread Whirle Poole in." The heavy stresses at the end and the removal of "in" to the end of the line simulate the experience of damnation that he fears. Taylor has reached the bottom-most point of the infernal regions, from which he can now rise. This happens again at that point in his story when he fears he will be rejected as a client of Christ the Advocate: "My Papers do contain no pleas that do/Secure me from, but knock me down to, woe." Rhythm and syntax again dramatize his fear. His syntactic distortions have him in the clutches of evil, which innovates his movement toward the good, an inert state of "smooth praises." When Christ is introduced as a possible advocate for a guilty man, Taylor cannot keep himself from simulating in his rhythms his heart's excitement over the prospect ("Joy, joy, Gods Son"). He even simulates the actions of Christ the smithy/carpenter making his own cross and nailing himself thereto ("Nails made of heavenly Steel, more Choice than gold/Drove home, Well Clencht, eternally will hold"). The vigor of his new happiness is in these lines.

There are some interesting theological implications of the imagery and form of such a poem. Taylor is dependent on the sin-to-song structure, for example, in order to convince himself of the possibility of hope; having made a poem with that structure, he can go on believing that his life has the same direction. He begins with the vision of a personal hell, for he feels that an individual needs the mediation of evil in order to go beyond his confines. Without it growth would be impossible and the possible abolished. It is to evil that he owes the style of his meditating. It is evil that confirms him as an individual, whether he likes it or not. (It is after all actually the Lord who "handle[s] mee . . . In Wrath"; that is, it is God who works through evil to bring him to Him.) The brief descent into hell in such a poem is a stimulus. He therefore cherishes simulating the torture. But then he ends with the sound of hope—no doubt a feature that language added to his faith. The harmony of form represents Taylor's imagined harmony with his God. His religious experience begins where cacophony and distortion leave off, where his abilities to sing, pray, and write begin. The poem ends not with any fulfillment but with mere hope, a kind of circular exercise, for to Taylor that is as far as man's straining toward salvation can go.

Further, the poem itself is an artifact, an artifice, a fabrication, a lie. Its little drama of salvation is sheer illusion and it is written to continue that illusion. Taylor's illusion-making poetry is a good example of Perry Miller's comment:

> Puritanism sees illusion in the visible universe; it requires men, as long as they are in the flesh, to act as though the illusion were real; it punishes them if they take illusion for reality.[2]

Taylor cannot know of his salvation; he can only project its possibility by dramatizing his hope. This constitutes his role as a poet, a role that parallels the role he hopes Christ will be willing to take in pleading his case while knowing Taylor to be guilty. On Christ's part it will take the art of lying (an act of mercy) to get him free: "Gods Son's the Sinners Advocate/Doth plead the Sinner guiltless." Taylor's rescue of himself from the clutches of despair through an act of imagination parallels Christ's fabricating a case of innocence for a guilty confessor-client. Or perhaps it is that Taylor hopes—whimsically, of course—that Christ will imitate him in his sinning/singing: "My Sins make thine." Which means that Christ, taking note of the little drama Taylor has constructed in his poem, will make out of it a real drama of saving Taylor from sin. Taylor is humble enough to admit that it is not himself but the divine in him that has authored his little poem, and if he can get Christ to claim authorship for his sins, his songs, then through poetry Taylor has turned illusion into reality! Taylor misused Scripture in this case; he read "Advocate" as lawyer, which makes it possible for him to have the pun *lawyer/liar* when he refers to Jesus "pleading the sinner guiltless."

That Taylor's poem is about the writing of poetry is suggested by the gestures of speech he uses throughout (references to crying out, chiding, pleading, advocating) and the technical terms of writing ("plaint," "Arguments," "Feet"). The "rough Feet" that become "smooth praises" in the course of the poem are, of course, Taylor's poetry itself, as are the "Papers" which are at first too lowly to offer God as a "plea" on his behalf but which eventually, through Christ's

pleading, become "pleas[ing]." The poem is therefore its own subject; it is a poem about itself as a poem.

In the poem there are a number of mixed and unclear metaphors in
which Taylor finds the artful magic of Christ at work. On the anvil of
life Christ can somehow hammer atoning nails out of flesh and blood
that will hold man eternally. He can somehow use his blood for
money to buy Taylor off from his debts. He can somehow dig
arguments out of his grave. Dying he can somehow live. These make
little sense. It is left to Christ to make them more than mere fanciful-
ness. His atonement is the missing factor in the making of meaning.
The very metaphors themselves are therefore dependent on the illusion created by the poem itself to save them from ineffectuality: the
saving Christ saves the poem from confusion and silliness. It is as if
Taylor himself is dependent on the poetic creation of such an illusion
to make his faith strong. The skill with which he is able to create that
illusion would possibly have been evidence to him of his spiritual
worth. The form of his poem is therefore of primary importance to
him. Though over the years he would often fail at his work of
sustaining his faith by means of poetic form and imagery, he would
succeed often enough, to his satisfaction, to justify the method.[3]

Such analysis makes the best case for Taylor as a considerable poet.
He is not an artist in any important sense, for he made himself
conscious of only those poetic means that would move *himself*. These
are interesting, though, for the ways in which the style reveals something of the man. He was apparently conscious of what he had to do
to move himself to where he desired to be.

His poems show Taylor to be a conventional religious thinker.
How he is different is in his use of poetic style to achieve deliverance
from his naturally troubled soul. His poetic style makes it possible for
him to invent sin and torment, to enjoy self-loathing, to be a fanatic
of rottenness and rescue. It justifies him to himself as an invalid in
ecstasy. In such simulated terror he finds his delight and takes a first
step toward deliverance. The form that he gives his language gives
substance to his desire for such deliverance; it keeps him from
metaphysical despair at his inability to adhere to being. To him, there
is more substance in a line of verse than in his own unreality. He turns
to words, pursues them, for assurances. He identifies his substance
with theirs, his success with theirs. He takes his language seriously;

by it he seeks his salvation. The fiction of the form of his words is truth to him. Taylor is thus a fanatic of words. This is a way of saying he is a considerable poet.

THE PROSE

Whether Taylor was a good writer of prose is another matter. More than anything else he aspired to being a writer of persuasive prose sermons and polemics, so one has to take it seriously in any consideration of him as a writer. Taylor's prose works are: a very short Diary, four series of sermons (three sermons from 1679, the *Treatise*, the *Christographia*, and two sermons from 1713), a Bible commentary fashioned in part out of sermons, his Church Record, several notebooks, a few letters, some scraps. Other prose manuscripts are in his hand but not from his pen. In this prose it is the public side of Taylor that one sees—the protestant, the assertive, the institutional, the pontifical in him—and that is much less interesting.

It was Taylor's work as a minister to make covenant theology crystal clear to his wilderness saints. In what he preached he tried to reason with them, instruct them, ritualize an ideology for them. But most of the sermons that he wrote and preached have more pedantry than clarity, more narrow piety than power to move others' minds. Eventually he seems to have seen the real audience of his discourses on theological matters in the university and clerical readers of theological treatises, and with such an audience in mind he wrote two long and impressive series of sermons as serial discussions of the hottest theological issue of the day, the Stoddardean heresy. These show that for the most part prose expression meant to Taylor definitions of truth rather than regenerating anyone's life. He obviously lived after Peter Ramus and before George Whitefield.

In his prose Taylor's verbal abilities unfortunately too often become mere verbiage. Like so many of his contemporaries, he fractures his faith, dissecting his beliefs until there is little life left in them. That is in part because his prose style is crowded and stiff. It is a product more of industry than of verbal competence or intellectual skill. Only occasionally do the attractive crabbedness and thorny diction of his poetry show in his prose.

Perhaps the most important prose piece by Taylor—important
from the point of view of a discussion of the tone of much of his
poetry—is a sermon Taylor delivered on 27 August 1679, when
required by his ministerial call to make a public statement on the
working of God's spirit in his life.[4] This personal testimony is the
earliest and the most self-conscious of his extant sermons.[5] In it he
moves easily, as he does in his poems, from scriptural citation and
definition to an account of the effect "of this work [of conviction]
upon mine own heart, with all humility." As in the poems, he gives
personal examples in praise of both "Soule abasement" and "Infinite
Grace," always careful to link the events of his own life with those of
Christ's. He is explicit about what he calls "Originall Sins [tes]tifying
influences" and the resulting "Guilt and filth": "My own heart was a
burden unto myself: . . . my heart being such a Prison of Naughti-
ness, and an Akeldama of uncleaness. . . ." But this is for the purpose,
as it is in his poetry, of showing how he came to take an apocalyptic
interest in Christ: "This I found that by how much I grew the more
offended with myselfe by so much the more lovely, and longed-after
did Christ appear in my eye."
     The sermon takes the form of the structure of many of his poems.
Taylor attempts to find ways of talking with confidence but without
presumption about the ways in which he might become "united unto
Christ savingly." He finds his strongest link, as he does in his poems,
in his hope that the personal affection he has for Christ is a form that
sanctifying grace has taken in his life. He feels he can justify his
position as minister to Westfield on that basis: the "indearing
rapture" he experiences toward Christ "indeare[s]" him, he feels, to
the members of his congregation. To exercise the "raptures," as he
does in poem after poem, is his way of becoming one with the saints
of the town. As lovers of Christ they become united through "the
Spirit called Love." To have "looked within doore," as Taylor calls
the meditative exercises which resulted in his poetry, is to have
looked in the doors of his church and found delight in becoming
familiar with "all the wayes of God." In this manner the poetry and
the preaching were to him one exercise, the service of his heart and his
friends one service.
     This is a delightful sermon, one that makes most of his others
coldly exegetical by comparison. But still there is little of his imagery
here and no drama or intensity of hope. Even in such a sermon as this,

Taylor does not do what he can in his poems—convert dogma into personal experience, or project a self beyond that which he was known as being, or make a spectacle of his fears and hopes, especially no spectacle of himself doing combat with himself. His prose is hardly therapeutic, has little of the energy, is not creatively asperous, the way his poetry is. At least in his poetry his obsessions are made interesting.

This is true as well of the other two sermons that Taylor delivered on that day in August of 1679 when the church in Westfield was organized. In the "Profession of Faith" that he offered his congregation, Taylor had the opportunity to let his prose soar, but the dogma he intended to explicate for them prevented him from esthetic considerations. Only occasionally, as is the case in most of the sermons we have, are there moments when the analogies become attractive conceits:

> The Ultimate Influence of heavenlie Glory upon the Soule . . . sets the Soule a singing forth the Praises of the Lord God having made the Soule such a glorious Musicall Instrument of his praises, & the holy Ghost having so gloriously strung it with the golden wyer of grace, & heavenly Glory having shored up the strings to sound forth the Songs of Zions King, the pouring forth of the Influences of glory play upon the Soule Eternall praises unto God. & now the Soule begging to sing forth its endless Hallelujahs unto God. If it were possible it would fly in pieces under its glory if this glory got no vent. & therefore it being filled with glory for Gods glory it falls to singing most heart-ravishingly out the Glory of God in the highest strains.[6]

and his rhetoric is capable of a little drama:

> Ay, but Soule[s] here [in hell] are such, but not a few onely but a whole dungeon full, a whole Hell full of such ugly things of roagues, Spirits, ghosts, & Divels! & not only so, but here is now nothing but such!——& not only so but al——roaring, yelling, frying, crying, tering, rending, frothing, foaming under the wrath of the almighty, trembling, Oh! dreadfull sight, oh hidious screech! Oh what company is here, but this is the society that inhabit eternall plagues.[7]

The other of this pair of sermons, Taylor's "A Particular Church is

God's House," is conventional in outline but so full of his learning (a full two-hours' worth) as to lack any excitement or coherence. Its purpose was ostensibly to stir the interest of his little congregation in preparationism, but its effect would have been otherwise: to impress them with his learning.

The eight sermons which make up Taylor's *Treatise Concerning the Lord's Supper*, written and preached in late 1693 and early 1694, are his most coherent work in prose.[8] They hold together and build on one another as if intended for a book and not merely for delivery on sacrament days. There is a consistency of tone in them resulting from the single metaphor of "the wedden garment" (one's visible spiritual worth) that they explicate. They are overweeningly repetitious, however, and defensively contentious. While they supply valuable theological information for an understanding of several of the Meditations, they reveal little of the personality behind them. At a few points they make good reading because of the personable style; Taylor is here eager to help his listeners/readers *enjoy* the communion. Taylor is trying to make his own joy, his own exercising of heart, contagious. When he does allow something of the color of his own personality into the argument, however, it is merely an aside:

A multitude of carnal thoughts, or worldly ploddings about the things of this life. This is a burden to the spirit of a child of God. Oh! I am so thronged with carnal thoughts, I know not what to make of myself. I find I am called to set mine affection on things above, and not on things upon the earth, and Christ saith, "take no thought for tomorrow, but let tomorrow take thought for itself" (Matt. 6: *ult.*), and David saith, "when I awake I am still with thee." But alas, I find it otherwise with me. I am overrun with evil and carnal thoughts. Where I have one thought of spiritual concerns, I have twenty laid out upon the things of the world. Truly this is the condition of God's children here in this life. While we have these bodies of clay to look after, and are betrusted with the concerns of families, towns, and public duties in our hands, they necessitate our thoughts; so that we lay out a great deal of our contemplative substance all the day long upon them, and are constrained to put off spiritual concerns with some transient ejaculatory thoughts. But as for this matter, I say, you are not to draw upon your conclusion in this case from these thoughts. For while we are in the flesh this is the fruit of our labor.[9]

But for the most part, of the impersonability of this prose one might have to say as Emerson does of the preaching style of the formalist in his Divinity School Address, "He had no one word intimating that he had laughed or wept, was married or in love, had been commended, or cheated, or chagrined. If he had ever lived and acted, we were none the wiser for it. . . . There was not a surmise, a hint, in all the discourse, that he had ever lived at all."

The fourteen *Christographia* sermons that Taylor wrote later (between 1701 and 1703) are his most concerted attempt at a grouping of his sermons on a single subject.[10] He possibly saw them as his best defense of orthodox Puritanism's Christ and possibly as a book to all the Christian world. Together they make a comprehensive portrait of *Taylor's* Christ, a portrait the learning and form of which should have been impressive to his congregation and colleagues. Over against the work of Taylor's antagonist, Solomon Stoddard, at whom they were directed, they come off in superior form. They ought to have given Taylor the stature in the Connecticut Valley, indeed in the entire colony, that he desired.

But it is difficult to imagine how anyone, short of Solomon Stoddard himself, could have sat through them. Only on rare occasion can a vernacular or individual language (language, however, that appears often in the poems) save a sentence:

> [Christ] will prick his heart veane to let a grace-drop of blood thence to fetch out this freckle from thy face.

> God hath utterly befoold this Subtill piece of hellish policy.

> The Quakers . . . belch out the most horridst blasphemy against the Person of Christ, that ever was uttered as an Opinion.

> Thou are under Coverbarn, and the Glorious Wing of the Fulness of Christs Grace will alwayes Cover thee with its gracious and all reviving Shade. He will hide thee with his Effulgent feathers, and under his Shadow thou shalt sit in all Safety.

> They tip their tongues with the language of Zion, but their hearts are as flinty as Sin Can make them.

O! methinks this Should indeed make thy Stony heart to fly apieces, and to Sinke within thee.

Their Crowns are too oft bedotcht with filthiness. Whereas Christ's Crown is glorified with holiness.

And occasionally a few of Taylor's exhortations parallel the colorful language of his poems:

And in greate desire after these Treasures of Wisdom betake yourselves to Christ to partake of them. Where Should the Hongry man goe for good but to the Cooks shop? Where should the Thirsty go for water but to the Fountain? No man will let his bucket down into an empty Well if he be aware of it. No man will Seek Riches in a beggers Cottage. He that would be Wealthy must trade in matters profitable. So if thou wouldst have Spirituall Treasures, trade with Christ.[11]

But these are exceptions. Unlike Cotton Mather in his prose, Taylor did not find a style for his *Treatise* and *Christographia* sermons that was congenial to his erudition nor a language entirely appropriate to both his convictions and his ambitions. It was probably enough to the Westfield settlers who listened to these sermons to have been satisfied by the *fact* of his erudition, his earnestness, and his enthusiasm. There is some consolation in the possibility that this was not the style of his regular preaching, which may be better represented by his "Day of Judgment" sermon.

The devices that Taylor uses to make his writings important as sermons, however, unfortunately often almost destroy them as interesting literature—the fulsome repetitiousness, the anxious scriptural citations, the technical language, the exhaustion of subject, the dutiful complexity of argument. When Taylor reduced a cosmology to discourse, it was a severe reduction. Though it may be wrong to expect his style to soar, to be sure it seldom soars.

Taylor's prose nevertheless shows how he worked himself up to the pitch of some of his poems. In the poems he often applies to himself what he advocates in his sermons that his listeners should do—look inward and find in one's filthiness the need for the work of a savior. These poems naturally follow hot upon his explication of his text, his doctrinal conclusion, and his application of "uses." His prose has some of the same discipline of joy, some of the same extravagance of language, some of the same imagination of his poems, but not at all very much. His prose can hardly explicate the poems, where it is the poetic form itself and how he is moved by it that is his subject. To be sure, the meaning of the poems is inextricably related to the doctrine of the sermons and their dogmatics gloss the poems' imagery helpfully, but the poems for the most part go beyond the prose in their therapy, their drama, and their revelation of personality. What Taylor's poetry has that the *Christographia* sermons lack is the use of language to create religious acts (they are explanatory where the poems are themselves a kind of action, a reenactment of the processes of salvation), the use of language to make love to what he believed in, the use of language to reconcile personal experiences and doctrinal requirements. That is why there seems to be so much more of his soul in the poetry than the prose.

The sermons on church discipline that Taylor preached in 1713, the last of his sermons that have come down to us, show an even greater defensiveness of the church and his conception of his role in it. They are more self-righteous and cantankerous in tone and more rigid in both doctrine and style. His subject in them is how to deal with actions and persons offensive to his will:

> Oh! the Patience of Christ to an offending Disciple! oh! the Pains he is at to bring him off from his Sin & reduce him! & oh! the Obstinacy & impurity of Sinners here will they expose their good names, Reputations & esteems to open Shame before they will turn from their sins? How will they withstand all means of Grace, teare Christs tearless Coate apieces, & cast fire into the temple, & raise an hellish dust & Smoke in Gods house to darken the Way of Sion, & to Smoother & Choake Such withall as come thither before they will fall down under their faults & confess their Sins![12]

His style is that of a jeremiad, for he fears the decline of the New England experiment; the New England cities are full of "Adulterors, Drunkards, Theeves, Murderers, Oppressors, Cursed Swearers, Liars, Cruell Unmercifall Witches, Dealers with Divells, & some Excommunicates."[13] His solution to this decline is simply redoubled covenanting (that is, a revival of interest in the civil oath implied in the preparation for the Lord's Supper), and the discipline necessary to maintain the standards of the elect. His approach is more legalistic than ever before and so is his language:

> Christ doth give forth Laws by which his Kingdom is to be Regulated. No Kingdom can be regulated or govern'd without laws. Christs Kingdom is the best kingdom which is. Hence it must be ennobled by the best laws which is.[14]

This is a far cry from the poetry he was writing at about the same time:

> When thou, my Lord, mee mad'st, thou madst my heart
> A Seate for love, and love enthronedst there.
> Thou also madst an object by thy Art
> For Love to be laid out upon most Cleare.
> The ruling Stamp of this Choice object shows
> God's Beauty, beautifuller than the rose.
>
> (2.116)

In the one, the institution is the most important factor; in the other, the individual heart. Taylor in the pulpit was often a different man from Taylor at his meditating.

An important relationship does exist between the doctrine in Taylor's sermons and the doctrine in his poems. But there is another kind of light they provide. Occasionally they tell, if only in passing, what Taylor thought about a few matters connected with the writing of his poetry. His few comments on esthetic matters in his sermons show some of the ways he thought about his poetry while concentrating on his theology.

What they tell first of all, of course, is that Taylor was a Puritan regular in being *suspicious* of human imagination and the arts. He was sure that the "Wisdom of this World . . . is but low, and little, and but of a little Concern and lasts but a little While,"[15] and to him, "all the excell[ent] things in all the World: in Heaven, and in Earth done by Sai[nts,] and Angells of God; are but dull drudgeries, and lifeless pa[inted] Cloaths. . . . All our pensills in all their draughts attain not to anything of the Excellencies of Christ's operations . . . and considered *per se* they are nausious."[16] Man's arts were to Taylor by and large insufficient for the communication of spiritual matters. He felt that grace, for example, is "Communicated [in] . . . a Spirituall Nature, and therefore not Communicated in a Naturall Way."[17] His religious intensity/anxiety taught him that "Grace excells all Metaphors. The varnish laid upon it doth but darken, and not decorate it: its own Colours are too glorious to be made more glorious, by any Colour of Secular glory."[18] To Taylor there is a clear distinction between art and religion: the one is the device of man, the other is of God:

> Christ calls it his Doctrine, . . . Doctrine not negatively, as if Divinity was not an Art, or Science, as well as other Arts, but Emphatically its a Doctrine in that, whereas there are such clear footsteps of other Arts, & Sciences imprinted in the fabrick of Nature leading blinde Nature to gather up the Systems of those Rules thereof, & to hold out the same without any Super-naturall teacher, yet Divinity cannot be so learned; but God himselfe must teach it himselfe or else it had never been Disco-vered.

He recognized that "Grammar, Rhetorick, Logick, are peculiarly conversant about the Essence, Grace, & Argumentative strength of Speech" but also that "none teach us to live to God of all of these" as divinity does.[19] It was natural that he should be suspicious of the conventional ways of the poet.

To Taylor, furthermore, art tends to pervert reality and truth, for it has the devilish ability to create "an Artificiall Union" between unsuitable things, such as writing that projects man into the trans-cendent or that images forth the divine in the objects and beings of the fallen world. In creating such harmony out of the naturally dishar-monious, it tells lies.

> There are no unsuitable things [that] will unite [to the person of Christ] unless they be first fitted, whereby their unsuitableness is done away. In all Unions, the things United reject union where they remain unsuitable one to the other. There is an Artificiall Union, as in any piece of Art. Suppose, in a Watch, Building, etc. the Matters to be set together and United must be first fitted, and framed So as they Will joyn together. . . . But there is no Humane Nature [that] is fitt to be United to the Person of Christ. All flesh hath Corrupted its Way.[20]

An art that "joyns things together according to the Rules of any Art" is the work of the fallen mind of man.[21]

Yet in this Taylor sees a creative possibility; he will through poetry create the *illusion* of an "artificial union" of himself and his savior. Though it is a lie since he cannot know for a surety his election, still he is free through poetry to imagine the truth of the possibility of such. In this way poetry provides him with the opportunity for hope.

The "various forms of speech" are in fact important to Taylor's faith. He has no quarrel at all with language when used for "signs" of factors in his faith:

> 1. The sign is used for the thing signified, as Circumcision for sanctification. 2. When the thing signified is the name upon which the Bread & Wine is said to be Christs Body & Blood. 3. When the effect of the thing signified is ascribed to the sign, as Regeneration the effect of the Washing in Christs blood is ascribed to Baptism. 4. When the property of the sign is ascribed to the thing signified, as the breaking of bread, unto Christ. 5. the property of the thing signified is ascribed to the sign, as when the Bread sacramentall is used for Spirituall.[22]

Taylor no doubt felt that such a list would discipline his use of metaphoric language, when in reality it would free it, given the intensity of Taylor's imagination, for the creation of extravagant types, puns, and conceits.

Taylor shows himself in his few comments in his sermons to be of two minds about the art of writing. He had both reservations and excitement about the religious possibilities of such a literary matter as imagery. When he wished to be pejorative about an idea he seriously questions, he used such literary terminology as "metaphorical," "synecdoche," "typical," "allegorical"—terms which today would be considered a writer's way of getting at his truth. On the one hand something might be "*onely* Metaphoricall" or "metaphoricall and *not proper*," but on the other hand, it could be a means of realizing truth. He is suspicious of all literary devices yet recognizes in them great relief for man's spiritual desires. In a 1679 sermon he calls the denial of scriptural metaphors "but Rhetoricall Atheism." No doubt it was such interest in the power of metaphor that led him to his poetry.

In one of his *Christographia* sermons, Taylor writes that he believes that God "sets it [the truth] before us by that word proper to [the children of men], but metaphoricall to him." That is, God speaks through metaphors, which man with his fallen abilities takes literally, but which man must learn to understand not merely literally but metaphorically before he can know them as a communication of the truth.

> All Languages admit of Metaphoricall forms of Speech, and the Spirit of God abounds in this manner of Speech in the Scripture and did foreshew that Christ Should abound in this Sort of Speech, and this Sort of Speech never was expected to be literally true, nor Charged to be a lying form of Speech, but a neate Rhetoricall, and Wise manner of Speaking. . . . This form of Speech is a truth Speaking form, Convaying the thoughts of the heart of the Speaker unto the hearers in Such words as are apt to do it metaphorically and wisely.[23]

Metaphors—really, all types of imagery and symbolism—were to Taylor the means God uses to bring together things of the world and things of God as tenor and vehicle, while keeping them distinct. To concern oneself with metaphoric writing, therefore, is to concentrate on the mysteries of God. Therein is a kind of union of man's little understanding of God's great truth. To Taylor, from God's point of view the metaphorical is a way of communicating after a worldly fashion, and from man's, it is a way of realizing something of the divine. It is metaphor which makes language sacramental to Taylor. "Thou dost use/This Metaphor," Taylor says to his God, "to make thyselfe appeare, In taking Colours. . . . (2.101) In the various forms of symbolism he used, he saw, as he did in the sacrament of the Lord's Supper itself, a representational union of himself and the divine. Tenor and vehicle, sign and the thing signified, made that illusion a valuable experience for him.[24] The metaphors of poetry were mere illusions of spiritual union, but illusions that encouraged hope.

Words were to Taylor, then, mysterious things full of life in their inherent forms. He would therefore as poet worry his key words until he got beyond their surface, using them often as puns, as conceits, as types, or as yielding meaning through spelling, etymology, or allusion. In metaphorical form, words were a way Taylor saw of transcending nature. Words that simply correspond with natural facts stand in the way of apprehension of the supernatural. Yet to Taylor God had provided the way of metaphor, whereby man might, if sufficiently spiritually imaginative, use the things of nature to realize supernatural things. Nature itself does not provide this avenue to the divine, but metaphorical language does. In the artful metaphor, therefore, God and man may meet—if not in reality, then at least in art, an "artificiall union."

Taylor also took metaphors as working like New Testament parables; this is, not clarifying so much as putting one's understanding to a test: if one has ears to hear and eyes to see, then through the intellectual effort required of one, he has proved himself worthy of the kingdom. That which is "parabolical" to Taylor is "a dark account and enigmatical," a language device part of which God makes explicit to all but part of which meaning he reserves to himself and those who are one with him.

> Natural things are not unsuitable to illustrate supernaturals by. For Christ in his parables doth illustrate supernatural things by natural, and if it were not thus, we could arrive at no knowledge of supernatural things, for we are not able to see above naturals.
>
> God hath a sweet harmony of reason running the same throughout the whole creation, even through every distinct sort of creatures; hence Christ on this very account makes use of natural things to illustrate supernaturals by, and the Apostle argues invisible things from the visible. So that on this account there is argument enough, if we have but skill to take it and use it aright.[25]

Metaphor is therefore seen by Taylor as a language game that works according to one's faith. It is one of God's ways of revealing the elect.

In a sermon in 1679 Taylor told how metaphors simulate spiritual relationships. The very structure of a metaphor was to Taylor of significance. "God would teach us something thereby," he believed.

> If [God] would teach us any thing by these Metaphors, then there must be some Analogy, & Suitableness in the Metaphors to the thing given us by these Metaphors. And therefore that which is most pertinent in them to their being, & end, must be granted to be in the thing designed by them. Now then as they Cannot be without their parts be joyned, & Combined together which Combination is their form. So they hold out that in a Church, which is the meaning of them, there must be Such a Combination together of its parts, that answers this their joyn-

ing & What is this Combination but a Covenant. For nothing else set the parts together visibly, but a Visible Covenant.

The illusion of apt metaphor was to Taylor therefore proof enough of the possibility of union of man and God. The uniting of disparates was the reason for using metaphors. To Taylor, metaphors do not so much teach truths as represent in their structure how faith/imagination can conjoin man and God. The form is the message.

> There are Some Metaphors the Spirit of God useth in this Case to intimate unto us the Form itselfe of any Church Visible. . . . Its a Metaphor borrow'd from Artists that joyn things artifically together with Glew. & the Spirit of God borrows it to import the Marriage Covenant . . . and for the Church Covenant.

The work of the metaphor-maker, the poet, is artificial and yet truthful in its conjoining of disparates, for this simulates, through the form of metaphor itself, the relationship of God and man.

> The Spirit borrows some terms of Nature, to intimate this unto us by. . . . It properly imports Such a joyning, & Compacting to gether as is that of the joynts by it[s] nerves, or Sinews. & altho' this imports the Union of the Soul stands in unto Christ, & the Spirits Uniting one member by these Nerves to an other: yet, as a Visible body it implies the Nerves of that body as Such joyning each Member to its place in the Body. And what doth this import but Such a manifest joyning of every member to this body a Church as another is joyned to that, or the other. & what can this be but a Covenant. Now then its cleare that a Church Covenant suites the very design of Scripture Metaphors.[26]

Taylor's attraction to metaphor was therefore both personal and theological. It was a structure the magic of which unites God with his church and a man with his God. Art, despite his disclaimers to the contrary, was therefore absolutely essential to Taylor's faith.

Synecdoche, another technical term that Taylor discussed in his sermons, works much the same way. Since man cannot understand the whole of the universe, all of the divine, or the fulness of Christ, or even entirely know himself, he must concern himself with only a part of the truth. Life is therefore a series of synecdoches. The fallen man will see only the part, but the elect (that is, those capable of great imagination and "right reason") will be able to deduce the whole from the part. If something is *mere* synecdoche, it is insufficient, but if through intellectual effort it has reference beyond itself, then it works synecdochically, leading one to the truth. As a poet, Taylor was to remember this, as Emerson was, in using the Eaches of his world to represent the Alls. The Each is by itself worthless but the right mind can deduce from it the All.

Such literary concepts as these few in his sermons were to Taylor's mind also concepts of life. To Taylor, life itself was a work of art, an artificial union, the forcing together of disparates by artful means. Life, Taylor wrote in one sermon, is not "natural" or "Spirituall" but "Metaphoricall"; that is, it is false and superficial and insufficient but suggestive of a full life:

> Christ is the Life, and all life, and all fulness of Life. If you would have Life naturall: you must have it of him. If you would have Life Spirituall, you must have it from him. If you would have Life Eternall you must have it from him. If you Would have Life Metaphoricall, a flourishing prosperous State, a Virtuous, and pleasant Life: If Towns, Societies, Churches, and Families, etc., would be in a peacefull, pleasant, glorious, aimiable, Lovely, Thriving, Flourishing State, and Condition, they must go to Christ. . . .[27]

Life is likewise to be understood as a synecdoche, merely a part of the whole scheme of existence, and as a type, merely a thing without meaning until linked with its antitype, the other world.

As with the uses of such in literature, they are not to be taken seriously in and of themselves. Like life itself, they have no meaning except as they are related by one's imagination (one's faith) to the whole truth. The art of art is therefore suspect to Taylor. Any poetic device is, as life itself is, "a poore, weake, beggarly, Inefficacious and foolish thing," as Taylor put it, and yet God works through such things, Taylor felt, just as he works through a man's life and the world, to test him and draw him to Him.

Working at writing, Taylor would therefore feel, with reason, that he was meditating on the meaning of his existence, the workings of his salvation. And the style of his poetry—with its heavy reliance on God-man-linking metaphors, synecdoches, and types, as mentioned in his sermons—is itself an analogy of Taylor's concept of existence and God's relation to man. In these ways his poetry was, for all of his fears about its artlessness, appropriately artful.

These few references to literary matters in his sermons, along with those which show his singing resulting from his sacramental joy (discussed below), reveal how naturally imbedded in his religious affections his tendency to write poetry was. This meager poetic theory, to be sure, was not the intent of any of his prose. His purpose was to define and praise his Lord.

Chapter 5

Gods Determinations: Taylor's Monument to the Covenant

The Voice of th'Turtle's heard o'rland within
For th'Gospell Golden Trumpet loud'gainst Sin
In Gospell Sermons Gospell Preachers make,
Painting the Hellish nature sins do take.
And Absolute need to be freed there from,
If otherwise Perdition follows there upon.
They also teach the right way to escape,
And to avoide the dread Eternall Lake
And this accursed thing; Christ & his grace
The onely means to help us in this case.
                    "A Valediction to the Whole World"

The largest consideration in this discussion has been given to Taylor's meditative poetry (and the light shed on it by both the facts of his life and the features of his sermons) and we must return to it as the best work that he produced. But some consideration must also be given his two lesser, if much larger, works, *Gods Determinations* and *A Metrical History of Christianity*. Like the *Preparatory Meditations*, both are collections of poems carefully unified by tone and argument, though interesting as poetry in a very different sense.

Gods Determinations[1] is the poetry of a man in love with his church and its members. It is poetry of piety, poetry of praise for a plan of salvation, evangelical poetry of covenant theology, the work of a poet-minister. Not exactly merely the versified doctrine that Louis Martz finds nor the best guide to Taylor's poetic achievement that Norman S. Grabo insists it is,[2] the poetry of *Gods Determinations* is, more moderately, an appealing call by Taylor to his congregation to believe and belong.

Taylor uses what skill he has to give his piety some drama in this long work, suggesting as his Meditations do that he conceived of his faith for the most part in active, dramatic terms. It suggests that his Puritan faith was made alive by conflicts between forces of good and evil, in fact, by life conceived as "Combat." The structure of the poem is more nearly that of narrative than it is dramatic or didactic,[3] as suggested by the four stages of the title:

[1] Gods Determinations touching his Elect:
[2] and the Elects Combat in their Conversion,

[3] and Coming up to God in Christ
[4] together with the Comfortable Effects thereof.

(GD 384)

Its purpose is to show the Puritan plan of salvation in action. Just as the Meditations show the individual Puritan actively engaged in a determined scheme of salvation, warming cold theology with his personal agonies and desires, so *Gods Determinations* shows the elect collectively engaged in becoming full members of the church. Within the static form of the Fall, a condition of which Taylor is a consistently morbid apologist, his hope of salvation was an active factor, as he is trying to demonstrate in *Gods Determinations*. The work is Taylor's testimony of the progressive, humanistic, liberating features of conservative Christianity. For all of its narrow parochialism, it is the best poetic defense in American literature of covenant theology.

The work, a 2,107-line series of thirty-five interlinked poems in eleven different verse forms, was not circulated or submitted for publication, as far as we know, in Taylor's lifetime. It is the work, however, in which Taylor is most conscious of a specific audience. Its audience is one Taylor needs to convince of the glories of conversion.[4] The issue that Taylor is taking on is the perennial ministerial one of a lack of converted membership, and it would have been easy for him to have been bitter about New England's failure to replenish itself with saints, or derisive of the laziness of the half-way members in Westfield, or argumentative with the Stoddardean dissenters of the valley. Instead, he chose to put his poetry in the form of elaborate praise of a plan and hyperbolic hope for his New England neighbors for succeeding at the plan. Quite the opposite of Wigglesworth's *Day of Doom* or Mather's *Magnalia*, two works with much the same purpose, Taylor's work is a tease glorifying the Day of Grace to come.

Its address to a particular audience of a particular time is, however, the main feature which gives it historical, and not much universal, importance as poetry. Its tone can easily put one off. While Taylor no doubt intended it as a comprehensive statement justifying God's ways to man, it succeeds only in describing the late seventeenth-century New England minister's ways toward half-hearted believers.

Gods Determinations is drier than Taylor's meditative poetry

because the drama in it is thinner. The tense conflicts of man's life are
spread out and dogma allowed in where it is kept out by the anxieties
of the persona of the Meditations. The institution of the church itself
almost entirely replaces the soul of man as the stage on which life's
dramas are played out.[5] What is alive in this work is the church, and
that is, in outline, dull. Taylor tries to counterbalance the dogma with
allegory, narrative, dialogue, and most successfully, with humor. The
doctrine of his poems was sweet to him, and he tried to create a tone
and a language for *Gods Determinations* that would be pleasing. In
Gods Determinations Taylor is taking on the task of making dramatic some ideas that are both well known and foregone conclusions.
He hopes to make them sweet. If he entertains the members with his
sweet verse, he believes, he will convert them. Their delight in the
language of his verse would amount to acceptance of the hard terms
of salvation he sells.

The Taylor of *Gods Determinations* is not the Taylor of either the
Meditations or the *Metrical History*. Here he is somebody else. In his
Meditations, Taylor uses poetry as a means for playing a role;
language made escape from his public self possible. It is the most
successful—and the most romantic—feature of his poetry. But in
Gods Determinations he is more nearly himself, minister at Westfield.
There is something of Taylor in each of his allegorized speakers in the
work—Justice, Mercy, Satan, Christ, Soul, and Saint—but the main
voice is Taylor's own, energetic, self-righteous, optimistic, pontifical,
wordy, witty. Whatever the epical, allegorical, dramatic, or lyrical
pretensions of much of the language of *Gods Determinations*, it is
mostly the preaching Taylor that we hear.

What is imaginative about his point of view in *Gods
Determinations* is Taylor's ability to play simultaneously preacher
and members of the congregation being preached to. In this one
work he can be both the individual struggling to know his election (a
voice that is sometimes close to that of the Meditations):

My Sweet Deare Lord, for thee I'le Live, Dy, Fight.
    Gracious indeed! My Front! my Rear!
    Almighty magnify a Mite:
        O! What a Wonder's here?

Had I ten thousand times ten thousand hearts:
    And Every Heart ten thousand Tongues;

> To praise, I should but stut odd parts
>   Of what to thee belongs,

                                                    (GD 418)

and also the minister working to encourage him in that struggle:

> Perform the Duty, leave th'event unto
> His Grace that doth both in, and outside know.
> Beg pardon for your Sins: bad thoughts defy,
> That are Cast in you by the Enemy.
> Approove yourselfe to God, and unto his
> And beg a pardon where you do amiss.
> If wronged go to God for right, and pray [,]
> Hard thoughted Saints [,] black thoughted thoughts away.
> Renew your acts of Faith: believe in him,
> Who died on the Cross to Cross out Sin.

                                                    (GD 444)

His voice does not go to the extremes it does in his meditative poems; we hear neither the anguish nor the ecstasy. For all of its variety, the tone is a more moderate one, one appropriate to Taylor's story of mankind making its way via the church from fall to glory without the sinful extremes of either excessive pride or excessive humility.

The story of *Gods Determinations* is the old Biblical-Puritanic-Miltonic narrative of fall and salvation, though with a marked New England difference. "The Preface," really an integral introduction to the whole of *Gods Determinations*, begins the work, conventionally enough, with an epical statement of thanksgiving for the joyous abundance of the Creation and the benevolence of the Creator (the "Infinity," the "all"); it outlines the structure of the Puritan universe in terms of simple extremes (high and low, light and dark, all-sufficiency and insufficiency) and ends with an announcement of the dilemma that gave a Puritan's life its vitality: with the Fall, man has become "Darker by far than any Coalpit Stone" and therefore stands in need of "Glory." The Puritan struggle from fall to glory, Taylor wants to inform his audience at the outset, is not only vitalizing but also man's only means of glorifying God: "Through nothing man all might him Glorify."

Taylor gives his story a setting by first describing the fallen condition of man; it is the frame for the evolving drama. "This poore fallen mans estate," to Taylor, is best described in terms of an overwhelm-

ing military assault of satanic forces on man and his resulting panic.
"Armies of armed terrours" reduce him to a madman, a child, a
"Lifeless life": "he liveth in/A Dying Life, and Living Death." As part
of this setting, two ballooning personifications, a raging Justice and a
perfumed Mercy, determining forces of man's fate, debate man's
savability in military and commercial terms. Justice represents the
satanic side of the divine (man must be attacked for his guilt) and
Mercy the savior side (man can be bought free of his guilt) that make
up man's determined condition.

The unique feature of the setting is that from beginning to end,
however, it is really that of a New England church service, demand-
ing that we see the entire debate over man's salvation in *Gods
Determinations* not on a cosmic scale at all but an ecclesiastical one:
Taylor wants a full house of testifying members. This is suggested by
his play throughout on the word "coach." His audience is one that
must be "Coacht along," achieving salvation through him as their
minister. The church itself is a "Royall Coach," a churchhouse with
scarlet canopy, silver pillars, golden-paved floor, and lined "inside
o're with lovely Love." And then once thoroughly in the church, the
congregation is encoacht for heaven:

> For in Christ's Coach Saints sweetly sing,
> As they to Glory ride therein.

(GD 459)

It is only in *the* church and *in* church and *under* Taylor as minister,
and especially through the "mighty sumptuous feast" of the sacrament of the Lord's Supper, that salvation, as the entire work argues,
is possible. If we are anywhere specific in the poem, we are in church,
and the scope of the poem is diminished by this small stage. *Gods
Determinations* is remarkable for being good poetry made from the
narrowest of perspectives.

When man appears in this setting in Taylor's narrative, "this Lapst
Estate," he comes on first as a childish, inconstant, lost player of
parts. His costume is filthy rags: "He [in] his skirts with Guilt, and
Filth out peeps." His makeup makes an exaggerated mask: "He . . .
out peeps/With Pallid Pannick Fear upon his Cheeks." He walks on
as, "at very best,/A Cripple." His gestures are pathetically melo-
dramatic: "He . . . With Trembling joynts, and Quiverring Lips, doth
quake." His speeches stutter and annoy, "tabbering on the Drum

within the eare." His stage-presence is poor: "His spirits are so low they'l scarce afford/Him Winde enough to wast a single word/Over the Tongue into one's eare." His part is altogether pathetic: "[His] tale at last with sobs, and sighs [he] lets goe." (GD 398–400)

Over against man's silly character we have, of course, the various personifications of God's love, and that transforms the narrative into one filled with hope. In the love which membership in the church offers (the offer, as Taylor would have it, of a free and pleasant ride to a heavenly feast), man's life takes on a pre-planned possibility that his natural fallen condition does not afford. If he is hungry rather than nauseated at the call to eat as the Lord bids, his life then has a dramatic possibility—and the possibility of drama. Though weak, man has in the church and its sacraments a prevenient love that gives him worth. Of God's determinations (his will) there are two that dominate Taylor's story, just as he believed they dominate a man's life: the Fall and God's love.

The main plot in Taylor's story—coming after setting, character, and conflict have been introduced—centers on getting the predestined elect converted, that is, in the coach and at the feast. It is a subject only a minister would attempt to elevate to the level of poetic drama. "Grace . . . calls them all" to full church membership, "and sweetly wooes," but only "Some won come in, the rest as yet refuse,/And run away." Those who flee are pursued by Mercy and Justice; some are caught and the others cornered. One way or another one's election finds him: grace, like it or not, is irresistible.

The plot thickens when Satan starts raging at and Christ starts pleading with the congregation of elect. It is not very thick, however, since neither can have much effect on God's determinations for the elect, except to move them to its recognition of itself: "Gods Mercy taking place,/Prepared Grace for us, and us for Grace." In the contest Satan loses, of course, both ideologically and dramatically. He fumes and puffs but has no mind; he is alternately trite ("Soon ripe, soon rot. Young Saint, Old Divell") and sophistical ("The Law must breake before the Gospell binde.") Christ, on the other hand, is successful because he sings in his lyrical lines to attract the elect: it is Taylor's own approach. Satan is needed as prod to make the drama go, to provide conflict ("His barking is to make thee Cling/Close underneath thy Saviours Wing"), but there is much less drama when Taylor drops him from the story at midpoint. Satan's prodding effect is seen when he tries to influence the emotions of the various sorts of saints—distinguished in Taylor's poem by their submission to the call of their election—and is successful in moving some of them to the two debilitating extremes of their saintliness, excessive pride and excessive humility. The souls of the saints are able to withstand most of Satan's assaults—doubt of the reality of one's conversion if too easily made, suspicion of man's thoroughly perverted will, nausea at man's filthiness, annoyance at man's laziness, worldliness, and hypocrisy—but they fall quite easily into the two sins of saintliness: self-satisfaction and self-denial.

The drama of Taylor's story becomes less, however, as it centers more on the saint in his congregation, which is the direction of the narrative. Satan is virtually removed from the scene (with his "Ath'istic Hoodwinke") and Christ finishes singing his love songs ("Peace, Peace, my Hony, do not Cry"). The soul of the saint is left to carry on a long series of dialogues with itself over the issue of the desirability of conversion, and Taylor comes in as long-winded, but gentle, admonishing minister. The great issues of man's salvation have been brought down to this; what began with the Creation in Taylor's scheme has finished in the meeting house at Westfield (which he then identifies, rather presumptuously, with heavenly glory). That is the structure of *Gods Determinations*—and of much of Taylor's thinking—and it is esthetically disappointing.

Taylor's congregation has become too smug and too timid to convert as he wants them to: this is what he has been working around to saying. His congregation is caught in the characteristic Puritan dilemma that Hawthorne loved to dramatize, between the Scylla of presumptuousness and the Charybdis of despondency. Either they have "A Forward Will joyn'd with a froward minde" and are smug or have become timid with their "Low esteeming of [them]selves." Both attitudes are destructive of the preparationism Taylor held as the keystone to real faith in New England. The one encourages a self-satisfied arrogance that prevents working at discovering God's will and one's worth; the other brings on simple discouragement:

> Converts new . . .
> Stand gazing much between two Passions Crusht [:]
> Desire, and Feare at once which both wayes thrust.

> (GD 455)

In the soul's dialogues with itself, hope and mercy win out, but not before it has had several Jobean quarrels with the flesh ("thou [hast] become . . . A Slave unto a Durty Clod of Clay") and with God Himself ("We humbly beg, oh Lord, to know our Crime/That we thus tortur'de are before our time"). Taylor is, however, on the side of simple orthodoxy; the faithful members of the Westfield congregation (personified as "Saint" for Taylor's story) are the main force bringing the soul to strong faith. They move him to the moderate faith Taylor is advocating, working as a congregation might work on a reluctant believer, encouraging him in his soul-searching, disciplining him in his sinful tendency, loving him until he is like themselves.

The climax of Taylor's narrative of the progress of a Puritan's soul comes when he is brought into full church fellowship. It is then that the voice of the persona of the Meditations takes over briefly:

> I strove to soar on high. But oh! methought
> > Like to a Lump of Lead my sin
> Prest down my Soul; But now it's off, she's Caught
> > In holy Raptures up to him.
> Oh! let us then sing Praise: methinks I soar
> Above the stars, and stand at Heavens Doore.
>
> (GD 451)

This suggests that if the Meditations were to be inserted into the scheme of salvation that makes up Taylor's narrative in *Gods Determinations* at any point, it would be here, near the end, that they belong. The desire and anxieties of the individual believer are what Taylor is best at dramatizing.

This preparational meditating is cut short, however, by the intrusion of the ministerial Taylor into the narrative to bring it to its close. The last five poems of the work show Taylor looking down on his congregation of saints, glorying in their conversion, their unity, their charity, their faith, and smiling happily at them. Harmonious singing is his metaphor for the salvation they have achieved. To demonstrate this theme of congregational unity at the end, he brings together his main metaphors from throughout the work: the "Almighty ALL," the lowliness of man ("Can I ever tune those Melodies/Who have no tune at all?"), the church as coach and feast, and the overwhelming sweetness of Christ, grace, church, and heaven. All of these are dominated by the singing—the saints', the soul's, Taylor's own. And

the whole story ends with the scene of Taylor leading his congregation in singing hymns of praise. In this way they "rise" to glory.

It is curious to find that the purpose of this poetry was to move
colonists to church membership. Though it is instructive to find this
to have been one of the motives for poetry in seventeenth-century
New England, it is hardly one of the usual purposes for poetry in the
canonized history of our literature. Though at the end of the poem
the saints transcend the world as they ride to glory, this is hardly
poetry of anything like mysticism.[6] And because the issues of the
work are tied to a place and time, it is not quite poetry, either, that is
descriptive or analytical of Puritan doctrine.[7] It is best thought of as
congregational church poetry. From his perspective, Taylor no doubt
thought he was writing something less than epic or dramatic poetry
but certainly more than mere sectarian verse. Yet that is the final
result. For him a poetry that directed one into the church was a
poetry that directed one to the fullest life and the only salvation.
Perhaps this suggests that Taylor's view of public poetry was too low,
too issues-oriented, quite provincial.

There is one point in *Gods Determinations* in which Taylor mentions a floral setting that is "Disciplinde / With Artificiall Angells" but
which he hopes to make "by Art Excell." One might well believe that
that was his intention with this sectarian verse: to turn the artificial,
the formal, the schematized into the excellent, the delightful, the
inviting, the desirable, by the efforts of art. He wanted to dignify the
covenant with poetry. He wanted to make it sweet.

In this light, the formal features of *Gods Determinations* are
relatively insignificant except as they make an analogy. The pleasing,
formal correctness of the poems of the work is really what the work is
about. The ragged, craggy primitivism of the Meditations would
have been improper, indecorous, too informal for a work of literature that must represent the scheme of salvation in the church. The
institution, not the individual soul, has become the focus of religion
for this work—though Taylor would have argued there is no
difference. The greater respect for precise rhymes, neat couplets and
quatrains (for the most part), balanced arguments, and the well-
planned direction of the narrative suggests the institution of the
church itself. The reading of *Gods Determinations* trains one for a
sweet acceptance of—not God, life, or self—but of the scheme of
salvation that the church represents.

But perhaps this poetry has its importance not so much in taking us back effectively to the Connecticut Valley of the 1680s with that era's concern for maintaining the covenant,[8] as in showing one example of the hard work of the first century that went into what Hawthorne, Melville, and Emily Dickinson were to identify as the very grain of the American character: the creating of a morbid, hope-filled self-consciousness, an alert and anxious attention to spiritual nuance, a life-dominating watchfulness, a spiritualized masochism. When Taylor writes,

> Poor Soul, Come then begin:
> Make known thy griefe: anatomize thy sin.
> Although thy sins as Mountains vast do show,
> Yet Grace's fountain doth these mountains flow.

> (GD 434)

the "darker" side of American literature has its beginning.

The darker side is, in Taylor's hands, humility ritualized, self-searching formalized, and in an idiom that had remained virtually unchanged for more than a century. How it became built into the early New England character we can never entirely know. But we do have the example of Taylor, working artfully to implant it firmly. This effect was not made by the daily facts and tensions of the colonists' lives themselves but by the literature, and Taylor is one of the makers of this darker side. The paradox is that this emphasis should have resulted from works, like Taylor's *Gods Determinations*, that are so sweet in tone and pleasing in their earnestness.

Almost all of Taylor's writings were an impassioned defense of church covenants, particularly of visible preparation for full membership. For three decades he worked to move his congregation—if not, by extension, the whole of New England—to a concern for the quality of one's attitude toward one's determined soul, a concern for one's acceptability before the highest spiritual standards, a concern for the ways in which one's personal life fulfilled the covenant of the New England settlement. Gradually he became "an island of orthodoxy" in New England, however, though no one had worked harder and longer—and, if his writings are an accurate indication, more exclusively of other interests—to establish this dark feature in the lives of the colonists.[9] *Gods Determinations* is a monument to that effort.

Chapter 6

A Metrical History of Christianity: Taylor & the New England Legacy

this world doth eye thy brightness most
When most in distance from thyselfe. . . .

(2.21)

Taylor should be known for prolixity rather than paucity of output. He has, for example, eight whole sermons on one Biblical metaphor, no fewer than 468 now-published pages defining the divine corporeality of Christ, some 220 poems on one ordinance of the church, the Lord's Supper, and, most prodigious of all, a single poem of 19,864 lines on the horrors of Christian history to the sixteenth century, his *Metrical History*.

That Taylor could sit on the American frontier in the latter part of the seventeenth century and compose so many lines of verse for a poem on medieval history is surprising. The rest were making new lives for themselves and dying of adventure while he was making doggerel with which to hold on to a world that was near an end. He probably intended its publication to the faithful and faithless of his time, but it was never finished. It is easily the longest poem in the first century-and-a-half of the history of American literature.

The manuscript of his long poem (nearly half the verse he wrote) he bound up in 1710, and it passed from descendant to descendant for almost two hundred years and then was found in an attic in Enfield, Connecticut, in 1905. It came to the Redwood Athenaeum in Newport, Rhode Island, in 1933 and then to light in 1957.[1] The title page and the first leaves are missing, as are quite a number of leaves from near the end. For purposes of identification it has been named *A Metrical History of Christianity*—not a very Tayloresque title.[2] It should be known as *Taylor's Book of Christian Horrors; or, New England's Legacy*.

The sources of the poem are the *Magdeburg Centuries* (*Ecclesiastica Historia Integra Ecclesiae*) by Luther's pupil Matthias Flacius (1520–75) and the *Actes and Monuments* of the diligent Protestant martyrologist John Foxe (1516–87). In the seventeenth century, these were two of the most reactionary writers of church history from a Protestant point of view. Taylor had the first six volumes of the former and the three-volume 1610 edition of the latter in his extensive library. Out of these sources Taylor made a poem that documents, in catalog fashion, the pagan and Catholic persecutions from the year 35 to 1101 and then the emergence of Protestantism in the sixteenth century.[3] Most of his poem is a paraphrase, at beginning and end, of Foxe and, for the body of the work, a rendering into English and into verse of large sections of the *Magdeburg Centuries*.[4] But the often awkward and sometimes colorful language as well as the elaborate uses of historical facts and figures to praise God's justice, patience, and grace are largely Taylor's own. It is a poem which describes a side of Taylor that is bickering, crude, verbose, maledictory, excessive, and full of love of a stern God.

Taylor's name is nowhere on the manuscript, yet his stamp is everywhere. It is on the devotion with which the world is mistrusted and the devotion with which God is praised. It is on his Puritan penchant for extravagant language and his insatiable desire for the apocalyptic. It is on the scatalogical denigrations ("tumble him in stincking sincks") and the sexual language of redemption ("The Heavens send Jerusalem/New like a bride adorned down then/Heart Ravishingly"). It is on the use of Justice vs. Grace for a life-organizing device, as in *Gods Determinations*, and the celebration of faith as an esthetic apprehension of the things of the world and the things of God, as in the *Preparatory Meditations*. His stamp is on the Leicestershire dialect (as seen in his rhymes: whereby/destroy, thick/yet, woe/do, drought/brought) and the archaic diction ("for feare his sight/Should run a Snick-Snarles," "forth springd rich beams of light," "Her glory out so bright rubd up hereby"). It is on the earthy images ("Waggon loads might here/Be Summed up," "But now to turn from Roman Dishwater," "Africa, thy glory too doth pickled ly,/In briny tears") and the incongruent levels of usage ("Grace, Patience, Justice, Rich Efficiency/and Truth Divine trod under foot/By Wickedness, shine sparklingly,/This makes my Hymns thus toote"). It is on the mixed metaphors and the homely conceits and the contentious ministerial humor and the eagerness to use language to show his delight in the hard matters of his faith.

Taylor's authorship is, then, unmistakable. There was no one else in early New England who would have made such a poem. It is marked throughout by his curious and impatient temperament, and his reputation in American literary history is marred by its macabre monstrousness. Yet for all of the marks of identification, the poem was written by a different Taylor from the Taylor of the Meditations. It will for that reason perhaps be all the less interesting.

When Taylor wrote his *Metrical History* is difficult to establish. The extensive use to which he put Flacius in his 1679 sermon "A Particular Church is God's House" (where he calls his source the *Magdeburgenciun Centuriators*) and the absence of any further use in his other prose suggests that he may have made the poem sometime before he began the writing of his Meditations in 1682. He put his Flacius to a different use for that sermon—for examples of pre-parationism in the early church—but he quotes and paraphrases some of the same material in both works. This appears to have been the period when he had his most serious interest in Christian history.[5]

Taylor's purpose in writing the poem is in part Flacius' and Foxe's—to fight the threat of Roman Catholicism.

> Oh! Monstrous Elves! Curst Papists! Bloody Fry!
> Shall Malice Stifle all Humanity?
> Oh! Firy Serpents! Hellish Crew! nere Cloi'de
> With Blood, and Fire! Venom Unsatisfide.
> Those Sparks that fly from Martyring flame will fall
> In burning flakes from Hell upon you all
> Unless you do repent.
>
> (P. 412)

To be sure, the Catholic threat was extremely remote from New England at the time, but, as with Communism today, it gave a Puritan a name and a place for his devil.[6] But Taylor had an additional—and more important—purpose. His main hope was to get the faithful to stay faithful, by demonstrating how many saints and martyrs had given their lives for the church.

> history doth thus complain
> There was no day wherein no man was slain.
>
> (P. 6)

The suffering, even martyrdom, of the saints of the New World was, we might believe he felt, simply an extension of God's justice, patience, and grace in the events and lives of the Old. In minatory fashion, Taylor wants the mighty examples of the past visible to his own people:

> These were some Organs of those glorious Beames
> That Grace did scatter in her shining gleams
> Ore all the World more Choice than golden streames
> > Our souls to save
>
> That in these Rayes we might attracted rise
> In Soule above the Pavement of the Skies
> Unto the Palace of Eternall joyes
> > In blissful Waves.
> > > (P. 102)

and he wants the horrors of the past taken as mighty warnings:

> Those that reject the Gospell Grace shall finde
> The Sword of Justice is for them design'd.
> > (P. 5)

Christianity occupied Taylor's own depths, and he hoped to prolong its career with the anxieties it would provoke and the solutions it could awaken in others. It was no doubt comforting to juxtapose over against the disorders of the world the coherence of Christian troubles and tribulations.

A reason for putting his historical materials into verse was to give them an entertaining form, as with the writing of *Gods Determinations*. That is the function of his rhythm and rhyme. The result is for the most part dull doggerel, for the form dominates his subject (Taylor will say almost anything to secure his meter and rhyme), but Taylor wanted to make the catalog of persecutions and martyrdoms that he relates *attractive* to his wilderness saints.

> Sweet Truth I come at last to Kiss thy Hand
> > With maimed Sapphicks crippled
> My dull Pentameters do stand
> > Wrinckled and rippled.
>
> I in thine Honour do ingague my quill.
> > My very Heart I truely mean.

These muddy puddles to fulfill
Thy Holy breathes Veans.

(P. 314)

He felt that giving lists of historical events a pleasing form would
make it easier for his wilderness saints to delight in the hard will of
God. His own faith was strong in this regard—he had moved his own
religious affections with the sensuous devices of his *Meditations*—and he felt that he could move others with something
of the same. As a Puritan trapped in an esthetic suspicious of the
sensuous, Taylor was doomed to failure in his efforts, as Wigglesworth was with his *Day of Doom*, yet for years he tapped out his lines
and hunted for his rhymes in order to make the hard will of God more
delightful by means of his verse. Poetry thus assisted his ministerial
duties.

At a few points in his long and disjointed narrative, Taylor is
capable of rendering his material fairly interesting. For example, he
gives a number of the dying martyrs lively conceits:

[Knight Sebastian] bravely said,
As white bread for the royall Table's made
By bolting fine the floure from bran, intire
And use of Water baking't then with fire
So I[,] ground in the mill of th'Word Divine
Within the Church and sifted in the fine
Lawn Sive Repentance and wet well also
In Baptism, bakd with the firy glow
O'th'Holy Ghost, a Christian right am made,
If then this Loafe again in finest trade
Be ground and wet afresh and better bee
I'le do what shall seem good to thine and thee.
This answer though it silenc't him a while
Yet soon he 'stroyes him by another wile.

(P. 113)

His homely language often adds humor to his characterizations:

Then Heliogabalus that greedy gut
In the Imperiall Throne of gold did strut,
The Miror of Excess, the Prodigy
Of Gluttony and filthy Ribauldry,
His Cloaths of Gold and costly Silks, his Shooes

Glistered with pretious Stones they did, did use
To ware no garment twice nor twice one fare.
Sometime they for his palate did prepare
The tongues of Popingais, and birds that sung
Most sweetly for him disht up, to him come
Five thousand Fowles, six thousand fishes lie
Serv'd at one Supper up (oh! Luxury).

.   .   .   .

                          and when he
Learned by his Wizzards that his death should bee
By violence silk halters got he did
To hang himself, and Golden Swords to rid
Himselfe therewith.

.   .   .   .

And border'd too with pretious stones from which
He is assaild then ment himselfe to pitch
Down headlong and destroy himselfe. At last
He's slain, dragd through the town, in Tiber cast.

                                          (P. 32)

Taylor even shows himself capable of versifying doctrinal arguments
interestingly:

Pelagius an Englishman up dresst
His dirty Cookery in East and West
That man was born with nature pure from sin,
Not Adams falt or stain was found in him,
And that his Will was free and also could
With offerd grace get glory, if he would.

                                          (P. 107)

Taylor's macabre humor also assists him in making the hard will of
God acceptable. Though he catalogs many of the horrors of Christian history with a heavy solemnity in his poem, Taylor is often
frivolous about "The Dismall things" of the past. It is the form his
own delight takes in the way God's will works itself out. Cosmic
disturbances are exciting occasions. The terrors of the globe are
events in a divine comedy. Killings, rapes, deposings, disfigurings,
diseases, burnings at the stake, genocide—all are a marvelous carnival. Chaos and confusion are directed by the delightsome will of
God. The smallest sadism restores his faith.

Because of this eagerness to delight in his God, it does not bother Taylor to describe the "Bloody Colours" of history with grotesque humor. When for example the Alexandrian Amachius martyred a number of Christians in 365, Taylor says they were

> rosted on the gridiron, Whence they spake
> With Valient Courage to him, on the Grate
> Wouldst thou eate roast meat, Amachy, turn first
> Us on the other side, lest that for rost
> We seem to be halfe raw unto thy tast
> And thus this doome they nobly embrac't.
>
> (P. 72)

Justinian's cruelties in 528 are similarly made light of:

> [He] did well begin
> A cruell punishment on varlets fling
> And upon Pederasts, for off he parde
> Their Genitalls as things that might be sparde. . . .
>
> (P. 168)

He enjoys laughing over the mean and depraved:

> Another filthy trick at Rome was this
>   They tooke her that was taken in
> Playing the Whore and forc'd much worse amiss
>   They beastly use in Stews, and ring
>   A bell while there they do the thing.
>
> (P. 88)

Taylor's witty language betrays the delight he takes in the productive providence he sees in such hellish things:

> With Envy, Malices Curdling into Curd
> And Whea the Gospell Dary up to fill
> The Serpents Cheesfat presst with hellish skill
> In Cheeses for his Table. . . .
>
> (P. 103)

After relating many such cruel matters with some relish, whether expressly for "the Gospell Dary" or otherwise, Taylor can rejoice:

> And thus we see the milke white glorious streams
>   Of justice shining in these Instances. . . .
>
> (P. 187)

He reminds us that such things, though horrifying to man, are
supposed to be understood delightfully, for that is the way they were
intended:

> we'st finde
> Gods Patience in the Same most clearly shin'd
> The glory of it now doth seem so thick
> As if he did alone delight in it. . . .

(P. 77)

In these several ways Taylor hoped to attract his wilderness saints to
a reading and understanding of the will of God as revealed in
Christian history.

Beyond whatever purpose Taylor might have had himself for
writing his poem, one may find it of interest today only in its view of
history. Here we find out something about the Puritan mind. Taylor's
historiography is representative of New England's: it has none of the
Renaissance historian's interest in the past for its own sake but all of
the medieval historian's interest in the past for the sake of his theology. Though looking for a Puritan view of history through the pages
of Taylor's *Metrical History* may make one more interested in Puritan pathology than in Puritan theology, still one may learn something
about the relationship between the image of time and the image of
place in their minds, that is, the relationship between what they
thought they were doing as Puritans in the New World—or at least
what *Taylor* thought they were doing—and the rest of Christian
history before them.

Lacking faith in vertical revelation, Taylor read history, whether
Biblical or secular, as horizontal revelation—and one of the main
revelations of truth available to man. The divine shines through
history, so Taylor felt he had discovered, in three ways—through
what he calls God's Justice, God's Patience, and God's Grace. These
gave his poem its organization and made a definition of the will of
God for him. The poem therefore becomes an example of man
apprehending God through human and natural history. This could
have been its main importance to Taylor, just as the hope of apprehension of the divine was the motive behind his Meditations.

Taylor's dominant metaphor for this revelation is what he calls
"Shines."

And thus we se Gods glorious sparkling shine
    By various Providences gleam.
Though sometimes Clouds do seme to dim the time,
    Yet soon the Beams of justice beam
    With Wisdom, Patience, Grace a stream.

                                                (P. 88)

The metaphor of a shining light is the main unifying device of the poem and it shows, as it does in Edwards, how Taylor longed for the discoverability of the divine in some physical feature of the world. Light to Taylor is to be found everywhere in this dark world if one has the faith wherewith to see it. In this quasi-Lockean view of history, God emanates forth as light on certain events and persons, and the man of faith, the justified man, is made receptive to that light through his faith. Just as the sun shines forth on many objects of the physical world and the eye of man beholds them as it is intended they be seen, so the light of God shines forth on the past and the spiritual eye sees the meanings intended. This is of course to Taylor an intellectual process, rather than the sensuous one it was to be later with Edwards, and one in which one seeks out those items of the past which best justify his convictions. The historian, as usual, reads the past in the light of his assumptions and justifies them thereby. History to Taylor, as it shines forth to his intellect, is therefore not something to forgive or to wake up from, as it might be to a modern historian, but something to read as proof of one's faith.

    Sections on the Shine of Justice, the Shine of Patience, and the Shine of Grace balance each other through most of Taylor's poems. For the most part each of these has its own stanza form (the *a b a b c c* stanza of the Meditations for Justice, couplets for Patience, and a more mellifluous *a a a b* stanza or the *a b a b b* stanza for Grace); each tends to have its own sound pattern (cacophonous, stern, and more lyrical, respectively); and each has its own light imagery (from dark to light). They are to Taylor three ways of justifying the ways of God to man. They are the three faces of God.

    By the Shine of Justice, Taylor means the God that scourges man and scours the earth, a cruel Yahweh that deals in perversion and punishment, an executioner and monster that destroys what he creates and condemns what he loves. In the figure of Justice, Taylor assigns God all the inhumanity he can imagine. To Taylor, "The Glorious Hand of Justice" is awesome and thrilling, a devouring fire, a fury that torments us. It is the form that, to him, God's own righteousness takes:

> Oh Justice Glorious, let all adore
> Thy Shining Beams scatterd the World all o're.
> Thou writest thy Glory oft in blood, in Fire,
> In water, Plagues, in Cruelties in Ire,
> Sometimes in Glory greate, and evry way,
> That all may yield unto thy Scepter sway.
>
> (P. 268)

For the section on Justice in his coverage of each century, Taylor uses his greatest poetic energy. It is obviously the side of the Puritan God of which he stood most in awe. This is seen in the fact that after lists of murders, wars, rapes, treacheries, and general destruction in each century, early or late in medieval history, Taylor can exclaim with self-satisfied, almost sadistic, glee:

> Now Justice hath her glory pollisht bright,
> Wherein her balance Stands with Equall Weights.
>
> (P. 350)

He delights in the horrors of history wherein justice is done the enemies of pure Christianity:

> Oh! Justice Bright, who will not thee adore?
>   Thou certainly, although thou long mayst stay,
> Wilt call the Wicked out to pay their score,
>   Or wilt thyselfe give unto them their pay.
>   Thou greatly art abusd under thy name
>   Much Wickedness doth pass. Oh! fy for shame.
>
> But now thou comest and blanchest thy white line
>   Quite through these darksom Clouds, dost shew thy hand
> Pure White as Snow: and that no vile design
>   Can smut thyselfe though some may thinke thee tan'd
>   Ile kiss thy milke white hand and thee adore
>   Because thou keepst for all an Eaven Score.
>
> (P. 42)

Thus Taylor's insatiable love of carrion, cruelty, and convulsion in his sections on Justice—and the obsession was widely Puritan—is the love of a God of arbitrary and absolute power, whose word is as fire, who destroys in order to establish his own glory, who as a figure in history must be respected on his own violent terms. From a non-Puritan point of view, of course, this could be seen as a love of Satan. And history then becomes an account of the devil in the world.

A second face of God in history, the Shine of Patience, is barely distinguishable from Taylor's concept of Justice:

> How should such glorious Grace in folds of Shines
> Displaid, drill all mens Lives to Holy Lines?
> And make the world like Candent Iron, or
> The Globe of Glory shine in Graces war?
> But if it be abused, or Disdain'd
> Can Vengeance sleep or Chalterd be restrain'd?
> Gods Patience then must shine as bright, so long
> As such bright shining Grace abusd bears wrong.
> And thus it plainly is while out doth blaze
> Errour, and Tyranny under these Rayes.
>
> (P. 28)

This is the God that allows, even creates and promotes contentions, heresies, and tyrannies, and also visions, healings, miracles, and other delusions—all of which Taylor calls "Patience exercised by Lying Wonders"—and all for His own amusement and entertainment. This is God seen as trickster. He often wears the mask of Satan, if only to amuse Himself, though also to provide the good with opposition. It is a secular form that the divine takes, a way that the hell of this world has heavenly purpose, even the way that Christ is at work *in* the Anti-Christ. Apparent evils are to Taylor in reality "Shines of Glory [that] Glorify. . . by their bloody Spur." Only the man of faith can see behind the mask to the glory underneath. He is not fooled by the ways of the world he finds in human history. He sees purpose in the hellishness. From this point of view, history is an account of the evil appearance that the reality of goodness often takes.

> God rules and will Secure his Glory though
> Things seem[in]gly run counterbuff thereto.
>
> (P. 314)

What to Taylor is profound and virulent in his faith is not the loving

divine but the demoniacal. God works in sadistic ways his wonders
to perform!

The Shine of Grace, on the other hand, is a sweeter chracterization
of God:

> Thy Grace, sweet Grace, is glory sparkling bright
> > That glorifies the Day wherein it shines
> In radient beams of blessed Gospell light
> > That fly from Holy Lips of true Divines
> > Not mudded with the dirt of sinfull times.

(P. 319)

It is the God that brings apocalyptic hope out of destruction, that
makes martyrs out of men, that leads the world to its orgasms of
glorified suffering—all to his own glory. In this form the divine
appears in the world in that which "Advance[s] Christs Cause,
secure[s] his truths, destroyes/His foes and puts an end to
Tyrannies. . . ." Though not entirely distinguishable from his concepts of Justice and Patience, the Shine of Grace paints the stern face
of God acceptable colors. Taylor's faith made him see all things in the
most hopeful light, and whatever proved the truth of his convictions,
however horrible or depraved, gave him reason to take pride in his
God. All is a "glorious Exercise" of God's will.

Satan is sweetness and light from this point of view. It is as if, once
he has given God a satanic function in human history (the Shine of
Justice) and once he has become aware that this is not the true nature
of God but only the way he must appear in this kind of a world (the
Shine of Patience), the Puritan becomes convinced that given this
kind of existence, the satanic God is the most believable, the most
relevant, the most justifying of his own piety, certainly the most
admirably virulent and productive, the most powerful.[7] This security
is comforting to him and it can therefore be thought of as a shining
forth of grace. The just and patient God, though satanic in shadow
and act, is to him sweet.

There are two other personifications of God in Taylor's poem
—Divine Efficiency and Divine Truth. These are brought in midway
in the poem and play roles overlapping the others in Taylor's course
of events. In both, God appears in the form of "things that hap not
ordinarily," that is, in the special providences of nature that often
stirred the Puritan's scientific curiosity and often convinced him of
the variety, colorfulness, and versatility inherent in God's power.[8] In

this we see that Taylor's view of history is not that of the anthropologist—he has, after all, little use for the normal, the mythic, the mundane—but that of the writer: history is the unusual, the bizarre, the surprising and shocking, the phenomenal. The high points of the past are to Taylor not only human accomplishments but also the accomplishments of the supernatural in such natural phenomena as earthquakes, floods, comets, fire storms, famines, plagues, deformities, diseases. He catalogs thousands of these in the course of his poem, each more curious and awful than the last. For instance, in the fourth century:

> At Antioch there plainly did appeare
> > The sign now of a Cross not Comet like
> In heaven having a larg, thick yet Cleare
> > And shining body of abundant light
> > Stretcht fifteen furlons long out in the skie
> > And answerable too in breadth, men spy.

> An Earth Quake now did shatter·many towns
> > Nice, Perinthus, Constantinople, sore
> And others too, Arsatius of renown
> > Foresaw urgd to repent, was scorn'd therefore,
> > God ruind Nice then by this Earthquake, nay
> > Fire that fell down did it in ashes lay.

> The following yeare Constantius when he dide
> > At Mopsus Wells of a strang Apoplex
> As out he went 'gainst Julian who tride
> > Now for the Empire and to play the rex
> > An Earth quake stroy'd Constantinople sore
> > And injur'd many Eastern Cities more.

> Now Julian th'Aposte wares the Crown
> > And in his scepter Vileness doth prevaile,
> Dread Earthquakes rise, throw many buildings down.
> > All things within or out doores safty faile.
> > Sore Droughts, hence scarcity of fruits up springs
> > And persons hungry eat unwholsom things.

> . . . .

> Presages 'fore this Pious Emp'rour dies,
> > Were dreadfull, Earthquakes, Rains, Dark fogs each way,

A great Ecclips 'for Pentecost surprize
    Did all the World with feare of th'judgment day.
    A Troop of Locust now about which pray're
    Cast i'th'East and West which spoild the aire.

He that beholds these things, and such as these
    Will easly see how Justice Wares her shine
In glorious Scutchons. These are golden fees
    Put in thy hand to plead her case divine
    These arguments will quite Confound all those
    That rise gainst Justice up her wicked foes.

                                                (Pp. 82–84)

And in the seventh century:

Ten dayes together fire in heavens shines
    Some say an Iris, all deem Dooms Day's nigh.
Pope Deodate dies: and for four month's time
    Th'Elements seem to breath Rome's Desteny.
    Storms thunders, Lightnings, Men, and beast do rue
    And all fruits; yet pulse spring again, ripe grew.

A Comet like a piller all aflame
    The Heavens Shew, Locusts in troops out goe
Ore Syria Mesopotamia tame
    One Callicike of Heliople, who
    Fled: saw in waters fire to burn with which
    The Romans burnt the Saracen fleet as pitch.

A mighty Earthquake shakes Mesopotame
    Much Spider-Web from heaven fell that houre
Wherein they Monothelatism tame.
    Vasupius did burn, and out did poure
    Its fires, and Ashes. And all green things 'noy.
    The Saracens Ceise Africk. Carthage stroy.

Plague, famine too pest Syria, Lybia.
    The next yeare blood is rain'd in England.
The Sixteenth day of Aprill they say
    The Moon did seem like blood till Cocks Crow. . . .

                                                (Pp. 232–33)

There is not a page in the poem where Taylor does not make history out to be an astrological spectacle, a geological carnival, a gossip's sideshow, a chaos. Taylor believes in the correspondence between such natural turmoil and human fate, believes indeed that science and theology are one: they meet in the subject of history. The terrors of the globe are presages and punishments, terrifying to relate or to anticipate and awe-inspiring to one's faith. These are God's communications to man, and a history of such phenomena is the account of God's dealings with man. Taylor's sometimes scientific eye was one searching constantly for the sight of God. The medieval view of history made it possible for him to find Him in the natural phenomena of the past.

Some of these phenomena are what Taylor calls "the excrements of time," that is, the special moments of justice and grace in a fallen world. Taylor enjoys groveling in the scatological language of these horrors. Some things, he admits, are "too shamefull for us to be told," but he tells all he can, for he is convinced that the world is God's dungheap and foulness is man's fate until he is redeemed from the Fall. Much of the *Metrical History* could be called Taylor's Scatological History of the Church, so interested is he in what strange things rulers voided, what monstrous births have been produced, what physical deformities have been created by God, how many notables died when their testicles were cut off or their innards gored or their entrails removed and tortured a hundred ways. Human history is to Taylor like "the Whore [who] on beast back in her hand / A Golden Cup held full of Filth." To him "It hath a long While filling been but yet / It will hold more." (p. 401)

In the MeditationsTaylor is eager to detach himself from the rottenness of the world, but in the *Metrical History* he reveals himself as a lover of it. Scatological language is used for the descriptions of man's wickedness, the descriptions of man's ideas, and the descriptions of God's justice. That makes it all-pervasive.

> He [Arius the Heretic] feels a Flux, asks for a Cuss-Johns-
> grace,
> And meets with one behinde the market place.
>
> He on it fainting sits and Voids his guts,
> His blood doth flush down then abundantly,
> His small roaps then come trailing out, out puts
> Much blood with's spleen and Liver; Death thereby

> This Cuss-Johns at Constantinople was
> Which folk in scorn did point at as they'd pass.
>
> (P. 81)

> When that the Arians an harlot bought
>   To Charge Eustathius the bishop choice
> Of Antioch of being with her naught
>   She rotted of a filthy sickness th'price
>   Of her Vile Wickedness, rotts quite away.
>   God will not let such pass without their pay.
>
> (P. 82)

> His unckle Julian with Chamber Lee
>   Profan'd at Antioch i'th'temple there
> Th'Communion Table, and Euzoy, when he
>   Reproov'd him, he him boxt about the eare
>   Then soon his guts did rot and's Excrements
>   He upward through his mouth, not downwards vents.
>
> (P. 83)

>   I come to Errours Hogshead now whose broach
> This Centrey had, wherewith it did approach
> And tap the same drawing her Canfulls thence
> Up to the brim all foming frothy, Hence
> I'le poure out that of Heresies, and brew
> It well with that of superstitions hew
> Now in my Urinall thereby t'divine
> The very Simptoms of this sickly time.
>
> .   .   .   .
>
> But while these nasty Dunghills send out reecks
>   Patience doth shine with lovely Cherry Cheeks.
>
> (Pp. 211–12)

The intention of the scatalogical in Taylor's other poetry is apocalytic—that is, it shows the world to be so foul that it needs a redeemer—but in the *Metrical History* there is little mention of redemption. All the world is excrement, disease, and deformity.

There is some of the scatological in both Flacius and Foxe, but most of it in the poem proceeds from Taylor's own predisposition toward anal esthetics. It comes quite easily to him to befoul the very world he belongs to. The facts of the world work against his spiritual desires, yet he is stoical about the excremental form that God's grace takes, even excited by the variety and entertainment it provides. To him, Adam fell so that man might have the life he has and man is made in such a way that he is able to find joy in his life. So an excremental existence gives the Puritan a certain kind of joy. In the scatological, we see the paradox of a Puritan's loathing of that which he enjoys and delighting in that which he loathes.

Following the example of Flacius and Foxe, Taylor saves his best obscenities for satire of the Catholic "antichristian Christianity" that he hates.

> Peters Chair at Rome begins to Crack
> By two plump Popes that croud in't bum and back. . . .
>
> (P. 105)

To his mind the church is best characterized in terms of "Romish trash," fly-blowed superstitions, a "Holy Sty," posteriors and waste. Unusually strong in his paranoid nostrils is "the Reech of Rome,"

> Whose pot is wallopping untill its Scum
> Runs in the firs, foists of each Popes Sweet bum.
> That do perfume the aire breized ore his Sea
> Some hold their nose thereat, come out, away. . . .
>
> (P. 295)

The scatological often makes Taylor's anti-Catholic spite hyperbolic. He is not content with the facts against the church the way Foxe was, nor with Protestant doctrinal claims the way Flacius was, but must often make out of his opposition to the church a dirty joke.

> The Writers pens now most are of such Vean
> As pewk out Elves of such a monstrous sise
> That Gibbits Faith, and Reason takes for lies.
> A drop of Which my pen bibd up and grew
> As Physickt, sick, and up again did't spew.
> And for the reader's sake a drop or more
> I now attempt to vomit as before.
>
> (P. 149)

History is to Taylor a drama of opposites. Christ opposes Satan. Good is possible only after Evil is experienced. And the reformed congregationalism of England and New England is pure by virtue of its difference from the filthiness of Roman Catholicism. So the scatological has a faith-promoting function.

Whatever form Taylor's God takes in history—whether personified as Justice, Patience, or Grace, or projected in the form of natural phenomena, or imagined in excremental metaphors—his God is the God of Luther and Calvin: aggressive enough to reawaken faith, demoniacal in his love, indispensable as an enemy. Taylor's uses of history in this poem show that before he can believe in the reality of salvation he must first have a perception of hell. Heaven comes afterwards as corrective and consolation. The presence of the satanic God in history, because it substantiates the world as hell, invigorates the Puritan movement toward its millennium.

In this light, Taylor's poem may be about New England Puritanism after all, even though it is never mentioned. History was to Taylor made up of the bones of saints leading up to the Protestant—and the Puritan—Reformation. Because it was left unfinished, we do not know what Taylor intended for the end of his poem, but the martyrs at the end are all English and Protestant and some of them are the heroes of the early Puritans, suggesting that Taylor was leading up to a climax with stories of the Puritan saints, and possibly including those in New England.[9] Taylor could calmly document the horrors of Christian history, for they led to the Reformation and then to The Light That Is New England and so were entirely justified. His poem was possibly meant as just such a justification.

In this, Taylor is seen to conceive of a kind of negative salvation: the awful fate of the world redeemed by the Puritan saints in the wilderness of America. The poem may have been conceived in such an attempt to graft Puritanism onto the events of history. Certainly Taylor was not above such a nationalistic obsession. If it is a poem showing Taylor haunted by the place of New England's example in history, it is then consistent with his sermons and poems, almost all of them defensive of the orthodoxy of the New England Way.

Where a mystic can leap outside of the world, Taylor, admittedly a captive of time and the world, endures and writes about the movement of time toward an end, a golden age—possibly Puritan New England. By and large, he saw the present as stasis, the end rather than the beginning of history, and all action as existing in the past. He at no point betrays an awareness of the end of history, however, for that would announce the end of the satanic, the very factor that invigorates the static condition of the past and makes the idea of a golden age possible. The cycle of successes led New England to conceive of itself as participating in such a destiny.

As a conservative Christian, Taylor found his theodicy in history. For him, history was to be explained by the Incarnation and by the revelation of God's design. For him, it moves toward a final redemption which justifies the entire panorama of human futility and chaos. From his vantage point (in the New England Zion) the falls and recoveries of human history are justified as being preparations for some final stage of salvation (like that of the New England Zion). The view reveals Taylor's submission before historical determinism.

Still, for all that it reveals about Taylor as poet and historian, the poem is embarrassing. Though its roughness of form is, as with so much that Taylor wrote, its most notable literary quality, it is in style an almost completely botched work. The doggerel makes it extremely dull. Taylor has difficulty maintaining his Justice-Patience-Grace pattern. He stumbles with his material at the end (" In this Sad Catalogue Some gleanings are/Pickt up, and out of place. . . ." "Story! Where art? What hath God Caught thee by/The Foretop Thus?"). And eventually, when he no longer has Foxe and Flacius to lean on, he gives up the poem altogether.

Furthermore, for all that it reveals about the Puritan view of history, the poem is annoyingly antihumanistic. Taylor's is a view of human history without human accomplishments. He recognizes no art or literature, no human justice or mercy, no inventions or ideas, no achievement or progress in all the world. All is, instead, God's will working itself out in the cruelest of ways: man's ugliness as God's art. The world is crap on which a few flowers of Puritan color will grow. This is the legacy that Edward Taylor saw for early America.

Chapter 7

Preparatory Meditations:
Towards a Wilderness Baroque

Of all the enjoyments of this world,
the enjoyment of this temporary life is
enjoyment of the choicest thing.

Treatise.

In contrast to *Gods Determinations* and his *Metrical History*, Taylor wrote his *Preparatory Meditations* out of the motive of personal hope, joy, and despair. Though perhaps he did not recognize it, the devices he used in these poems to move himself made them the poetry by which he is best remembered. His personal needs led him to superior esthetic ends.

That in the hallowed wilderness of early New England a few flowers of profane metaphysical wit should bloom, however sparsely, is no small miracle for American literature. Anne Bradstreet brings Christ's atoning grace wittily into her kitchen. Philip Pain, as he faces death himself, piously puns on the terms of man's mortality. Benjamin Tompson makes heavenly things comic. The anagram-mists and elegists jest their loved ones on to glory. Edward Taylor, in the midst of his meditative moments, puns about the Bread of Life that he needs. Cotton Mather baroques his way ingeniously through the history of New England's soul.

In the use of a wilderness baroque in his *Preparatory Meditations*, Edward Taylor was by no means alone. He is a climactic figure, just as Jonathan Edwards was, in the tradition of using features of the baroque in finding a way of expressing delight in what he believed.

One way of defining the shift from a baroque period of poetry in a nation's literature to a neoclassical period is to note the movement of the central interest of the poetry from metaphor to rhythm. In the earliest poetry of New England, the distinguishing feature is metaphor. In part because of the metaphoric needs of the theology, but mainly because of the personal needs of writers in the New World, it is imagery rather than structure, rhythm, or even idea that gives Puritan poetry its quality.

The passage of the baroque system of metaphor to the New World, at least its humbler ingenuities, was easy. There was often an intimate link between the "fantastic" poets of England and the emerging culture of the colonies—almost a cross-fertilization. Among the many literary practices which passed over was one which was not merely a poetic fashion but a literary means for delighting in those hard principles that drove the Puritans to make the passage in the first place. More than a fad or fashion, more than a literary convention, there appear to be personal reasons for baroque in the wilderness, reasons why metaphysical wit sometimes appears at the Puritan's most serious moments: personal disaster, communion, death.

It is not difficult to show how some of the early American verse fits into the tradition of metaphysical wit. The pious puns and wittily macabre memento mori of clerical verse, the surprising ingenuity and playfulness, the emphasis on confessional states of mind, the intellectuality of extended analogies, the heavy metaphorism and dense lines and experiments in rhythm and rhyme—all were part of a tradition which the Puritans inherited. Maybe it came easiest to mind and hand.

The philosophy of this tradition of wit, as Austin Warren has pointed out, is Christian, supernaturalist, and incarnational. It develops out of

> a philosophy which admits of miracle and transcensions of common sense, hence of surprise; its aesthetic, by appropriate consequence, endorses bold figures verbal and imaginal, such figures as the pun, the oxymoron, the paradox, the metaphor which links events from seemingly alien, discontinuous spheres. It likes audacious mixtures,—the shepherds and the magi; the colloquial and the erudite. If it provides ecstasies, it allows also of ingenuities. . . .[1]

By the middle of the seventeenth century the use of conceits and other fantastic poetic devices for spiritual fervor was, along with plain and other styles, an established convention. The meditative character of

Puritan preparationism required a meditative poetic mode. The amplification of religious affections required amplified language. The delight in the Christian comedy of salvation required a language of personal delight.

But for all the points of correspondence, New England theology and the American experience made this wilderness baroque different from British baroque. For one thing, where the tradition had been largely an aristocratic one, in American hands it becomes less and less so; courtly conventions become domesticated, manners become primitive. Further, because the theology did not hold to the integrated, mysticized universe of the Loyolan or Anglican meditative poets, the baroque conventions in the New Zion, even though practiced only a little, are taken less seriously as ideas. And too, the more meiotic view of man and the world on these shores and the corresponding greater amplification of God and glory make for a more self-conscious style, a narrower function for poetry, and what Charles Mignon calls "a more limited range of metaphoric possibility."[2] Passage to New England and conversion to the New England Way made a different kind of baroque. Written for other, humbler, more personal, less literary reasons—though also, as I want to show, for the most part for more indulgently joyous reasons—this wilderness baroque must be seen on its own small stage and with its own lights and props and language.

In many ways the age prepared for the wilderness baroque of Taylor's *Preparatory Meditations*. He would not be out of place. Even though there was much about congregational Calvinism that should have denied to the Puritan writer the services of wit, the theology and the new life in the colonies demanded it. He needed a particular mode of expression for his spiritual delights. Of these delights Perry Miller writes:

> Living was a serious business, and those who took it gaily here would come to reckoning hereafter. What made it supportable to them was not the incidental amusements along the way but the one engrossing joy of the saints' communion with the God who had made them and had redeemed them. . . . Worldly pleasures, even when permissible, turn pale before heavenly ones, and unmistakable limits were set to Puritan cheer. It could

not ever exceed a "seasonable cheerfulness.". . . . Men were
made believers by an inward gladness, and they found in their
beliefs the supreme source of joy and an inexhaustible delight.[3]

Whatever its need in England, metaphysical wit served a different
purpose in New England. In the Calvinists' (and Americans') view of
the world as being a hard and dark condition, there were few
pleasures. A humble wit was, however, one safe pleasure, not one of
much significance to be sure but nonetheless one which could help a
writer keep his chin up, express his delight, catch his fleeting, minor
ecstasies. In his consciousness of his afflictions, it helped him bear his
crosses a little better. As with a writer like Anne Bradstreet, life had
"toys (not joys),"[4] and for someone fascinated with literature and the
uses of language, metaphysical wit was one of life's more serviceable
toys. Play with it and one is cheered a little in the darkness. Use it and
one can feel his delight in the obstinate truths about his hard earthly
lot and his risky otherworldly possibilities. Make a game of it consistently, as Edward Taylor was to do in his *Preparatory Meditations*,
and one puts himself imaginatively into the bliss to which his faith
raises him out of the world. It was of importance mainly in the
Puritan's more serious moments. Calvinism was to the Puritan poet,
after all, delightful, life a comic tragedy, judgment sweet, death and
the eternity to come bliss. How could he be grim for long about such
things? Before retiring John Cotton liked to sweeten his mouth, he
said, with a piece of Calvin.[5] The Puritan poet in America sometimes
found it to his liking to sweeten his Calvin with a little bit of wit.

Metaphysical wit was also productive in New England verse, small
as the production was, because it assisted in adding the warmth and
affection of Puritan home life, the personality of individual lives, and
something of the actual daily power of early American society to the
cold logic of the theology and the earnestness of the history being
made. Though he recognized it only seldom, wit offered the Puritan
poet a means for being himself, perhaps more than when he wrote in
"the plain style." Fantastic imagery freed him from imitation and
convention a little and provided opportunities for extending the rigid
forms of his beliefs to include himself and his own experience. With a
sense of humor and a sense of language, he could, through the device
of witty metaphor, help his life play vehicle to the tenor of truth.
Metaphysical wit was in its way one more small factor in the long

move toward an American individualism made from personal perceptions of the world.

Though there is the danger of seeing a world of significance in the baroque in the wilderness (it is after all only one of a number of styles which characterize Puritan writing), one other characteristic should be noticed. If metaphors are momentary games, games in which there is some measure of individuality, then it was possible through the imagination and a little art to construct metaphoric situations in which, as in prayer, man and God come close to each other, if only in a simulation. In contradistinction to the theology, which in the main keeps God far above man and man far beneath dignity, the wittier poetry manages a superimposition, a mingling, of two concepts of the human and the divine, without any attempt to explain one by the other. A number of the Puritans called their poems meditations. And at some of their most introspective moments, with their conceits and packed lines, they imagine some kind of relationship, whether in the form of God caring for the dying and dead or in the form of the worthy imaginatively elected/seduced by Christ. It was merely a game, but an exercise of the imagination, of the spirit, in playing at communion—not forbidden, of course, because the theologically sensitive and esthetically astute writer *knew* it was play. As in the case of creating a little wit and managing some individuality in an impersonal system, the game of half-mysticism-through-fantastic-metaphor was a kind of compensation for Calvinism. What the church had not allowed for, this little bit of metaphysical wit in the poetry of early America tried to provide. However insignificant, contrived, and hyperbolic it appears to us in our own time, the Puritan's delight in the metaphors he concocted was an added dimension to the life of a Puritan.

The history of Edward Taylor's interest in metaphysical wit is well known. As a lover and friend he wrote preposterous verse acrostics, as a mourner he wrote punning elegaic verse, and as a minister he made what he preached into conceits. In his love poems of 1674, for instance, the anticipation of his sweetheart's affection moves him to conceits (his heart strings become the golden threads of a love knot and the cloth of "Loves brightest Mantle") and moves him to picture poems, with doves, hearts, triangles (the Trinity), and circles (love) made by his excited words:

This Dove &
Olive Branch to
you
Is both a Post &
Emblem too[1]
These for M[y Dove]
Tender & Onely [Love]
Mrs. Elizabeth [Fitch][2]
at her father's house in
N[orwich]

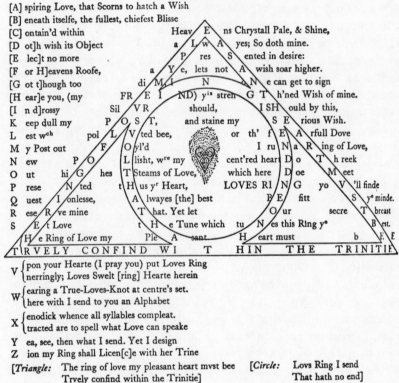

[A] spiring Love, that Scorns to hatch a Wish
[B] eneath itselfe, the fullest, chiefest Blisse
[C] ontain'd within   Heav E ns Chrystall Pale, & Shine,
[D] ot]h wish its Object   a L w A yes; So doth mine.
[E] lec]t no more   a P res S ented in desire:
[F] or H]eavens Roofe,   a Y e, lets not A wish soar higher.
[G] ot t]hough too   di M I N e can get to sign
[H ear]e you, (my   FR E ND) yᶦˢ stren G T h'ned Wish of mine.
[I n d]rossy   Sil V R should,   I SH ould by this,
K eep dull my   P O S T, and staine my   S E rious Wish.
L est wᶜʰ   pol L V ted bee,   or th' f E A rfull Dove
M y Post out   F O yl'd   I ru N a R ing of Love,
N ew   P O L lisht, wʳᵉ my   cent'red hear D o T h reek
O ut hi G hes T Steams of Love,   which here D oe M eet
P rese N ted t H us yʳ Heart,   LOVES RI N G yo V 'll finde
Q uest I onlesse,   A lwayes [the] best   B E fitt S yᵉ minde.
R ese R ve mine   T hat. Yet let   O ur   secre T brest
S E t Love   t H e Tune which tu N es this Ring yᵉ B est.
H e Ring of Love my   Ple A sant   H eart must   b E E
TRVELY CONFIND WI T HIN THE TRINITIE

V { pon your Hearte (I pray you) put Loves Ring
    nerringly; Loves Swelt [ring] Hearte herein
W { earing a True-Loves-Knot at centre's set.
    here with I send to you an Alphabet
X { enodick whence all syllables compleat.
    tracted are to spell what Love can speake
Y ea, see, then what I send. Yet I design
Z ion my Ring shall Licen[c]e with her Trine

[*Triangle:* The ring of love my pleasant heart mvst bee   [*Circle:* Lovs Ring I send
Trvely confind within the Trinitie]   That hath no end]

Similarly, in his funeral poems, Taylor's voice amid this sorrow is often cheerful. When his wife Elizabeth died in 1689, for example, he wrote a happy "mournfull Poem." His extravagant praise of his wife's virtues ("In Hyperboles her praises dress") and his enthusiastic faith in her immortality and election made a certain amount of conceiting appropriate:

What shall my Preface to our True Love Knot
Frisk in Acrostick Rhimes? And may I not

Now at our parting, with Poetick knocks
Break a salt teare to pieces as it drops?
Did Davids bitter Sorrow at the Dusts
Of Jonathan raise such Poetick gusts?
Do Emperours interr'd in Verses lie?
And mayn't such Feet run from my Weeping Eye?

(P. 473)

This is the case as well in funeral poems on friends and colleagues. His funeral extravagances include such items as an acrostic on the name of Francis Willoughby; attractive exultant phrases ("Glories flowering Pot," "Graces Garden," "Glory's Hall") anagrammatizing the name of John Allen ("The GRACES ALL ON Allen showing bright/Are calld ALL IN to bed & bid God night"); double acrostics and quadruple acrostics "whose Trible is an anagram" on the name of Charles Chauncy; and witty dominant metaphors:

But now Deaths Cickle hath thee reapt, Christ Corn,
Whom by bright Angells art to's Granry born.[7]

None of these make the poetry any better. They merely show the cheerful attitude of a man of faith.

Wit is everywhere in Taylor (really much more than in the other poets of the period) and in widely varying forms. His verses written in England and at Harvard show he might have done passing well at satire. He admired the satires of George Wither and Robert Wild. His topical poems are full of sarcastic jibes at Quakers and Catholics. He could not write love verse without playing with words or funeral verse without conceiting.

Though his meditative poems are of a different order from these, it may have been the sheer fun of such playing with language that taught Taylor how to use language in his Meditations for the purpose of enjoying his God. In them Taylor was skillful in turning the minor and tortured ingenuities of the time into something personally significant.

Few of the commentaries on Taylor's wilderness baroque give it the kind of esthetic significance it deserves. To his critics it has been variously: merely an imitation of a British fashion, merely evidence of ecstatic violence, merely brightly decorated doctrinal sophistry, or merely odd tone amid cold structure.[8] But because his poetry was written largely to satisfy personal needs, his baroque style has to be seen from the point of view of the personal needs it satisfied. Because Taylor was in large part a man of great hope and joy, his metaphysical wit must be seen for its contribution to his cheer. And because there is not anything Taylor did which was not integral to his theology, his need to conceit and his humor must be seen in *its* light.

In what way should one have to think of that in Taylor which is bizarre, sensuously vivid, tough, and witty as being part of a meditative-metaphysical-baroque tradition? To hold over against him the criteria derived for an age, a style, or a temperament, and see how his shadow falls, may define him without illuminating him.

That aspect of Taylor's style that is baroque has its roots somewhere, of course, and has parallels in instructive places—in the Loyolan theosophical tradition, in the Ramist and DuBartasian conventions of language, in George Herbert's example and Richard Baxter's encouragements. Harvey Gilman says rightly, "Taylor's simultaneous acquaintance with and freedom from the several traditions of seventeenth-centry devotional poetry enabled him to employ with no sense of anomaly any and all of the technical devices and structural features of metaphysical and baroque poetry which had flourished two generations before in pre-restoration England."[9] While references to tradition, convention, and milieu flesh out Taylor's esthetic, the danger is that in any comparison, Taylor will be seen more for what he is not. He had personal needs to be met.

Louis Martz has provided the best approach for realizing the philosophical and theological justifications for Taylor's baroque. His approach is historical: religious forces from the Reformation and counter-Reformation converged to give Taylor a familiar style.[10] From the meditation movements of the sixteenth and seventeenth centuries there undoubtedly came to Taylor: an order for his thoughts, the opportunity to use language in his search for signs of grace, the practice of dramatizing theological points, the justification for his desperate colloquies with God, the freedom of a colloquial style, and a way of accepting the symbolism of earthly things. As a comparison with his other verse shows, the discipline and formal rules of meditation, more than anything else, made Taylor into a real poet. This cannot be emphasized too strongly.

But the mysticism of the meditative method is missing from

Taylor's style.[11] For a methodically meditative man, Taylor is gross and excessive in both attitude and style. He either did not know how to practice Loyolan meditation or he practiced it too well. The loathsomeness and the loveliness are in too high a key. In theory Loyolan meditation is a morbid duty, but Taylor's is much more *joyfully* morbid. The strong ingredient of his delight makes a difference.

Of the many handbooks for meditators in the period, Samuel Willard's *Some Brief Sacramental Meditations Preparatory for Communion at the Great Ordinance of the Supper* (1711) is the only one we know Taylor knew (by the time he might have read it, however, he had written most of his Meditations), and the meditative process it recommends is for New England Puritanism an unconventionally joyous one: "thou art to affect thy self deeply herewithall . . . to inflame thy love, thine admiration, and draw them forth to [Christ] with most endeared obligations. . . . Rouse up then, thou dull and sluggish heart of mine; Cry aloud to the Lord to enlighten thine eyes, that thou maist see the beauty and glory of a Crucified Savior, here exhibited to thee."[12] There is an encouragement toward delight here like that which one finds in Taylor.

Taylor's sacramental poems are meditative constructs in the tradition in which Martz finds him a place, to be sure. But the tradition dominates his ideas and the structure of his poems without having a great deal to do with his language, where his main interest as a poet lies, or the final effect on Taylor himself, which is not so much either transcendental or self-revelatory as pleasurable in a masochistic way. For all of the tradition that appears in his poetry and is important, there is in Taylor a disregard for the stages or sequences of the conventional process (at least at Martz outlines them); there is a heavy metaphorism and sensuously exploited imagery distrusted by the pious; there is an indifference to communication of his experiences; and, finally, there is the wit. These do not entirely fit the scene. Wit and fancy and excessive imaginings, especially, have less of a place in the Loyolan programme, are really subversive of it. The progression of the purged soul is in Taylor's poems an oddly joyful one, one that, because of the witty language used, includes the feature of enjoyment as a way that man in this hard existence becomes one with his God. Unlike the meditating regulars of the tradition, Taylor is not really very seriously psychoanalytical either: though he tries, he cannot know, finally, either himself or his God very well; he cannot resolve his anxieties for they are out of his hands; he can know no grace, only anticipation. Dominated by such fate and such futility, all that is left for him is to enjoy *imagining* that he can. And for that he is, in his poems, not a conventional meditator but a poet. So though an heir to Martz' tradition, through his baroque language and dogged adherence to dogma, Taylor is somewhat outside it, or at most an anomaly within it.

The approach of Rosemond Tuve in codifying the limits of Elizabethan and metaphysical imagery has become another way of reading Taylor's baroque.[13] The approach is a causal one: into Taylor's life came the example of Robert Southwell, Herbert, Quarles, maybe even Donne, Vaughan, and Marvell. They seem to hover over him like the muses. Miss Tuve's criteria for them work also for him: the liveliness of image, the functional sensuousness, the delightfulness achieved through compression and richness, the witty forcefulness of radical language, the discipline of efficacy and significance and appropriateness. The long list of technical features of the style—*mimesis*, *allegoria*, *parabola*, *descriptio*, *amplificatio*, *tapinosis*, *catechresis*, etc.—can be found, mechanically, to make up the form if not the substance of Taylor's poetic technique. The whole line of development toward dramatics in baroque poetry genuinely includes him, if unawares. Without the spirit of Herbert, Taylor would not have been a poet.[14] The style of metaphysical wit that he inherited or fell into was to Taylor apparently the most hopeful strategy for a self-deprecating lover of God like himself.

But in the final analysis Taylor does not do very well when seen either in the light of the critical documents of the period or the requirements of the standard genres. The Tuve approach overlooks a man's theological and psychological predilections, and without those a poet like Taylor is only mechanically a metaphysical. The approach implies full knowledge of conventions and fully conscious participation in poetic fashion—two assumptions we cannot make about Taylor. And the approach wants an audience's affections to move and an accepted decorum to satisfy—neither of which Taylor's sacramental poems had.

The criteria of the baroque movement in poetry in Europe are in large part irrelevant to Taylor's baroque. He begins by assuming that his language *will* be indecorous; how could his works or images ever do justice to his theme? The illogicalities and inconsistencies and awkwardness would have annoyed those mindful of proportion, beauty, and decorum. Taylor is simply too narrowly, repetitiously, doggedly doctrinal for the school: the drama of salvation unfolding within him is his sole interest. And where is there much irony, paradox, obscurity, complexity, intellectual subtlety, or logical difficulty? He is all deprecation and glorification. He is all dogma and pun.

Comparison of Taylor with Miss Tuve's English metaphysicals is not very profitable.[15] While he imitates them, uses images from them, and parallels their devotional practices and their esthetics, beside them Taylor most of the time falls embarrassingly short. But that is perhaps because he is a very different personality with other predilections. Also, where they are fantastical, Taylor seems funny. But that is exactly the point: Taylor's fun with language reflects his delight in his subject, the Lord's Supper. Why shouldn't he talk to himself in the happiest language he knew? Over against the sweetness and intellectual toughness and activity of his English counterparts, Taylor is primitive. The causal approach explains only part of what moved Taylor and what fired his wit. The Loyola-Baxter-Hooker structure of reality limited him artistically as much as it formed him; the Herbert-Donne tradition was as far beneath him as it was beyond him.

There is a danger in testing Taylor against an age's total style, for he is both a manifestation of broad tendencies and at the same time an isolated eccentricity. Even if he did have the traditional resources, he ignored much that was important to the art of the period and had some few tricks of his own that the age would have laughed at. The historical and stylistic coherence that one can make out of the seventeenth-century meditative-metaphysical-baroque tradition in poetry includes him only tangentially.

There may be still another way of getting a sense of the significance of Taylor's style in the *Preparatory Meditations*, especially that baroque part of it, by observing the esthetic extensions of his theology. It is one thing to see how a man's work fits standard molds and quite another to sense what his own motives for his work were, to watch the shape it naturally takes, and to hear him commenting on it. It is doubtful whether Taylor knew or even cared about the cultural climate or literary tradition we reclaim for him. He had his spiritual exercises to do and he may have simply used whatever scraps of form he had around his mind in order to do them. There would then have to be some other justification for the baroque in him.

The baroque does not appear in everything Taylor wrote. Except for the few love poems and funeral elegies, for the most part it is the style of only Taylor's sacramental poems. That fact shows perhaps that he did not have the same enthusiasm for his other subjects. For his narrative of church membership, *Gods Determinations*, and for his semi-epic of Christian history, *Metrical History of Christianity*, a drier, more "reasonable," more public style sufficed. But for his private devotions at the time of celebrating the Lord's Supper, Taylor needed the "lively colors" of the baroque. It is as if a lesser Milton knew in private a way of expressing to himself his greater joy.

We can be sure that the language of Taylor's Meditations has its origin in his obsession with the Lord's Supper—in the doctrinal acceptance of it, the purgative but exhilarating preparation for it, the sermons in defense of it, and, most important, the delight of personal involvement in it. The style of the Meditations derives from the joyous state of mind Taylor was in at the sacrament and when he wrote about it.

The most serious occasion in Taylor's life was the Lord's Supper—almost every six weeks throughout his life in the American Wilderness. In a number of ways it was also the grimmest: "Stay from the feast, and wrath comes upon you. Step into it [uninvited], and wrath comes upon you. . . . Come to the wedden without the wedden garment, and it will be to your destruction."[16] Yet so great was his preparation for it ("We are always to be purifying ourselves from all filthiness both of flesh and spirit"), the sense of worth that he had from it ("The main design of it is a design of grace"), and the exclusive right he felt he had to it ("holy things are for holy ones") that he talks about the sacrament as a thing of delight, joy, excitement. "Be of good cheer, Soul. Here are choice things for thee."[17]

In his *Treatise Concerning the Lord's Supper* (1693–94), which was his most elaborate argument against changing the requirements for admission to the sacrament, Taylor describes at length the state of soul necessary to a communicant and the difference grace makes in his life. Much of the *Treatise* is dead serious because Taylor is talking

about the state of the soul necessary before approaching the Lord's
Supper. But whenever he comes to talking about those who, full of
grace, actually participate, the language becomes a language of delight, for then one achieves "a right spiritually festival frame of
spirit. . . . See that you get, and mentain a festival frame of spirit
spiritually," Taylor preaches. "See that your spirits be in trim. Be not
morose. Keep thy heart with all diligence."[18] He speaks of the sacrament as "good cheer," a "celebration," a "feast of fat things," a
"gospel wedden supper . . . [wherein] appears God's delight
abundantly."

> Here is royal entertainment, noble society, and hearty welcome
> with sweetest familiarity imaginable. Oh! what sweet, what
> heart-ravishing and soul-enlivening delight will here be unto
> thee? Christ will stay thee with flaggons, comfort thee with
> apples according to thy prayer (Cant. 2:5), and draw the canopy
> of love over thee.[19]

So serious is the ordinance to Taylor that he rejoices in the occasion to
the point of physical excitement. And accordingly his language
moves from syllogism and exhortation to description and extended
metaphor. "The blossoms of the greatest joy and rejoicings flourish
upon the branches of these actions forthwith carried on."[20]

Of the separate rhetorical stages of each of Taylor's spiritual
exercises—the imaginative opening of the scriptural text to affect the
memory, the exposition of doctrine to affect the understanding, the
evaluation of details to affect the sense of duty, the exhortation
affecting the will, and the expression of stirred affections—his writing of his sermons, as Norman Grabo has shown, appears to have
often satisfied the last.[21] His poetry, then, was often the climactic
point of his joy, the point at which he himself must show himself
stirred. The language in it needed to go beyond that of the sermons,
needed, in fact, to apply his ideas to his own life and to involve his
"stirred affections." The extending of the sermon's metaphors led
Taylor quite naturally into a baroque style, for while "meditat[ing]
upon the feast," he would want to describe his feelings "in lively
colors." And the witty, joyous extension of the images (most of them
Biblical, worn, trite) gave him opportunity to exert/insert his individuality, his thought, his self. This was true application.

It dispels much of one's preconception of this wooden minister in the wilderness to hear him exclaim in the *Treatise on the Lord's Supper*: "Of all the enjoyments of this world, the enjoyment of this temporary life is enjoyment of the choicest thing." On such an occasion Taylor is one with Ecclesiastes: life is by and large made up of meaningless matters ("Truly this is the condition of God's children here in this life"), there is little time for the spiritual ("Where I have one thought of spiritual concerns, I have twenty laid out upon the things of the world"), and he who has the ability to *enjoy* "the fruit of our labor" has perhaps the gift of grace.[22] Any special moments of enjoyment may be moments of special grace. As with Edwards, delight is the form that salvation takes.

Though in the *Treatise* Taylor is attempting to find a basis in logic for his conviction about the exclusive rights of the justified, his affection, like Jonathan Edwards', often takes the form of an *esthetic* epistemology. It is not that the sacrament itself is beautiful ("it [is] but paint that will rub off and not abide"[23]) but that some spiritual-esthetic sense already in oneself has been affected, like that which Edwards calls "the *beauty* of holiness."

> Now it is the Father's design to set out the Son as most lovely, and therefore He celebrates the feast for this end. He is the lovely rose of Sharon, and glorious lily of the valley. He is altogether lovely in everything, lovely in His person, lovely in His natures, lovely in His properties, lovely in His offices, lovely in His titles, lovely in His practice, lovely in His purchases and lovely in His relations. And in all these, and all other things, He is altogether lovely.[24]

To the advantage of his interest in writing poetry, the sacrament was for him an esthetic experience more than it was a matter of austerity of spirit.

It is natural then that Taylor should say that his delight in the Lord's Supper is the source of his own songs, his own poems of delight: "This rich banquet makes me thus a Poet." (2.110) When one is saved, then he can sing. "Oh! the joy that spreads itself then over the soul. Oh! how it then is filled with singing."[25] When he feels that he has "accomplished" his election, then from his pen can come "sweet heart-ravishing melodies, musics, and songs of a spiritual nature," until as poet/singer he lives in "the very suburbs of glory."[26]

In such a state of joy Taylor wrote his Meditations. And the devices of a meditative-metaphysical-baroque style, perhaps better than anything else, gave him a way of living and reliving that which was most joyous, most serious to him.

Since Taylor's baroque language must be seen as more than convention and contraption, as, instead, a function of his earthly enjoyment of things divine, perhaps Jonathan Edwards' esthetics provides the best way of understanding the language of delight—his wilderness baroque—that is fundamental to his poems. In his emphasis on beauty and sensibility in the celebration of the Lord's Supper, Taylor anticipates Edwards in a number of ways, is perhaps the true Edwardsean poet.

Taylor's poems show that he believed with Edwards that divine excellence is better felt than defined. In his "Treatise on Grace," Edwards writes:

> The first effect of the power of God in the heart in regeneration is to give the heart a Divine taste or sense; to cause it to have a relish of the loveliness and sweetness of the supreme excellency of the Divine nature. . . . He that is once brought to see, or rather to taste, the superlative loveliness of the Divine Being, will need no more.[27]

In subject and style Taylor shows that he inclines toward Edwards' belief that it is beauty that is the law of the moral and spiritual world. He shows this when he exclaims in *Christographia* sermons six and eight on Christ's sufficiency:

> We See what attractives there are in Christ to draw Sinners to him, and what unreasonableness there is in men, that betake not themselves to him. . . . All the Sovereign attractives to draw persons unto him are in him. O most lovely Jesus! O most wonderfull One! O most necessarie unto the Sons of men.

> He that you are espoused unto and so intrested in is one, and the onely one who is full of all glorious Grace in all its glorious Fulness. You are a member of his Body, a branch of his Vine Stock, and What can be more refreshing than this? Here all the Fulness, and Excellency of Grace is yours. Hence ariseth unspeakable delight.[28]

In order to understand the poetic language that Taylor would find necessary as a suitable vehicle for this esthetic side of his theology, it is necessary to understand that in Edwards' ontology the will to conform to the divine (the "stirred affections") is the same as the apprehension of beauty. Beauty is not in the eye of man but in God. Beauty, and its attendants enjoyment and delight, are to Edwards the form that God's communion with man takes. Edwards makes beauty a means of redemption:

> The reason why gracious affections issue in holy practice, also further appears from the kind of excellency of divine things, that it has been observed is the foundation of all holy affection, viz. their moral excellency, or the beauty of their holiness. No wonder that a love to holiness, for holiness' sake, inclines persons to practice holiness, and to practice everything that is holy. . . . That which men love, they desire to have and to be united to, and possessed of. That beauty which men delight in, they desire to be adorned with. Those acts which men delight in, they necessarily incline to.[29]

In such a scheme the Edwardsean poet would be one who has a passionate interest in conforming the subjective order of pleasure (one's delight) to the objective order of beauty (God). He does not lack passion, but rather has a passion for seeing things as they are and responding accordingly, and his language is appropriate to his passionate delight in the objective order of beauty. Taylor's Meditations, for one example, are fairly redundant with terms for God's attributes apprehended sensuously. This does not necessarily assume any man-God coincidence, even fleetingly; such dangerous waters of thought were avoided by admitting the disparity between God's fulness and man's meager abilities to apprehend the beauty. More than any other writer in early America, except Edwards, Taylor clearly sees God's beauty as His prime communication and recognizes his own delight in that beauty as a minimal form of communion. That is, after all, what the *Preparatory Meditations* is about: delight is the form that man's salvation takes—and in a language appropriate to that delight.

For Edwards, as for Taylor, beauty is available only to the man who is inclined, only the man capable of being engaged in the things of God, only the man of sensibility, the elect. Only spiritual persons are capable of "being's cordial consent to being"—Edwards' definition of both beauty and love of God. Taylor also described man's relationship to God, in one sermon, in terms of "Consent."[30] Of the role of this sensibility in Edwards' esthetics, R. A. Delattre writes:

> Edwards tried to understand all things in relation to God. In settling upon beauty as the most distinguishing perfection or attribute of God he chose a concept that enabled him to conceive of God in objective, structural, and ontological terms and at the same time to make it philosophically (and not merely dogmatically) clear that (and why) God can be fully known only if He is the direct object of enjoyment—that men's knowledge of God is in part a function of his enjoyment of Him. . . . God cannot be adequately known without being enjoyed. For beauty is objective with respect to the self, and yet it is available only in and through the enjoyment of it. It is not discernible to the indifferent eye. Though indifferent men may know many things about it, they do not and cannot know beauty itself.[31]

Since beauty is not contained in man himself or thing itself and is not self-contained in God either but in the benevolent communication, effulgence, and radiation of being to being, then, according to Edwards, when a man like Taylor in his poetic role as seeker finds beauty in God and delights in that find as he does continually in his Meditations, Edwards would feel with Taylor that God and man have interacted through the factors of beauty and delight to become one.

> Those affections that are truly holy, are primarily founded on the loveliness of the moral excellency of divine things. Or (to express it otherwise), a love to divine things for the beauty and sweetness of their moral excellency, is the first beginning and spring of all holy affections.[32]

Taylor can be shown to have believed with Edwards that beauty, along with virtue and holiness, does not come from "the consent to beauty" but from "the consent to being"; that is, not from that which is beautiful (harmony, proportion, conventions, ideas, works of art and literature) but that which beautifies (God). Edwards calls the concern with harmony and proportion "secondary beauty."

"Primary beauty," on the other hand, lies in man's consistent conformity with other being (that is, God) and his enjoyment is a sign of his spiritual sensibility. From Edwards' thinking it would follow that to make great poems is of secondary consideration, but to identify within oneself the ability to consent to the beautifying One, the bestower of beauty, is primary.

  Though admittedly strained as he applies it in his poems, this is precisely the logic of Taylor's poetic practice: it is the delight in God and the attendant language of delight that is the "art" of his poetry, not the form that his work takes and not the forms of his language:

> entertain me with thy Spirituall Cheer.
> Which well Concocted will make joy up start,
> That makes thy praises leape up from my heart.
>
> (2.106)

This distinction of Edwards between primary and secondary beauty helps one understand Taylor's interest in writing a poetry in the *Preparatory Meditations* that in and of itself did not interest him. Primary beauty is man's apprehension of and delight in the things of God, which delight acts (this is my own metaphor) like an electric current: as soon as consent (generally in the form of faith, love, or hope) is given to God, the resulting "charge" gives man grace and God glory. This is accomplished through the device of human enjoyment. But secondary beauty is different:

> There is another, inferior, secondary beauty, which is some
> image of this, and which is not peculiar to spiritual beings, but is
> found even in inanimate things: which consists in a mutual
> consent and agreement of different things, in form, manner,
> quantity, and visible end or design; called by the various names
> of regularity, order, uniformity, symmetry, proportion, harmony, etc.[33]

Because he was an idealist and because he would not understand the platonic relationship between a secondary beauty and a primary beauty that Edwards has, Taylor would have an interest only in the plane of the primary, a consent to the beauty of God's being. Taylor would also hold that any emphasis on secondary beauty can lead to private systems of belief apart from faith in God. Secondarily effective poetry could become a form of dissent from truth, leading to one's taking more delight in one's creations than in the created beauty, more in one's discoveries than in Christ discovered, more in his own experiences than in experiencing Christ, his beauty and fulness. Secondary beauty will not necessarily produce primary beauty; art does not necessarily lead to faith. It is in itself no sure sign of primary beauty. Taylor simply hopes that possessed of primary beauty he will also possibly be capable of secondary performance; that is, that his faith will affect his art positively. Regarding the baroque language of his poems, odd as it may seem, Edwards' distinction shows how Taylor's extravagance of language can be significant without being any good!

Edwards reasoned further that, to be known, true beauty must be experienced or encountered firsthand, for it is available only in the personal enjoyment of it. Enjoyment means the beauty is immanent and being is immediate. Being is available only through enjoyment, not through reflection, perception, or understanding. True to such an esthetic, Taylor is in his poems struggling for an enjoyable encounter and seeks enjoyment rather than understanding, since he feels, with Edwards, that God is encountered as a reality according to the degree of one's joy.

With these principles in mind, listen to the characteristic Taylor voice. Hear how his theology, like Jonathan Edwards', becomes a matter of esthetic consideration. Just as Edwards suggests, beauty connects him to his God and delight is a sign of grace. Taylor began his 1679 "Profession of Faith" with the announcement of the esthetic nature of his faith:

> The Christian Religion [is] that which having its Spring Head in Christ runs with Christlike influences from Christ into the Soul tinging of it with a smack of Christ, & as Spirituall Magnetick attracting of the heart & affections to God in Christ with devout Design there to abide. & hense it is called Divinity in that it is the Lesson the Divine Nature reads to us, & in our Learning of it we shall come to attain Divine Communication of Light from the Divine Minde, & of Grace from the Divine Goodness of this Minde. . . . Those gracious Influences coming from him upon our Souls so as to draw out the Soule Satisfying delight of God in

them to the felicitating of our Souls with the Divine Sweetness therein. Of this is sweet indeed.[34]

This esthetic is of course much more explicit in his poetry:

Lord, Cleare my Sight, thy Glory then out dart.
　　And let thy Rayes beame Glory in mine eye
And stick thy Loveliness upon my heart,
　　Make me the Couch on which thy Love doth ly.
　　Lord make my heart thy bed, thy heart make mine.
　　Thy Love bed in my heart, bed mine in thine.

(1.35)

This is not Puritan obsequiousness but a man believing *esthetically*, a man loving God in the only way that Taylor (and after him, Edwards) thought a man could love God—artfully. Within the Edwardsean esthetic that Taylor shared, beauty is also the measure of goodness, designating what is highest and most attractive in goodness. "The mind can be said to be sensible that anything is good or excellent . . . when it is so sensible of the beauty and amiableness of the thing that 'tis sensible of pleasure and delight in the presence of the idea of it."[35] Good cannot be fully known unless its beauty is known and enjoyed. "There is a difference between having an opinion that God is holy and gracious, and having a sense of the loveliness and beauty of that holiness and grace. . . . There is a wide difference between mere speculative rational judging anything to be excellent, and having a sense of its sweetness and beauty."[36] This describes Taylor in his poems, for he seeks to measure his worth by trying to enjoy the *beauty* of God and apprehending the sweetness of his faith, more than any other attribute or characteristic.[37]

Oh! let thy Beauty give a glorious tuch
　　Upon my Heart, and melt to Love all mee.
　　Lord melt me all up into Love for thee
　　Whose Loveliness excells what love can bee.

(1.12)

Taylor's excitement over the beauty of Christ and the baroque language necessary to the excitement are to him, then, a part of his sought-after goodness. Remote as the relevance may at first glance seem, it is through the faculty of delight and a lively language expressive of the delight that Taylor feels he participates in divine things. This is what Edwards calls "the enjoying faculty." It is, as Edwards schematizes it, the form a man's "consent to being" takes.

For someone like Edward Taylor who felt himself called to glorify God in his poetry, the ethical value of delight that Edwards was to make systematic is central to the articulation of his Christian vision. A hyperbolic style was one encouraged by the passionate joy he generally felt; therefore the elaborate comparisons, the far-fetched analogies, the rough rhythms, the puns, the excessiveness.

The excitements of wit and radical metaphor were, within this esthetic, the Holy Spirit in him, giving him, through delight in the beauty of Christ, his faith in God. For Taylor, as for Edwards, to have a way of delighting in the divine beauty was to stand surely in the presence of God. Language and wit gradually became Taylor's way of delight. The manner of his telling his delight in divine beauty is the manifestation of His presence. So, given the underpinnings of the esthetics that he shares with Edwards, Taylor's metaphysical strain (his language of delight) is fully justified. Would the tradition-bound meditators, the metaphysicals, and the British practitioners of the baroque have understood this?

The language forms that Taylor's delight takes are tricks from the metaphysical mode and are given quite different significance by his theology of delight. The *pun* in his poems, for example, often brings together something of God and something of man in witty conjunction; the fun of the correspondence of sounds or spellings and the consequent overlapping meanings represents the illusory delight of sacramental oneness. When he writes in "Huswifery," for example, "The yarn is fine. . . . Then *dy* the same in Heavenly Colours Choice," Taylor's free-form spelling makes for a playful illusion of oneness with God: Christ's death "dyes" man's "Holy Robes" so that man's heavenly existence will be delightful. In other poems, the Son is the sun, Christ's scent is sent to perfume us, the Cross crosses our lives, Christ the rose rises, awful man is offal, sin sings, prayers praise—so many, in most of the sacramental poems, in fact, that one becomes convinced of the enjoyment Taylor has in meditating on the communion of disparate things and the skill he has in exploiting the pun to represent that feature of his faith. In such puns Taylor appears superstitious of language, as if he believed that linguistic forms have hidden religious meanings. But it is the *delight* in the various correspondences that language offers that is important to him, not the miraculousness of language itself.

Catechresis, or far-fetched analogy, was another vehicle for Taylor's "consent of being to being." With such a device provided him by the metaphysical poets long before him, he could express his faith in the objective beauty of God by reacting wittily. Throughout the *Preparatory Meditations* Taylor's "consent" to Christ takes the form of witty analogies. Taylor's Christ is variously "A Box of Ointments Broke," "Heavens Golden Spout," "A Golden Stepping Stone to Paradise." The sacramental body of Christ is "Roast Mutton," God's "rich Love Letter," "Soul Bread," "sweet Junkets," "a lump of Glory," "Zion's pastry," "Heaven's Sugar Cake," and "griddle cakes," and the sacramental blood is wine, beer, nectar, and drippings from a roast. A simple analogy was not enough for Taylor; it had to be extended wittily to parallel the reach of his delight to God and to have a fuller sense of communion with divine things. The good feeling of his wit he could then take as the Holy Spirit in him making him one with God through the faculty of delight.

A conventional Biblical type like Christ as the Rose of Sharon (1.4), for example, is manipulated until it includes Taylor's delight in Christ in the extended analogy. It is at first merely "The Rose of Sharon which with Beauty shines. . . . The Fairest Rose that Grows in Paradise." Out of love for man the Rose blushes with the colors of the crucifixion, red and white, and the dew on its leaves is "Sweats of Glory." The atoning Rose then becomes in the course of its work of salvation a bed of roses for Taylor to lie in when he dies, a blood-red medicinal syrup which acts as a purgative for his soul ("When Dayly usd, doth never fail to Cure"), a distilled rose water which relieves "Heart burns Causd by Sin," and yet is still a rose which, after being mangled to thus save man, "rose up again/And in its pristine glory, doth remain." Because of the witty extensions of his faith, Taylor can hope in the end:

> My Dear-Sweet Lord, shall I thy Glory meet
> >   Lodg'd in a Rose, that out a sweet Breath breaths.
> What is my way to glory made thus sweet,
> >   Strewd all along with Sharons Rosy Leaves.
> I'le walk this Rosy Path: World fawn, or frown
> And Sharons Rose shall be my Rose, and Crown.

Such puns and analogies (particularly "rose" as a play on "resurrection" and the crown of rose thorns as a crown of glory in the last line) are to Taylor themselves a metaphor for the delight that makes God and himself one.

The much-quoted catechretic analogy "Who in this Bowling Alley bowld the Sun?" from "The Preface" to *Gods Determinations* works much the same way. In the entire poem Taylor is delivering himself of his thanks for God's condescending love to man for having made a delightful Creation for him, even though over against God's "All" it is as "Nothing." It is to Taylor ironic that as Creator God would stoop to being carpenter (itself a pun-allusion), stone-cutter, mason, designer, and tailor, all for the sake of worthless man. To Taylor, for God to have made the sun, like the other seemingly grand acts of creation, was as simple and meaninglessly entertaining as bowling. Yet the pun *sun/Son* makes this simple act of God significant for man's ultimate salvation.

> Who in this Bowling Alley bowld the Sun?
> Who made it always when it rises set
> To go at once both down, and up to get?

This simple act of sending the Son was God's game of salvation. Through the paradox of the crucifixion (a setting is a rising, a going down is a getting up, humility is majesty), man, though worthless, is included in the game, just as in Taylor's puns and analogies two factors are included in one language unit. Like most of the imagery in the poem, the bowling alley in this scheme is a uniquely appropriate figure for catching the form of delight that Taylor's faith takes: the alley is the All made diminutive (-ey); the reference to "*this* Bowling Alley" is pejorative (in two other poems, 2.18 and 96, the bowling alley is a place of sinfulness); the activity of bowling turns the creation into an insignificant act; yet the act was a bold ("bowld") one, for it brought light to the world (see also 1.13: "The Shining Sun of Wisdom bowling there"); and yet "nothing Man" sees the Son/sun merely as a dark ball, that is, he cannot perceive the light in him. Though the scheme of things (the construct of reality that his theology holds to) alienates him from God, through such wit Taylor feels reunited—imaginatively, illusorily, esthetically—with God. With such a witty device faith and art become one.

Similarly, the *conceit*, whether humorously brief or hyperbolically extended as a structure for a poem, is Taylor's way of reaching out again for God through "the faculty of enjoyment" throughout his

sacramental poems. His yearning for salvation was so intense that it
needed the most strained form of language he knew how to use. That
he could thus delight in the beauty that lay behind the severe factors
of salvation as he chose to believe them might even have been a sign
to him of his spiritual acceptability.

In Meditation 1.18, for instance, Taylor's delight in Christ's victory over man's sins breaks the conventions of language and breaks
out in conceits:

> The Fairest Flower in all Gods Paradise!
>
> Stept in, and in its Glory 'Counters all.
> 　And in the Belly of this Dismall Cloud,
> Of Woes in Pickle is gulpht up, whose Gall
> 　　He dranke up quite. Whose Claws his Face up plow'd.
> 　　Yet in these Furrows sprang the brightest Shine.
> 　　That Glory's Sun could make, or Love Enshrine.

The conceit lies in Taylor's play on the word "Furrows": it is both the
lines on the face (made by man's crucifixion of Christ) and narrow
trenches in a fertile field (where Christ can plant the seeds of salvation). Witty logic and punning language make it possible for Taylor
to go on believing and loving such a scheme. His metaphoric ingenuity on such occasions is evidence of his acceptance of the old
terms of the Puritan construct of reality—man is bad, God is good,
Christ saves, praise the Lord—and at the same time evidence that
Taylor can make room for himself within the construct. It is a way of
both delighting in and gaining individual freedom and dignity within
the system.

Conceits give Taylor a way of defining—or rather, imagining—his
place in a joyous scheme of salvation. Though he begins, as he does in
Meditation 1.6, by worrying about his spiritual worth ("Am I thy
Gold? Or Purse, Lord, for thy Wealth;/Whether in mine, or mint
refinde for thee?"), he soon finds a way through play on words and
witty extensions of metaphor that he can be considered for salvation
though worthless. He wants to be "counted" of worth, though fears
he may be found out to be merely "gold washt face, and brass in
Heart." He has no "touchstone" of his own that can make him
"Counted Gold," and so needs Christ who, in this case, is a minter
that puts a new "Stamp" on old forms. But man is so blind that he
cannot see "If thy bright Image do upon me stand." Eventually,

through the redeeming process that involves "Plat[ing],"
"enfoil[ing]," and "Superscrib[ing]" of "golden Letters," Taylor
hopes to become an "Angell," a coin, of God. It is the wit here that
makes any concept of grace possible. Only in the wit is the delight of
oneness possible to the imagination.

Conventional language was to Taylor obviously a human, therefore a fallen, contrivance of expression. He complains about the fact
throughout his Meditations. Only in leaps of logic and leaps of
metaphor—to human senses, of course, absurd and silly—could
truth appear. God's sense is nonsense to man and in nonsense God's
truth may appear. Language is earthbound, unexpressive, dead, but
the articulate fool-in-Christ, the poet, the conceitist, has greater
opportunity for making that connection with the divine that results
in spiritual delight. The "foolish" aspects of language may bear the
burden of truth. In place of choice and chance, wit works against fate
in man's imagination to provide opportunity for man and God to
meet. Metaphysical wit must have seemed to Taylor a foolish
rhetoric—but he thought of it as perhaps God's foolishness, God's
way.

Edwards seems almost to be describing the delighting Taylor of the
Meditations when he writes in his *Religious Affections*:

> He that truly sees the divine, transcendent, supreme glory of
> those things which are divine, does as it were know their divinity
> intuitively; he not only argues that they are divine, but he sees
> that they are divine; he sees that in them wherein divinity chiefly
> consists; for in this glory, which is so vastly and inexpressibly
> distinguished from the glory of artificial things, and all other
> glory, does mainly consist the true notion of divinity: God is
> God, and distinguished from all other beings, and exalted above
> 'em, chiefly by his divine beauty, which is infinitely diverse from
> all other beauty. They therefore that see the stamp of this glory
> in divine things, they see divinity in them, they see God in them,
> and so see 'em to be divine; because they see that in them
> wherein the truest idea of divinity does consist.[38]

On these esthetic grounds Taylor should indeed be added to the
Edwardsean tradition of American literary thought, as his conception of the role of delight in Puritan theology and his uses of the
language of metaphysical wit prove. As with Edwards, the Puritan
austerity in him is tempered by his sense of the beauty of things

natural and divine. In the Puritan stress on the enjoyment of divine beauty (his neo-Calvinism), Edwards was less of a pioneer than a perfector. For Taylor as much as for Edwards, the experience of the beauty of divine things constituted the most intimate and fullest communion with God. As the example of Edward Taylor and the example of Emerson suggest, this tradition in American esthetics begins earlier and lasts longer, is more pervasive and more funda- mental than we may have recognized.

It should be evident that Taylor's language—from his explosive ejaculations and hyperbolic dramatizations to his puns and ex- travagant conceits—participates in his holy delight, proceeds quite naturally from it, and helps greatly to sustain it. To see Taylor's wilderness baroque within such an esthetic as he obviously shared with Edwards is to place his wit back into the context of his theology where it belongs. And to see it as part of his theology is to give it an unusual significance for so quaint and contrived a convention of rhetoric. To be sure, it appears to have cheered him a little in his alienation from the divine, as it did other Puritans; it gave him a way of asserting himself within the rigid system of his poetry; and it served to stir his religious affections. But Taylor's practice of wit goes well beyond the other New England poets', as so many features of his poetry do, to provide him with a way of exercising his faith, a way of sustaining his hope, a way of loving his God. His language of delight ("the enjoying faculty")—however witless and corny it may often appear—gave him, though earthbound, an illusion of oneness with his God. More than anything else, it turned his *Preparatory Meditations* into the richest form of praise for his God that he could conceive.

Chapter 8

Preparatory Meditations: The Images of Salvation

*I felt in myself that high workings of Love
in one [hand and] of Griefe on another. . . .*
                              "Spiritual Relation."

The art with which Taylor pursued his ideas in the *Preparatory Meditations* is seen best in his imagery. A significant esthetic emerges from his metaphors, but more valuable to Taylor would have been the fact that an important eschatology is what his imagery reveals. That the *Preparatory Meditations* was intended by Taylor to be a unified work, in both thought and style, shows up in an exploration of its image patterns.

Among the various kinds of images of salvation in his poems, that scatological and erotic imagery that peppers Taylor's *Meditations* is most fundamental to his thought and most unifying to his art as a Puritan. Taylor obviously felt that his orthodox Puritan eschatology was best explored in such terms, for of all the various types of images in his poetry these are the most dominant. Taylor's vision of the fallen world and of sinful man often finds form in excremental language like the following:

A State, a State, Oh! Dungeon State indeed.
    In which mee headlong, long agoe Sin pitcht:
As dark as Pitch, where Nastiness doth breed:
    And Filth defiles: and I am with it ditcht.

.   .   .   .

I in this Pit all Destitute of Light
    Cram'd full of Horrid Darkness, here do Crawle
Up over head, and Eares, in Nauseous plight:
    And Swinelike Wallow in this mire, and Gall.

(2.77)

Oh! woe is me! Was ever Heart like mine?
A Sty of Filth, a Trough of Washing-Swill
A Dunghill Pit, a Puddle of mere Slime.

(1.40)

We've griev'd them [the heavens] by such Physick that they shed
Their Excrements upon our lofty heads.

("Upon the Sweeping Flood")

In contrast, Taylor's vision of salvation often finds form in erotic
language like this:

Raptures of Love, surprizing Loveliness,
    That burst through Heavens all, in Rapid Flashes,
Glances guilt o're with smiling Comliness!
    (Wonders do palefac'd stand smit by such dashes).
    Glory itselfe Heartsick of Love doth ly
    Bleeding out Love o're Loveless mee, and dy.

(1.14/15)

Thy Love that fills the Heavens brimfull throughout
    Coms tumbling on her with transcendent bliss
Even as it were in golden pipes that spout
    In Streams from heaven, Oh! what love like this?
    This comes upon her, hugs her in its Arms
    And warms her Spirits. Oh! Celestiall Charms.

(2.142)

It has been an embarrassment to some of the readers of the
Preparatory Meditations that Taylor was so worldly in his imagery
and a comfort to others that he can be so colorful in his orthodoxy.
But rather than being embarrassed or comforted by Taylor's
"bawdy" imagery, I would like to argue the extent to which Taylor's
excremental view of life and erotic view of salvation *are* his
Puritanism. And in the process, one can become convinced of the
artful unity of the *Preparatory Meditations*. The descriptions of
flatulence, defecation, diseases, seductions, and sensual pleasures in
meditation on the Holy Supper are not nods, slips, heresies, or
sublimations, but simply honest talk (in rather conventional
Biblical/Protestant/Puritan symbols) of how God's grace works.
    It cannot be said of such imagery in Taylor's poems, as it can of,
say, Shakespeare's bawdry, that the poet is thereby proclaiming his

manhood, revealing that he is worldly-wise, or showing himself simply frank and capable of compromise with "the world's slow stain." Though Taylor's individual excremental and erotic images are used by and large in the Meditations as if they are merely facets of cold dogma, the very choice of such language by Taylor suggests a sense of human balance and normalcy of sensibility of the sort that one enjoys (much more fully, to be sure) in Shakespeare. Taylor is withdrawn, intensely dogmatic, and private, however, rather than broad, healthily coarse, and unsqueamishly natural in his use of such language.

Nor can it be said of Taylor's images of salvation, as it can of Donne's grotesque and erotic imagery, that it reveals that underneath the skin he was both sinner and saint, idealist and realist, or a man gradually reforming his life. Taylor is, instead, consistently austere and overwhelmingly eschatalogical; the joy and sap of life did not fill him in the same way.

Also, where a writer like Swift used conventional Christian symbols of vilification to emphasize his misanthropic view of the depravity of man and the repulsiveness of contemporary life, as well as symbols of sexuality as expressions of hope, a writer like Taylor uses the same symbols for sin and salvation, but for a more plainly soteriological purpose. Swift damns the human race with its "strange Disposition to Nastiness and Dirt" in order to effect a catharsis, and Taylor, with a different theology, makes man stink so that salvation will smell sweet to him.[1]

In the Meditations, Taylor's excremental vision of life and erotic vision of salvation are characterized by existential endurance, evangelical introspection, and infallible hope. That makes him a different kind of writer. From the point of view of the psychoanalysis of history, Taylor is a Protestant fundamentalist of the purest, most analytical and honest kind.[2] And his scatological and erotic imagery proves that fact better than anything else.

As Taylor would have one believe in the Meditations, the world is a "Dunghill Pitt" where man in his fallen state has been corrupted by irrevocable and inscrutable guilt, and is therefore "with filth . . . all defilde." (1.31, 32) Such scatological imagery is not peculiar to Taylor, however. It is part of world culture from the Bible and Augustine through Calvin, Luther, and Puritan theological discourse. All of these taught Taylor to characterize man's condition in the language of filth.

In the Bible, beginning with the Levitical ceremonial pollutions, in which man is unclean from birth, unclean by association with forbidden things, and totally defiled through his sensuality, filth and deformity are made emblematic of man's state.[3] "We have all bene as an uncleane thing," Isaiah proclaims, "& all our righteousnesse is as filthy cloutes. . . . From the sole of the foote unto the head, there is nothing whole therein [in the body], but woundes, & swelling, and sores full of corruption." (1:6, 64:6) Men are "all corrupt," the Psalmist also mourns; "there is none that doeth good, no not one." They are "not washed from their filthinesse"; they have become as "dongue for the earth." (14:3; 83:10) Likewise, Job laments: "How muche more is man abominable, & filthie, which drinketh iniquitie like water?" (15:16) And much the same is expressed by Ecclesiastes: "I considered in mine heart the state of the children of men that God had purged them [that is, made them pure at first]: yet to see to, they are in them selves as beasts." (3:18)

Similar imagery emerges in the New Testament, especially in Pauline apologetics. "I thinke all things but losse, . . . and do judge them to be dongue," Paul writes to the Philippians. (3:8) "We are made as the filthe of the worlde," he continues to the Corinthians, "[and] the offskowring of all things, unto this time. (1 Cor. 4:13) Man is "defiled," he entangles himself in "the filthinesse of the world," he walks "after the flesh in the lust of uncleannesse," he has a "filthinesse of the flesh and spirit," and he is often not even fit "for the dunghill."[4]

Augustine, influenced by the Bible metaphors for sin and sinful world and by the Neoplatonic emphasis on "base matter," conceived of evil as privation of good and was therefore given to metaphors of decay, pollution, defilement, dirtiness, and the befouling of that which was originally pure and clean. In defining original sin, he speaks of "nature's corruption" and of "that impurity of [man's] which he has contracted in the stain of his birth, and which proceeds, not from the divine work, but from the will of man;—since also the impure spirit itself is a good thing considered as spirit, but evil in that it is impure."[5] Augustine was among the first of the Nicean and post-Nicean fathers, comments Portalié, to use the dogma in this pejorative way. "He calls the line of Adam a mass of slime; a mass of sin, of sins, of iniquity; a mass of wrath, of death, of damnation, of offense; a mass totally vitiated, damnable, damned."[6] Before we are born, he believed, we are "tainted with contagion,"[7] from birth we are "impure" and "Stained," we "defile" and "pollute" ourselves through our sins until we are "most filthy," and we must be "washed" and "cleansed" from our "uncleanness"—metaphors which explore severely the Christian drama of grace in terms of degeneration and regeneration.[8] To Augustine the business of grace was to purify pollutions rather than preventing perversions of nature, to cleanse vileness rather than creating goodness; and so the language of foulness became appropriate to any talk of salvation.[9]

Calvin's terms for man's state and estate, coming in large measure from the Bible and Augustine, are similarly excretory and decadent. His metaphors vilify man's alienation from God: being, property, and human action are all anagogically excremental. Therefore, the divine comedy of damnation and redemption, as he conceived of it, is relayed in analogies of filth and cleansing. To Calvin God's purity makes all things appear filthy, and by contrast the world and mankind (a condition in which the things of God have ceased to be pure to polluted man) are vile. In the estrangement from God, "everything in man, the understanding and will, the soul and body, is polluted. . . ." Through original sin ("the perpetual corruption of our nature") man is "most filthy." His actions are "pollutions," "contaminations," "infections," "impurities," "defilings," "moral maladies." His hands are polluted with rapine and murder, his throat is an open sepulchre, his tongue is vile, his lips are envenomed, his works are corrupt, and the inmost recesses of his heart are full of impurity. To Calvin such mortification brings purification, for the dunghill serves a salutory purpose:

> We cannot think upon that primeval dignity [man's prelapsarian state], without having our attention immediately called to the melancholy spectacle of our disgrace and ignominy, since in the person of the first man we are fallen from our original condition. Hence arise disapprobation and abhorrence of ourselves, and real humility; and we are inflamed with fresh ardour to seek after God, to render in him those excellences of which we find ourselves utterly destitute.[10]

Filth is therefore the glory of God (that is, it is by contrast a measure of God's transcendence and by contrast a deprived object revealing his benevolence) as well as the glory of man (that is, salvation is God's alchemical distillation of the soul from mud). Man is, in Calvinist logic, affirmed by such negation, for to be cleansed man must first be dirty, to be redeemed he must first be polluted, to live in heaven he must first experience the dunghill of the world. The Calvinist dirty language is therefore the language of grace.

These analogies of the filthiness of the sin-bound life also gave Luther specific metaphors for a scatological world view, as did his observations of the crude life of the times during the Protestant Reformation. To Luther the entire realm of visible reality—the world, the flesh, and all of men's works—is the Devil's, and the anal character of Luther's Devil made the world a filthy place. "Scatet totus orbis," he exclaimed. The Devil is a black and filthy *Scheisser*, he believed, an overwhelming force of foul flatulence and defecation. The world is therefore a "great privy" and the things of the world a "rain of filth." Man within the "gaping anus" of the world is the dung of the devil:

> We are nothing but a worm in ordure and filth, with no good or hope left in us, a loathsome abomination and object of scorn because of the loathsome stench and scorn for the sake of the cross.

Forced to live in a place of universal filth (a foul place of extreme alienation from God), man has his only hope in faith, and salvation lies only in resignation to the dunghill of this world (one must even "desire to be lost" in the filth!) The Devil's dunghill therefore works to man's (and God's) glory, for the Devil will "stink us and stab us with his dung" and God will use the filthiness to his own advantage: "The world and all that depends on you," Luther imagines God saying to the Devil, "shall be my manure-dung for my beloved vineyard." The language of anality therefore also becomes in Luther's hands a description of the workings of grace.[11]

This imagery from the affirmations of Augustine, Calvin, and Luther (among many others) effectively dramatized a dark world view to the mind of the Puritan. More than anything else, though, the use of the archetypes of foulness was encouraged by the doctrine of preparation within the meditative tradition of the seventeenth century. This is a doctrine dominating fundamentalist Protestantism from Calvin to Edwards which Norman Pettit has described as an imaginative and dogmatic process by which a man, although utterly depraved, might somehow predispose his heart to be wrenched from depravity to grace; it is a discipline which "fostered an element of doubt so that no man could claim to be regenerate without close self-examination."[12] Within this scheme of preparation, piety took the form of Paul's belief: "Godly sorrow worketh repentance unto salvation," with "godly sorrow" interpreted as self-vilification.[13] In this introspective exercise of preparation, an earnest man must make himself utterly vile so as to predispose himself for saving grace. He must bring himself to despair in order to force himself to see that Christ's and not his own efforts are the only hope for salvation. He must imagine himself so low that the anxiety of total worthlessness will check any arrogant enthusiasm in which he might claim salvation through direct revelation from God. Unless a man dwell on his corruptions intensely and imaginatively, he can never by true faith lay claim to love from God. We must "join with God in bruising ourselves," wrote Richard Sibbs, Puritan divine at Cambridge; we must "lay seige to the hardness of our own hearts and aggravate sin all we can"; we must make within ourselves a "spiritual emptiness" that God can fill with love.[14]

Within the New England Way, Thomas Hooker described this self-demeaning meditative process as the attempt to "track the abominations of our lives, step by step, until we come to the very nest where they are hatched and bred, even of our original corruption."[15] "No preparation, no perfection," he taught. "Never humbled, never exalted."[16] Most men, Thomas Shepard claimed, "are driven to Christ by the sense of the burden of an hard, dead, blind, filthy heart."[17]

Even within so wide a range of Puritanism as the thinking of Bunyan and Milton, these archetypes of foulness take on dramatic form. Bunyan characterizes the fallen world, natural man, and sin with the excremental imagery of the Biblical/Calvinist tradition. In The Pilgrim's Progess, for example, the best things of the earth are, in comparison with the glory of heaven, "but as a dunghill." Disobedient man defiles himself as in mire, and a sinner is a dog that licks up "its stinking excrements." "Original sin and inward corruptions," Bunyan thus says, "have defiled the whole man." It is significant to Puritan mythology that Christian's first experience on his burdened journey toward The Desired Country is in a place of filth—the Slough of Despond. Like all mortals, Christian falls into the mire of the world and is "well nigh smothered" in the muck made by all the "carnal and fleshly" sins of fallen man. The slough is the dunghill of this world through which a man of godly sorrow must make his way, and his sins are the excrement that he must leave to the world when cleansed by saving grace.

> This miry slough is such a place as cannot be mended; it is the descent whither the scum and filth that attends conviction for sin doth continually run, and therefore it is called the Slough of Despond; for still, as the sinner is awakened about his lost condition, there ariseth in his soul many fears, and doubts, and discouraging apprehensions, which all of them get together and settle in this place. And this is the reason of the badness of the ground.

Similarly, Christiana later experiences the "great stinks and loathsome smells" of unredeemed sins in the Valley of Humiliation. In Vanity Fair, the carnal sins of man are characterized not only by the language of commerce, games, and crime, but also by the language of filthiness: the people at the Fair "besmear" the pilgrims with dirt; the judges attribute their own "vilifying terms" to the pilgrims; and generally the way of the pilgrims through the Fair is "sometimes . . . clean, sometimes foul."[18]

In *Paradise Lost*, at the other end of the Puritan spectrum, Milton also uses Puritan imagery to describe man's predicament. The original "Maker's image" in mankind is "vilified" by "ungoverned appetite," for they pervert "pure Nature's healthful rules" to "loathesome sickness." Man's "polluting sin" is characterized by "draff and filth" and by the "sucked and glutted offal" of dogs, and salvation is described in terms of washing man "pure" from "stain."[19]

Though Puritan verse in New England during the first two generations is noticeably devoid of talk of the fallen state of man and the world, whenever it does turn on the subject, the imagery of vilification is again present. In Anne Bradstreet's debate "The Flesh and the Spirit," there is outlined the imagery of "things unclean" and "city pure." Philip Pain, as he meditates on his human lot in his *Daily Meditations*, revels in the "Dust Heap of Mortality." In *The Day of Doom* Michael Wigglesworth instinctively renders the Judgment as revealing "All filthy facts, and secret acts" of vile man. The devils ("Legions of Sprights unclean") and man's singular nature ("so

defil'd and made so vild") together make man foul, and the rank odor
of humanity invites God's purifying wrath. The flesh is "vile" and
"defiles" the gifts of God: the best of men go "Wallowing in all kind of
sin" and thereby bring themselves "to decay." At the time of judgment Christ must therefore "wash" men of their filthiness if they are
to see salvation.

The images of salvation in Taylor's Meditations are similarly
orthodox. At his hands, as at Swift's, the fundamentalist-Protestant
excremental view of life is described honestly and fully to dramatize
the construct of reality that we refer to as Puritan theology.

Through the foulest of imagery, Taylor succeeds in making the life
of man look bad:

> Unclean, Unclean: My Lord, Undone, all vile
>   Yea all Defild: What shall thy Servant doe?
> Unfit for thee: not fit for holy Soile,
>   Nor for Communion of Saints below.
>   A bag of botches, Lump of Loathsomeness:
>   Defild by Touch, by Issue: Leproust flesh.
>
> (2.26)

In the first of his *Christographia* sermons, Taylor explains this use of
the Biblical imagery of vileness and purification in defining human
nature. "All fallen Nature [is] defiled by the Fall," he says, and must
be "purged and cleansed by the Power of God."

> There is no Humane Nature [that] is fitt to be United to the
> Person of Christ. All flesh hath Corrupted its Way. Sin hath
> render'd all men Sinfull, Vile, and Abominable. Sin is an abo-
> minable thing in the Sight of God. . . . That his own Elect may
> be brought off from Sin, he sent his Son to deliver them from Sin
> to Sanctify them. . . .[20]

To Taylor, humanity is covered with "filth, and mire, Sins juyce,"
so thick and deep that man sinks to his ears in it. (2.78) The world is
"this dirty slough/We puddle in below and Wallow now." (2.138)
And fallen man, in his "life Animall," is but a cauldron of "Guts,
Garbage, Rotteness,"

> And all [his] pipes but Sincks of nasty ware
> That foule Earths face, and do defile the aire.

Yet God's electing love comes to the "Swine Sty" of the world and

"Cleanse[s] the house" that stinks "With marks and Stains of Sin."
(2.75) Throughout Taylor's poems, and particularly in the Meditations, such scatological definitions make up a dominant strain of his
poetry. It is a strain which debases the constitution and psychology
of man and reconciles him to the process of Christian regeneration.

With an excremental imagery as his way of exploring a universal
fall, Taylor's main concern is the role of one particular sinner in that
fall—himself. As he turns inward in the course of composing his
Meditations, Taylor finds his own heart "Fild up with filth." (2.70)
"In Guilt and Filth I wallow, S[c]ent and Smell," he complains.
(2.14) Convinced in this grim self-examination that he is "Unclean"
and "all vile," Taylor characterizes himself in poem after poem as a
man who is associated with those foul things of the earth from which
the spirit of God has departed. God requires purity, but Taylor finds
himself "fowle" and covered with "all filth, alas!" By virtue of his
human nature, he is "tumbled thus in mire." The excrement that
covers him typifies his outcast state; it cannot be washed off with the
strongest nitre or soap, but only by the "bright Chrystall Crimson
Fountain" of Christ's blood, which "washeth whiter, than the Swan
or Rose." (2.26)

In this severe manner, Taylor increases the weight of the burden of
his humanity, taking the most loathsome part of himself as symp-
tomatic of his low spiritual state in a graceless world. He thus creates
a persona in his Meditations who rolls in the muck of a world
without grace so that he may be cleansed of earthly things, who
bedungs himself so that he may be made pure, and who makes
himself wretched and sick so that heaven's physic will be necessary.
Hope is thereby affirmed over and over again.

But there is more than simple vilification in Taylor's use of the
scatological and other terms of corruption in his poems. Taylor is not
merely dramatizing man's humble state and confessing his own
humility. He is also celebrating—by contrast—the greatness of God.
He is showing how the gift of affliction (man's dunghill state) is
actually an act of divine love, and he is exploring an apocalyptic
eschatology in which man is befouled to justify Christian salvation.

From the beginning of the *Preparatory Meditations*, Taylor
analyzes his difference from the Divine in terms of foulness, and the
contrast in the images, while demeaning man, magnifies the glory of
God to Taylor's mind, just as to Jonathan Edwards' mind man's total

dependence on God magnifies the absolute and arbitrary will of God. For example, compared to the greatness of God,

> Were all the World a sparkling pearle,'t would bee
> Worse than a dot of Dung if weighd with thee.
>
> (2.34)

This is because

> this world doth eye thy brightness most
> When most in distance from thyselfe
>
> .   .   .   .
>
> My back is best, and dark side Godward bee. . . .
>
> (2.21)

While man smells like "stincking Carrion" and "Dunghill Damps," God is by contrast "A Pillar of Perfume" and "Sweetness itselfe." Man's flatulence makes God's hard grace smell sweet. (1.3) Man is "Becrown'd with Filth" in contrast to the flowers and herbs that crown God's works, and the ugly sight makes the flowers of grace look the more beautiful. (1.45) Taylor furthermore characterizes himself as sick and diseased but the Lord's grace as having saving salves and medicines, and the sickness makes the Christian plan of salvation seem all the more a redeeming remedy for his sins. (2.14) The divine is thus defined by its opposites. In a sermon in 1679, Taylor celebrates the glory of God that his foulness leads him to and convinces him of:

> Oh how have I matter of Humiliation, enough to make me abhor myselfe, and morn ly[ing in] dust and ashes . . . my heart being such a Prison of naughtiness, and an Akeldama of uncleaness, that I could not alow it a good thought. . . . Oh that he would take my hand and lead within the limits of that promise, Mat. 13.12. But this I found that by how much I grew the more offended with myselfe by so much the more lovely, and longed-after did Christ appear in my eye.[21]

To construct this human difference from the divine, Taylor draws on three sources for his terms (apparently the lowest and foulest he knew): barnyard and swamp imagery, toilet images, and the language of bodily disease. The structure of his thought is often defined by the way he moves in the course of a Meditation or a series of

Meditations from a barnyard scene to a garden scene, from a privy to a washroom, or from a sickroom to a physician's apothecary. Each move is a definition—by contrast—of saving grace.

Let me illustrate. The scene where a number of Taylor's Meditations begins is around a manure pile (like Luther's "world") or in a bog of filth (like Bunyan's Slough of Despond). References throughout the Meditations to sties of filth, troughs of washing-swill, dunghill pits, puddles of slime, fumes of muck, and wagonloads of manure paint his world loathsome. To warrant pity and to celebrate the mercy of God, Taylor, like Job, turns himself into a foul dunghill. He breeds worms, his thoughts are flyblown, and his heart is "the Temple of the God of Flies" (2.25), for in his wretched condition the dunghill of the world has to him become sweeter than any grace.

> A Crown of Glory! Oh! I'm base, its true.
>   My Heart's a Swamp, Brake, Thicket vile of Sin.
> My Head's a Bog of Filth; Blood bain'd doth spew
>   Its venom streaks of Poyson o're my Skin.
>   My Members Dung-Carts that bedung at pleasure,
>   My Life, the Pasture where Hells Hurdloms leasure.
>
> Becrown'd with Filth! Oh! what vile thing am I?
>   What Cost, and Charge to make mee Meddow ground?
> To drain my Bogs? to lay my Frog-pits dry?
>   To stub up all my brush that doth abound?
>   That I may be thy Pasture fat and frim,
>   Where thy choice Flowers, and Hearbs of Grace shine
>   trim?
>
>   (1.45)

But to counteract the world's foulness and Taylor's own sinbound life, which is "truely stincking . . . As Dunghills reech with stinking sents," God's grace comes over the "Dunghill Pit and Puddle Sin" with "Sweet Spices, Herbs and Trees" and with "Viands Sweet" and "Odorif'rous air." (2.63) Taylor imagines his private dunghill to be benevolently perfumed by Christ's atonement with allegorical flowers like Herb-a-Grace, Grains of Paradise, Angelica, Rose of Sharon, Herba Trinitatis, and many others that overwhelm his foulness. (2.62) Taylor's hope thus finds expression in gardens growing on dunghills, or fountains of atoning blood "wash[ing] away the filth in mee," or the sweetening of the foul air of "Sins Dunghill." (2.3, 70)

The filth that an earnest man wallows in in the barnyard of this world thereby justifies, Taylor hopes, the grace of God.

In a similar manner, toilet imagery was in Taylor's mind representative of the anality of man's state, and the contrast with the "Sweet Aire" of God made grace great. Like Luther's, this is a vision of the world and the human body as excrement:

> Now when the world with all her dimples in't
>   Smiles on me, I do love thee more than all:
> And when her glory freshens, all in print,
>   I prize thee still above it all. And shall.
>   Nay all her best to thee, do what she can,
>   Drops but like drops dropt in a Closestoole pan.
>
> (1.48)

In this frame of mind, Taylor finds himself from time to time "All fould with filth and Sin, all rowld in goare" (2.125), for he fears that God treats him like excrement:

> If off as Offall I be put, if I
>   Out of thy Vineyard Work be put away:
> Life would be Death.
>
> ("The Return")

Thus cast out from God and thus judged foul, mankind is but "A varnished pot of putrid excrements,/And quickly turns to excrements itselfe,/By natures Law." (2.75) Man fallen from grace is in love with his own flatulence, his "Stinking Breath" vitiates the world, his "intraills bleed," he gives foul suck to devils, he discharges "Insipid Phlegm," and he defecates on himself. (1.3, 9; 2.5, 27)

In the Meditations, the greater Taylor's sense of grace the fouler his sense of self. Yet man's natural filth, he believes, will be washed in "Zions Bucking tub/With Holy Soap, and Nitre, and rich Lye," because Christ's atonement is a cleansing grace. (1.40) In saving man, Christ must "imbrace/Such dirty bits of Dirt" and so must "Cleanse mee thus with [his] Rich Bloods Sweet Showr" (1.41; 2.27) In his psychology of religion, it is through this imagery of the excretory nature of humanity that Taylor gets most forcefully at the heart of the ruthless Puritan wisdom of the Fall.

Furthermore, looking inward, Taylor also finds himself innately and mortally sick. "Issues and Leprosies all ore mee streame," he

cries in Meditation 2.27. He finds himself "uncleane" because the
running issue of his mortality spreads like leprosy over all his life until
he is "all ore ugly." His lungs are "Corrupted," his skin is "all botch't
and scabd," his breath stinks, and he is covered with a "Skurfy
Skale." But Christ will come to cure his unclean body, he concludes,
with the miracle of his medicinal blood: "Here's Grace." His is a
"Diseased Soul" with "Spirituall Sores" that only Christ can cure.
(2.160) The cause of the sick world is, he finds, Satan: "His Aire I
breath in, poison doth my Lungs./Hence come Consumptions, Fev-
ers, Head pains: Turns." (2.67b) And as a result of his condition,
Taylor contracts a multitude of diseases and bodily ailments that
describe his foul state: he is "Consumptive," he has "Wasted lungs
[that can] Scarc draw a Breath of aire," he is full of "ill Humours"
that need to be drained out of him, or he has

> Lythargy, the Apoplectick Stroke:
> The Catochee, Soul Blindness, Surdity,
> Ill Tongue, Mouth Ulcers, Frog, the Quinsie Throate
> The Palate Fallen, Wheezings, Pleurisy.
> Heart Ach, the Syncopee, bad stomach tricks
> Gaul Tumors, Liver grown; spleen evills Cricks.

> The Kidny toucht, The Iliak, Colick Griefe
> The Ricats, Dropsy, Gout, the Scurvy, Sore
> The Miserere Mei.

So compounded is his sickness and foulness that he begs for relief
from Christ the Physician. He wants desperately to be purged of
wastes, to have his blood purified, his ears picked, his eyes quickened
by God's "Ophthalmicks pure," his mouth washed out, his scabs and
boils cleansed, his fistulas and gangrene treated, his swellings plas-
tered. "Heale me of all my Sin," he cries in anguish. (2.14, 67b)
Taylor learns that man must "Purge out and Vomit by Repentance
all/ Ill Humours which thy Spirituall Tast forestall" to get rid of "Filth
and Faults." (2.104) The gospel therefore acts as physic and God's
love as balm.

And so grace is again justified because it is desperately needed. The
foulest of barnyards, the filthiest of ordure, and the most severe of
diseases all construct the desperation of that need and celebrate by
contrast the power and benvolence of God.[22] From his human point
of view, if he is put off "as Offal,"[23] then to Taylor, "Life would be

Death." But from a divine point of view, the excremental state is necessary to the process of salvation, for to be bedunged by God is *part of God's grace*. Such a scatology of grace was for Taylor a way of probing through metaphor the necessary anality of rebirth. The symbolic manipulation of excrement or substitutes for excrement is therefore apocalyptic: dunghills produce gardens, excrement purges, sores bring salvation.

As he attempts to reconstruct the causes of man's foul condition, Taylor reasons (particularly in his poem "Upon the Sweeping Flood") that man was originally pure, but natural disturbances show him that the body of the world has become sick. Original sin and man's mortal sins have acted as a "physick" upon the heavens "To make them purg and Vomit. . . And Excrements out fling." The heavens are so grieved that "they shed/Their Excrements upon our lofty heads." Man's dunghill state is therefore God's judgment upon man's sinful ways. But in a further poem, as he observes the judgments of God, Taylor finds that the "Sweet Sun of Righteousness" shines "Upon such Dunghills, as I am," producing "putrid s[c]ents and rhimes, . . . Stincks/And Nasty vapors," and foul diseases, so that man will be humbled and beg for relief. (2.67b) God causes the filth in order to effect love:

> The Influences my vile heart sucks in
>   Of Puddle Water boyld by Sunn beams till
> Its Spiritless, and dead, nothing more thin
>   Tasts wealthier than those thou dost distill.
>
> .   .   .   .
>
> Yet when the beamings, Lord, of thy rich Joys,
>   Do guild my Soule, meethinks I'm sure I Love thee.
>
> .   .   .   .
>
> For when the Objects of thy Joy impress
>   Their shining influences on my heart
> My Soule seems an Alembick doth possess
>   Love [di]stilld into rich Spirits by thy Art.
>
> (1.48)

When God finds man in such a "sad state," Taylor writes in Meditation 1.8, he causes his "Tender Bowells [to] run/Out streams of Grace" on man. Out of love, and yet also in recognition of fallen man's low state and base deserts, God grinds up his "deare-dear Son" (this takes place in his bowels, the seat of both compassion and excrement), and the son then "runs out" of God's tender bowels in sacramental form down a golden path to man's threshold. This holy excrement is the bread of life, even "Heavens Sugar Cake," to filth-devouring man.[24] By analogy, the dunghill of the world too is God's sacramental excrement, a place of sorrow that is a gift of benevolence. The gift of affliction thus becomes an act of love, for dung is God's way of bringing man to Him. Suffering stirs affections, and earth becomes a stinking place so that man will turn his affections toward heaven.

But unlike medieval mystics, Taylor feels repugnance at all the loathsomeness he constructs in his Meditations. God is not associated in his mind with the idea of dirt, except by contrast. In this regard he is unlike most Christian ascetics: dwelling on the idea of dirty and disgusting things, such as phlegm or flatulence or feces, does not emphasize and enhance his nearness to God. His pervasive excremental imagery does not at all constitute the mystic's "dark night of the soul" or "Way of Purgation," as Norman Grabo implies, following the lead of Evelyn Underhill.[25] "I'm not/Pleased with my mud," Taylor objects; "Sin doth not tickle mee." (2.67a) Rather, Taylor's imagery of filthiness is eschatalogical. The motif of defiling/cleansing reveals the pattern that Taylor felt existence has, and though simplistic, it was for him an expression of profound hope. The imagery of his belief is parallel to that in the eschatology of the prophet of *Lamentations*: God has "compassed me with gall, and labour. He hathe set me in darke places, . . . therefore have I hope." (3:5-21)

Hope in the form of love-longing is the other half of Taylor's imagery of salvation: gold weds dung, Christ embraces dirt, Eros wins over Thanatos.

> I know not how to speak't, it is so good:
>> Shall Mortall, and Immortall marry? nay,
> Man marry God? God be a Match for Mud?
>> The King of Glory Wed a Worm? mere Clay?
>> This is the Case. The Wonder too in Bliss.
>> Thy Maker is thy Husband. Hearst thou this?
>>>>> (1.23)[26]

In this regard, Taylor's metaphoric approach in the *Preparatory Meditations* is an important theme, showing affirmation amid despair and trying to make a garden of bliss out of the dunghill. "Love," Yeats writes, echoing the Augustinian imagery of salvation we find in Taylor, "has pitched his mansion in/The place of excrement." This is the archetypal paradox of love in a fallen world.

When Taylor strikes an erotic note as he discusses his salvation—

Lord, let thy glorious Body send such rayes
   Into my Soule, as ravish shall my heart,
That Thoughts how thy bright Glory out shall blaze
   Upon my body, may such Rayes [to] thee dart.

(2.76)

—we are assured that the repression of life/world/self is replaced in his thinking by affirmation and desire. Yet such erotic imagery pervading the Meditations is not cathartic (that is, not a device for releasing sexual tension) nor ascetic (Taylor is not diverting his emotions into sensuous devotions), nor is it mystical and theoleptic (Taylor does not seek to be literally God-possessed). Rather it is semi-Dionysian— Christ the Lover is a god of joy, of healing, of fulfillment—in a way thoroughly consistent with Puritan theology. This erotic imagery is the sensuous apprehension of the possibility of new life—which was, after all, the true calling of a Puritan minister-poet.

Beginning perhaps with the Judeo-Christian allegorical use of the erotic Song of Solomon, the symbolic love-relation between God and man infused Christian imagery. Early Christian interpreters made use of the Canticles as an allegory of the love of Christ for his church (for example, Hippolytus, Origen, Jerome, and Augustine) or as an allegory of the mystical union of a believing soul with God or Christ (especially Origen, Gregory of Nyssa, Theodoret, and St. Bernard).[27] It is in this latter sense that Taylor himself exploits the sensuality of the Canticles in 76 individual Meditations.

The Song of Solomon was Taylor's favorite book in the Bible— erotic verses from it appear as his text most frequently in the Second Series and especially in his maturest years, after he was 70—because it, like his other favorite, the Gospel of John, offered a bulk of imagery which proposed a solution to the domination of despair in the world and in himself. The solution to the dunghill of the world

and the filth of the heart was, in its simplest anagogic form, passionate love—as symbolized first of all in God's (or Christ's) benevolent
desires for man and then by man's ardent desire for God.[28]

As a frame for his theme of love-against-death, the *Preparatory
Meditations* begins and ends with a series of poems based on Canticle
texts which Taylor read as celebrations of the Great Lover. The
passion between the maiden and Solomon the King becomes an
object lesson in the joys of love to Taylor, who in the course of his
Meditations caresses the body of the Lord with the eyes of his words
and who yearns to be the "seduced" Loved One. The King's position
as seducer and the maiden's descriptions of love as the most irrestible,
most precious, and strongest of all things gave Taylor an erotic basis
for his exploration of the psychology of a seeker and the logic of
God's pursuit of foul mankind.[29]

The Gospel of John was Taylor's second scriptural source for the
images of divine Eros that he conceived of as a solution to man's
dilemma. The 29 Meditations based on texts from John, as well as
many of his other Meditations, show an erotic exuberance that to
Taylor satisfied the demands that the burden of the Fall, the filth of
life, and the sickness of man placed on his own soul. Whereas the
imagery of filth best characterizes the limitations of human life to
Taylor, this erotic imagery conceived from the Canticles and John
best characterizes full life; that is, the reconciliation of earth and
heaven, death and life, man and God. In his erotic imagery, Taylor
attempts to effect such a unity of opposites, if only in the form of
poetic illusion.

John's concept of man as the passive Loved One and God as the
aggressive Lover emerges in such statements as these:

> There arose a question . . . about purifying. . . . John answered
> & said, A man can receive nothing, except it be given him from
> heaven.
>
> (3:25–27)

> The Sonne quickeneth whome he wil.
>
> (5:21)

> He . . . cometh downe from heaven, and giveth life unto the
> worlde.
>
> (6:33)

No man can come to me, except the Father, which hathe sent
me, drawe him.

                                                    (6:44)

Taylor proceeds to draw erotic analogies from such a relationship:

> God's onely Son doth hug Humanity,
> Into his very person.
>
>   (1.10, based on John 6:55)

> Gods onely Son . . . imbrace[s]
> Such dirty bits of Dirt, with such a grace!
>
>   (1.41, on John 14:2)

>   thou, my Lord, . . . shouldst take delight
> To make my flesh thy Tent, and tent with in't.
>
>   (2.24, on John 1:14)

> Thy Love-Affection . . .
> Brings Loads of Love to sinfull man all gore.
>
>   (2.31, on John 15:13)

> O let thy lovely streams of Love distill
>   Upon myselfe and spoute their spirits pure
> Into my Viall, and my Vessell fill
>   With liveliness, from dulness me secure.
>
>   (2:32, on John 15:13)

The allegorizing of the intimate and ardent aspects of Johannine
agape naturally led Taylor to the use of these erotic metaphors.
Medieval mystics from Dionysius to Jakob Boehme had done
much the same. The imagery of human love and marriage had best
expressed the fulfillment of life they achieved through ecstatic and
visionary union with the divine.[30] But Taylor's imagery is different
from theirs in being doggedly earthy. Mysticism, in its classical form,
belongs to a different tradition from the Puritan. Because of his
humility with regard to man's condition, Taylor never does achieve
the mystical state. While he yearns for transcendence, he never gets
off the ground—and this makes his spiritual desires all the more
painful and realistic. His are poems of desire and hope, not reports of
fulfillment. Earth the dunghill was to him, as later to Frost, the right
place for love.

In his own time, sexual imagery had of course become archetypal for love of the divine among devotional poets—as in Donne's image of Christ as ravishing Lover, Herbert's mild Lord that eyes and wooes the heart and creeps into the breast to kindle the love of faith and Crashaw's spirit of rapture in contemplation of the divine. But in none of these is erotic imagery used programmatically, as it is in Taylor; that is, as a consistent part of the dialectic of salvation.[31] In them, the erotic seems a public pose (hortatory, exemplary) or self-indulgent (a spiritualizing of the senses, a confusing of the exuberance of the flesh as spiritual transcendence) rather than fully meditative. Taylor's is a private struggle with the world, God's will, and foul self, rather than a preoccupation with a world beyond human experience. And the resulting imagery is more personal and primitive and earthy.

Erotic imagery was operative within Calvinism itself. Calvin, as he attempts "an accurate explication" of the meaning of the Lord's Supper, centers his attention on physical-sensuous aspects of the sacrament—such as flesh, body, embraces—rather than the purely mystical-spiritual.

> We embrace Christ by faith, not as appearing at a distance, but as uniting himself with us, to become our head, and to make us his members. . . . He also makes the very flesh in which he resides the means of giving life to us, that, by a participation of it, we may be nourished to immortality. . . . Here, then, we enjoy peculiar consolation, that we find life in our own flesh. . . . We know [we] can not otherwise be effected than by entire union of both body and spirit with us. But that most intimate fellowship, by which we are united with his flesh, the apostle has illustrated in a still more striking representation, when he says, "We are members of his body, of his flesh, and of his bones. . . ." That holy participation of his flesh and blood, by which Christ communicated his life to us, just as if he actually penetrated every part of our frame, in the sacred supper he also testifies and seals. . . . If, by the breaking of the bread, the Lord truly represents the participation of his body, it ought not to be doubted that he truly presents and communicates it. . . . If it be true that the visible sign is given to us to seal the donation of the invisible substance, we ought to entertain a confident assurance, that in

receiving the symbol of his body, we at the same time truly receive the body itself.[32]

In his blunt language, Calvin describes grace in terms of "a forcible seizure, a rape of the surprised will."[33] Such an emphasis could give a Puritan poet orthodox justification for an erotic approach to the sacrament.

Further justification came from the Calvinist meditative tradition of the prepared heart:

> By preparation [is] meant a period of prolonged introspective meditation and analysis in the light of God's revealed Word. In this process man first examined the evils of his sins, repented for those sins, and then turned to God for salvation. From conviction of conscience, the soul moved through a series of interior stages, always centered on self-examination, which in turn were intended to arouse a longing desire for grace.[34]

Though this process begins in self-vilification, its object is to achieve the "longing desire" for God's love. Such severe logic asserts that after a man sees in what need he stands for the favor and grace of God, God extends his love to man so that it may be reflected back again. This meditation on the love of dependence results in a "heart of flesh" to replace man's natural stony heart, and empties oneself to be filled with divine love. Though a man's "longing desire" cannot bribe, warrant, or create grace, it prepares him for the covenant promise of God's pure, unselfish love for man. A man prepares himself not mainly out of fear but in anticipation of divine love, and because of the dominance of this theme in Puritan thinking, the language of love, in the meditative tradition, becomes an orthodox response that is often intensely felt and often passionately expressed in strong erotic metaphors.[35] Thus, an intensely personal love-longing for salvation became a guiding esthetic in Puritan expression.

Puritan divines in New England often justified such imagery as essential to a proper celebration of Christ's love. There is the possibility, as Edmund Morgan has suggested, that their Christianity was a sublimation of sexual impulses.[36] Cotton Mather thought of the Lord's Supper as a "Love-Feast" at which one should experience a "Love-fire," and Samuel Mather, in his comprehensive exposition of the ordinance of communion, called it a Commemoration of the greatest love, which cannot be done as it ought to be, without the reciprocation of our most ardent and intense Love. . . . If we love Christ as we ought, he is our all. . . . If we do not come to enjoy him, and lie in his Embraces, we do not come with a right design, nor can we expect to profit.[37]

Likewise, Thomas Goodwin in *The Heart of Christ in Heaven Towards Sinners on Earth* dwells on the physical body of Christ with an erotic intensity imitating Calvin's.[38] In a sermon defending the sacrament against Stoddardean liberalism, Taylor himself proclaims the orthodoxy of the erotic in popular use:

All Union being a making One of Severall, lyeth in joyning things together. Our Lord Styles marriage Union a joyning together. So the Mysticall Union is a joyning the Soule and Christ together.[39]

Especially to a Puritan like Taylor, no happiness existed apart from such glorification of union with the divine.

Such imagery was to orthodox ministers in New England fully appropriate in expressing the natural inclinations of a worldly heart toward heavenly love. And it was fully appropriate in explaining the mortality of Christ: the Son of God could not have been produced on the earth, as Taylor says in his poem "The Experience," unless God and man had "Together joyn'd . . . Flesh of my Flesh, Bone of my Bone" and, through "enflamed" love, had consummated their love. But more important than these reasons, it was a theologically necessary imagery, in order to show God's love rivalling and excelling what Taylor calls the "Worldly Gayes" and "Carnall" passions of mankind stuck in the dunghill of the world.

Taylor's choice of erotic imagery shows that in the severe Puritan wisdom of his poems his emphasis, like Jonathan Edwards', is not on a God of wrath but a God of love. In an autobiographical confession of faith, Taylor clarified the semi-erotic language that his spiritual desires for a God of love take in his poems:

As for Love I can assert that I have been bound in this cord. Oh the outgoing of this Affection whether inriched by the Sanctifying grace of the Spirit called Love, or no, I say not, but hope it. Oh how it went breaking after Christ and longing for him, oh those inward heart panting[s], and musing[s] can testify. . . . This hath been mightily promoted in reading the history of Christ's passion, and So Love to the people of God. Oh, this I have had such a Sense of, that I could not bear to hear a word against them; but it was a Qu[i]ck thing in my heart that upon the entrance of a thought of Such into my heart as professed godliness in truth, my heart would be Surprised with an indearing rapture toward them, and hearing them set out as Such as Should Shine a[s] Sparkling Diamonds in the Ring of Gods glory. Oh how it did indeare me more, if it could be, to thee and, oh (me thought) that I was but one of them. And so I indeavored to be.[40]

The metaphors of love-longing are here, as in his meditative poems, expressions of God's love, the love of God, and the humble desire to be godly.

The scheme of Taylor's love meditations is simple; he tells it in his first poem in the *Preparatory Meditations*. God's love is so over-whelming that it "Cannot bee/ In thine Infinity, O Lord, Confinde." It is a pent-up flood. But this love is not satisfied until God, through Christ, has "Marri'de our Manhood, making it its Bride." Then, as in a marriage union, it finds release. The love desires of God are satisfied only when, after filling heaven up and overflowing hell, the veins of God the Seducer are conjoined with the veins of Man the Beloved. Then the love that God passionately finds outlet for in man through Christ can be repaid by man's passionate love of God. All the factors of Taylor's erotic scheme of salvation are here: God as Lover, man-kind as the Beloved One, the seduction, and the loving reaction in man that amounts to regeneration. Through such erotic terms, the doctrine of atonement is turned into poetic metaphor.

Taylor tells the whole story of atonement once again in Meditation 1.23, and again in erotic terms. So that he might be passionately "inflamde," Taylor says (now playing the role of a desirous woman, as he does in most of his Meditations), he prays for permission to peep into the "Golden City" of heaven to see how "Saints and Angells ravisht are in Glee." Yet he thinks that *his* affairs, *his* love of God, would teach them a thing or two: " 'Twould in fresh Raptures Saints and Angells fling." He proceeds to tell how passionate his own love is. Yet he has great doubts that "Man [can] marry God," for it is improper and unnatural that "The King of Glory Wed a Worm." So all that is left for him is "the Wedden in our Eyes"; that is, the passion, the desire, the flirtation. It is the lot of fallen man that his desires go unfulfilled. The reason is that the desires cannot be consummated simply as the result of man's passion; he is depraved, filthy, a worm. It is not until "Christ doth Wooe" and compels the earth-bound Loved One to true love that the two can be joined. God must first be a lover of man before man can be a lover of God. Then their love is consummated.

In characterizing God as the Great Lover, Taylor is probing the nature of a God who should seek worthless man. God so loves mankind that he puts on the appearance of a young buck "with the purest ruddy looks" (Christ as the young man of Canticles) who pursues man and takes him "in folds of Such love raptures" that man is seduced by love into the ability to love spiritual things. (2.116) Christ flirts with man with the eye of a lover—"this pert percing fiery Eye of thine"—and pursues him "in a blesst Chase . . . to fetch . . . My Heart and Love . . . in Hottest Steams." (2.119) The Lord's passion for man therefore arouses equal passion in man for God. But it is "Degenerate" for man himself to pursue God, except in desire and hope and love-longing; he must wait for Christ to come as Lover. Only when Christ takes someone for his Beloved will they be wed and man be ravished in glory. Since man cannot be saved until he loves God and since he cannot love God until God loves him and brings him to Him by force, election takes on the imagery of seduction, almost a rape of the will.

In his poem "The Reflexion" Taylor clarifies (again in erotic terms) the active role of God and the passive role of man in this love-relationship. Man's conduit pipes are stopped up with muck, Taylor says, and the phallic spade of God is needed to "Ravish" and clean out the pipes:

> what Ravishment would'st thou Convay?
> Let Graces Golden Spade dig till the Spring
> Of tears arise, and cleare this filth away.

Though this divine seduction hurts, causing tears of penance, it makes "sweetness" in the foul soul possible. That is, Taylor, like a virgin, can respond to the Lord's sexuality only after he has been ravished by God. At first he is feeble (therefore feminine), but after the divine rape he takes on a more active, masculine role, in imitation of Christ the Lover. He is then capable of love himself.

In his role as Seducer in the drama of salvation which unifies the *Preparatory Meditations*, Christ comes "forthe to Wooe," and because man acts like a whore, Christ pays her "Price" on the cross in order to procure and possess her. Through his atonement in the loathsome world, Christ flirts with mankind until he melts "all up into Love" and the whore is won over. (1.12) Angels assist in such divine seductions of the human heart. They come as courtiers to the earth and help Christ "inravish" the heart. (1.20) God also takes advantage of the imagination of man ("the Fancy") to flirt with his soul. He comes like a handsome lover and "wantons" with man, tempting him through his senses into union with him. Man blushes and backs off from the Lord's sensuous advances, yet the Lord continues to "come and Wooe him." (2.101) In these ways God overcomes the world.

"These Metaphors [that] we spirituallized," Taylor explains self-consciously in defense of his erotic descriptions, "Speake out the Spouses spirituall Beauty cleare" (2.151). And to show how desirable the Christ-Spouse of the communion is, Taylor constructs elaborate metaphors that ascribe great physical beauty to the Christ-Lover of whom it is a spiritually beautiful emblem. To lure man to him, the Lord, like the King of Canticles, adorns himself seductively. To Taylor, he is, as the long catalog of fleshly descriptions in the Second Series shows, lovely "all o're." He has a "Spirituall Countenance" with rosy cheeks that send one into "love raptures." He has piercing eyes of the "most Charming beauty." His mouth drips with "Myrrhie Juyce" that sanctifies through joyous kisses. His hands put one into ecstatic raptures. His bowels embrace lovingly. He is "from the toe to th'top Divine." (2.116, 119, 121, 122, 123a, 152) Therefore a man's love does not go anywhere but to the Lord: "Thy Loveliness attracts all Love to thee" because of his physical beauty. (2.127)

The sacrament of the Lord's Supper, as we have seen repeatedly, is to Taylor an emblematic communion in which man, when "enravished" in his affections, identifies himself with Christ the Lover. To Taylor's mind the Christ in that communal act is in his "Elementall Frame," virile and powerful—"The top of beauty," he says. There never was "So Beautiful a piece of manhood frame." And yearning in a spiritual sense to be virile and beautiful too, he "hunger[s] to bee filled with [Christ's] likeness." (2.99) This identification with Christ's beauty is not so much ecstatic transcendence, however, as it is that a man's longing to be virile has given

Taylor, as he meditates on communion, a metaphor for his desire to be godlike. Yet the almost-ecstatic language of desire emphasizes the tragic fact in Taylor's mind that all he can do is admire and yearn.

One mistake some critics of Taylor have made, however, in wondering at the orthodoxy of his erotic imagery is in seeing these fleshly descriptions of beauty as descriptions of only Christ's physique, flesh, and organs. But it is not so much the physical features of Christ that are being caressed by loving metaphors (as in verse growing out of Catholic tradition) as it is the beauty of the idealized self—the pure, beautiful, and beloved person that Taylor desires before God so passionately to be. In that elaborate catalog of descriptions taken from the erotic lines in Canticles (2.116–52), Taylor identifies himself for the most part with the young maiden rather than with the King; that is, with an idealized self whose attributes derive from God but whose identity is separate and passive, rather than with Christ's person itself.[41] He yearns to be the desired one, the attractive one, the Beloved of Christ. Fallen man's is a "Hide-bound Heart," his head "but a durt-ball . . . of tainted mould" to the side of the ideal, but Christ, by acting the Divine Lover toward him, can, Taylor desperately hopes, transform him into something beautiful, something worth saving. (2.118) It is not the mystical proximity to the body of Christ that to Taylor constitutes the sacramental act of emblematic communion (that would be spiritual pride), but it is the intense yearning to be beloved though hide-bound, saved though a dirt-ball, glorified though tainted.

When Taylor's metaphors of yearning go beyond fleshly descriptions of the Christ who is the source of spiritual beauty and descriptions of the idealized loved one with whom Taylor identifies his spiritual desires, Taylor comes to a use of the language of sexual consummation in a joyous celebration of the conversion from worthless selfhood to divine acceptability and regeneration. "Christ loves to lay the Beloved down" and with "lovely arms . . . Circle [her] about, with great Delight." (2.96) It is as if the soul goes into "Raptures of Joyes" until, as he says, "My Ravisht heart on Raptures Wings would fly." (2.93) Yet this is not erotic mysticism, but the expression of joy and delight in the possibility of salvation from man's condition. Taylor's desire for love is so intense that it is *like* sexual intercourse: "Thy Person mine, Mine thine, even wedden-wise." So he continually pleads for salvation in sexual terms:

"Make thou mee thine that so/ I may be bed wherein thy Love shall ly," for he knows that the only way for him to be saved is through the "down laying of myself"; that is, either through abject humility that is like being seduced, or in death as a kind of union with the divine. (2.79) Such "down laying" is a joyous experience, however, for it is the only way given to man to fulfill his desire for salvation. The language of seduction therefore assists Taylor in reminding himself of the joy, the pleasure, the dynamism of his spiritual desires.

Taylor's erotic images are varied as he seeks to suggest the joy of the love communion: a pearl put into a cabinet, wine poured into a cup, fiery arrows shot through the heart, bag-pipes filled with divine air, sparks of heavenly fire dropped into a tinder box, bellows blowing a fire, or key and oil in a rusty lock:

Lord, make thy Holy Word, the golden Key
    My Soule to lock and make its bolt to trig
Before the same, and Oyle the same to play
    As thou dost move them off and On to jig.
                    (1.25, 28; 2.92, 115, 129; p. 470)

For much of such suggestive imagery in the Meditations, Taylor finds it easy to make an erotic metaphor out of innocent Bible idioms, as he does with John 6:53 in Meditation 2.80: "Except you eate the flesh of the Son of Man, etc., ye have no Life in you." To Taylor "having life" suggested the appropriateness of the language of conception in explaining how God gives man a spiritual life. In the poem, Taylor is again the seduced Loved One, who, he says, has no life in her until she "be brought to bed" and "outspred" in the attitude of lovemaking. Then when seduced by the aggressive God that John preaches about, the soul is the womb and Christ is "the Spermadote" and "Saving Grace [is] the seed cast thereinto." Or in other words, God through Christ has holy intercourse with man, "Making vitality in all things flow" until in the womb of the soul "The Babe of Life" is conceived. If the Lord, Taylor concludes, does not make life in him (the seed cast into grace's garden), then his soul is "Spiritual[ly] Dead." Thus man is a fertile garden plowed by the Lord!

Concurrent with Taylor's hopes for God's enravishing love, however, are his more realistic fears that he is rejected as the Beloved of God. He is seldom "hugd," he says, and can "seldom gain a Kiss." (1.37) He is worried when Christ has kissed him but will not allow him to return the kiss; his emotions are aroused but frustrated:

> let mee lodge in thy Love.
> Although thy Love play bow-peep with me here.
> Though I be dark.
>
> (2.96)

The fault for this lies in himself, he concludes, for though his "ardent love in Christ [has] enfire[d] the Heart," his "Spirituall Eye" is "wholy dark/In th'heart of Love." He yearns for love, yet his fallen nature prevents it. He therefore often fears that Christ might lose his "ardent Flame of Love" for him, his "passionate affection," his "true Love's passion" with "its Blinks or Blisses," for he (Taylor) admits his inclination to love the dunghill of the world more than the Lord. He can find no evidence in his heart at times to "prove his marriage knot to Christ." It is a one-sided love affair, for Taylor finds himself incapable of true love. So he prays that in spite of his debased state, the Lord might make love advances to him continually. (2.97)[42]

The moment of conversion to God's love is, within Taylor's symbolic scheme, the moment when God the Lover, "Heartsick" for man, ejaculates "in Rapid Flashes" and "bleed[s] out o're Loveless mee." Then man breaks out "in a rapid Flame of Love," repaying the affection. (1.14/15) When espoused (chosen) by the Lord, man is "inravisht with thy Beauty's glorious glee," and then "Christ doth Come and take thee by the hand,/And to himselfe presents thee pleasantly [as]/A glorious bride." When Christ has brought beauty to man (that is, elected him) he is then fit "for Christ's Bed" (the communion). Christ proceeds to "Cover thee with's White and Red." (2.134) In this kind of triple entendre, Taylor's conceits bring together the imagery of sexual union, the signification of the communion, and the dogma of the atonement in a form expressive of the joy of his spiritual desires.

Just as the human and divine combined to create the Christ, so the love between God and man, as in sexual union, combines to make a new being out of excremental man: "One made of twoness Humane and Divine" in order to "compose a Third." (2.32) This is accomplished when, as Taylor puts it in one poem, Christ's phallic bellows blow on Taylor's coal "till/It glow" and "send Loves hottest Steams" on him. This warms him into intense affection, as to a new life. Then Christ fills his arms and Taylor's worship takes the form of

"Embraces." (2.6) The Lord, as in a bawdy Renaissance scene, "coms tumbling" on man and makes love "in golden pipes that spout/In Streams from heaven." (2.143) And man is born spiritually.

In this scheme of divine seduction, man's reaction to God's ravishing love is the ability to love—this is the newborn life in him. Being able to love amounts to salvation. When the "Warm Sun" of God's love melts the "numbd Affections," man breaks out "in a rapid Flame of Love" to God (1.14/15). This love is the "extasie," the "trance," the "glory" that Taylor then describes himself as being in—which, again, is not erotic mysticism but joyous, sensuous apprehension of momentary personal evidences of his salvation. The ability to love God is to Taylor the sure sign of his election:

> Hence I have power to Love and to desire.
>   These brave Affections Choose such Objects which
> Desirable and Lovely are t'infire
>   These bright affections that upon them pitch.
>   Such objects found by these affections sweet,
>   Desire draws in, and Love goes out to meet.
>
> (2.127)

Through love, Taylor exclaims, "thou hast made me all Divine." (2.32)

The erotic is therefore appropriate to a conviction of grace. The language of love desires shows a conviction that a divine energy is at work in oneself. To Taylor, the essence of man is his desire, and the quest of man is to find an object for his love. Man's condition, his dunghill state, works against such longings, yet his salvation lies in his ability to hold fast to his desires. The predominance of all this erotic imagery in the *Preparatory Meditations* shows with what joy he contemplates his fundamentalist belief that through desire man's condition is changed from one that is static to one that is dynamic.

Most important in Taylor's imagery of salvation that helps to unify the *Preparatory Meditations* is the contrast of the erotic with the scatological. The juxtaposition of the two throughout his Meditations makes an archetypal scheme contrasting, in personal terms, a man's desires vs. his humility before his estate, and, in cosmic terms, spiritual life vs. spiritual death. As Taylor sums it up in Meditation 2.120, because of the "Earthy Dunghills" and "dirty Earth" that dominate man's fallen state, it is necessary for the Lover-Christ to come "Enravishing" mankind, making the world "sweet and Beautious."[43]

In other poems, similar contrasts schematize Taylor's concern for the cosmic Christian drama of salvation. The King weds worms and gold weds dung. Christ embraces dirt. The Divine Lover kisses the vile and seduces the unclean. God ravishes man though he is filthy. Man is saved though a dirtball and glorified though tainted. Gardens of bliss bloom on dunghills. Though spiritually dead, man is loved into new life.

Summary

> Thy Love-Affection, rooted in the Soyle,
>   Of Humane Nature, springing up all ore
> With Sanctifying Grace, of brightest file
>   Brings Loads of Love to sinfull man all gore.
>   Here is greate Love. . . .
>
> (2.31)

In playing both sides of this archetypal scheme against each other and then resolving them in metaphoric forms that amount to a description of the conjuncture of the severe justice of God and the love-longings of man in the process of salvation, Taylor is following the admonition of Paul to the Colossians: " You must first "Mortifie . . . your members which are on the earth"; then "as the elect of God, holie & beloved," you must "put on tender mercie"; then will "the peace of God rule in your hearts." (3:5–15)

When seen as a unified work after the manner illustrated here, the *Preparatory Meditations* becomes a powerful affirmation of the eschatology of Augustine: "Inter urinas et faeces nascimur." To be sure, the Meditations are individual poems written on particular occasions in language that is varied and on a number of religious subjects. Yet throughout, there is a unity of imagery and tone in all of the separate poems in the series. They were written over a period of thirty years, and yet they work together as a whole to celebrate— even to create—that scheme of salvation which was Taylor's faith.

Chapter 9

Taylor as a Myth-Maker

All the Springs of Divine influences in the head,
shall be carried by the hand of Love down thro'
all the Secret Wayes and Chanells of
Convayances to every member of the body for
its Spirituall increase, and fulness.

Christographia

"Edward Taylor," Francis Murphy has written, "is the first of a great triumvirate of Connecticut Valley writers (the others being Jonathan Edwards and Emily Dickinson) who, born a hundred years apart, shared a common metaphor for experience: the burdens and joys of life under the Covenant."[1] At the one end of the traditions of the Connecticut Valley, Thomas H. Johnson argues, there was Taylor living a life of quiet usefulness and faith-promoting influence and at the other was Emily Dickinson, whose life and thought "is inseparably a part of the Valley tradition" that Taylor helped to start. "Had [Taylor] not lived in the Valley three hundred years ago," Johnson concludes, "there would have been a different drama."[2]

It is primarily in the myth-structure of that Connecticut Valley intellectual tradition, a structure of which he was an active pioneer and defender, that Taylor has a significant reach beyond his own life and time. For the biographical critic it is the substance of the life and work of the man. To his life it gave a definition, a foundation, fiber, bone, and blood, an identity, a security, a structure. Its dimensions, as we shall see, were assumed to be reality itself; by considerable skill, it was imaginatively imposed on the universe *as reality*.

All of Taylor's work is informed, even defined, by the Puritan structure for which he gave the testimony of his life. He cannot be seen without it or outside it or beyond it or beneath it. It defines him, he defines it. Whatever form his speech may take, it derives from the language of that structure. Whatever his delights and fears, they have their source in the Calvinist system of his belief. Interestingly enough, when seen as part of the myth-structure that it itself participated in making, Taylor's work has an importance to a tradition in American culture up to and including Emily Dickinson, not by virtue of its own power but by virtue of the mythic that it supported. By virtue of a mythic Puritanism, Emily Dickinson teaches one how to read Edward Taylor, and Edward Taylor is, in a way, a creator of that tradition in American literature that includes Emily Dickinson. They become part of each other's world, unwittingly and irrevocably.

Use of the mythic in discussing such a writer as Taylor implies that one sees how he imposed on reality a structure which he felt it had to have in order to be meaningful, a structure which corresponded in general with the organization of his own life, a structure which made an artist out of him. From the vantage point of these structuralist assumptions, Taylor's position in tradition and his contribution to a tradition become much clearer, as do the more controversial features of his writing—the privacy, the roughness of form, the coupling of the meditative and revivalistic, the freedom within terribly restrictive forms.

The mythic in Taylor is that abstract relation of things which would not let existence become meaningless, a system outside which his life would have no meaning, a structure which alone could provide his possibilities of meaning. The mythic in Taylor is the structure of *a priori* which attached him to society and tradition and at the same time encouraged a secure individuality. It is that which is most assertive, most powerfully provocative in his work, a pool, a reserve, a storehouse in his creative process. It is the principle of continuity, hidden but dominant, in him. It is the ordered system of values upon which the major features of his life are contingent, the outline of his system of thought, the latent content of his work.

The mythic in Taylor is the level of assumption and abstract law as opposed to the level of experience and concrete sensation. Material experience may not constitute meaning; meaning comes from the use of an ordered system of signs making up a myth-structure. The myth may remain unconscious; yet it determines conduct and expression. The mythic use of language presents a message by way of signs pointing to the primary level of meaning, a latent sense, a system of thought removed from action and experience. Expression actualizes the structure where the possible meanings lie. It is not at the level of expression that writing makes its sense but at the level of one's structured assumptions. At the one level is the means for one's expression to have the possibility of meaning, and at the other his own voice and speech; at the one his ideology, and at the other his experience; on the one hand, form, and on the other, individuality. The voice of a writer therefore has referents in a system of values and at the same time is an expression of personal experience.

The myth-structure that informed the life and work of Taylor is the Puritanism of the Connecticut Valley. That Edward Taylor's poetry represents this construct well should be fairly obvious. Without much strain, many of the fundamentals of Connecticut Valley Puritanism can be deduced in simplified form from the poetry that he wrote in defense of it. With only slight variations he is a thoroughgoing representative of it. It is the structure in which he moved and a structure that his life's work worked to move into the hearts of others. Of all the literature written within the confines of New England Puritanism, it is, I feel, most easily reconstructed and understood from his sacramental verse. This is a possibility that would have made Taylor's heart glad to hear.

Taylor found a kind of security in that dimension of the myth-structure which puts man down in order to lift God up. "This world doth eye thy brightness most/When most in distance from thyself." (2.21) To a mind like Taylor's everything else follows from this spatial contrast. It was a source of both security and anxiety, the cause of both the Puritan's feeling of aristocracy and his humility, the justification for believing that as things are they are right.

A second dimension in the structure of Puritan thought, one that is definitely platonic, also appears strongly in Taylor. Without the schematization of time and eternity and without the possibility of movement from the horizontal plane of things to the vertical plane, existence to a Puritan like Taylor had no plot, no adventure, no human purpose. Existence for him is a linear history and a process in time: "Life! Life! What's That?. . . . It from the Worlds Birth runs unto its End. . . . But oh! Sin found this Glory: Man hath lost it." (2.87) This is the basic drama that defines time and life to Taylor.

His writing poetry is itself a constant reenactment of the process of moving from the trap of time, the horizontal human plane, to the vertical where the divine exists. He is meditating repeatedly (however illusorily) on the justifications of this one best hope and imagining rescue from the static plane to a dynamic one (as with the "Wasp

Child with Cold" that Taylor identifies himself with, when "enravisht [he can] Climb into/The Godhead.") He tries to move in a poem from self-deprecation to thoughts of glory, from roughness of form to smoothness, from anxiety of tone to patience and peace. His whole reason for writing is to project himself in motion imaginatively from one plane to the other: "Inspire this Crumb of Dust till it display/Thy Glory through't: and then thy dust shall live." Taylor prays constantly for a change in status:

> thus my Soul Steps goe
> From Vegetate to Sensitive thence trace
> To Rationall, and thence to th'Life of Grace.
>
> (2.80)

The Puritan construct in Taylor's mind is not coldly static and time bound, nor rigidly and remotely cosmological, nor merely a matter of existential process and transcendental progress, but also a matter of what fills up time and eternity, world and infinity, self and Other —that is, the Puritan concern with a dimension of depth. The quality of the self that aspires, the quality of the aspiration, and the quality of that state aspired to—these are a dimension in his ontology as well. He showers the Divine with his most magnanimous and amplifying terms, not always merely in praise but in justification of his goals. He rationalizes his insufficiencies lest he have to live with them and change them himself. He dramatizes his pursuits to fix them meaningfully in his own mind. He invests his praise with the greatest obsequiousness, the descriptions of his life with the most self-justifying meiosis, and his desires with anxiety-removing dramatics—all to give depth to what he wants to do and believe and be. Holiness, beauty, delight, and happiness are the ways his theology taught him of suffusing the structure with substance. Taylor calls this an "Ebb and Flow" of warmth among Creator, Creation, and creature, a matter of sparks, a "mighty Tide" overwhelming all things. (1.1) The other, colder dimensions of the myth-structure that inform Taylor's faith required concentration on such factors of quality to give it its warmth and depth.

These are the ways in which Taylor incorporates the Puritan myth-structure into his poetry. There was a thoroughness with which he tried to hold to it as an ordered system; he stood, as he said in a sermon, "within the times of method and order" in his beliefs.[3] How

Taylor conceived of his convictions as an ordering of things is seen in his use of his curious word "Superstructure" in reference to his beliefs in both his poems and his sermons,[4] and there are other terms which reveal how the relations of things made his beliefs sure: "synecdoche" (the process of "Understand[ing] the Whole by the part," the interrelation of the individual and the All); "metaphor" (an allegorical juxtaposing of temporal and spiritual matters); "type" (the relationship of spiritual events in time, the schematizing of human history to meet spiritual ends); "beauty" and "sweetness" (the attractions between remote subjects and objects); "Hypostaticall Union," "Personal Union," "Inbeing," "Theanthropy" (the meeting of the far-distant points of divinity and humanity in the person of Christ). It should be obvious that Taylor was obsessed with this structure within which he lived and moved, for he felt that it gave him his life.

This myth-structure, of which Taylor is one of the more interesting representative voices, became a tradition that stretched to the time of Emily Dickinson and beyond. The Connecticut Valley was from the outset a defensively orthodox stronghold of the faith and at the same time a unique theological unit. There was, as Perry Miller has written, "an emerging difference of temper between the east and the west." By 1700, Western Massachusetts was, in anthropological terms, "a distinct cultural entity, with more ties down the river to Hartford and New Haven than to Boston or Salem."[5]

> New England was effectually divided into two realms. There were still, of course, basic habits maintained from Maine to New Haven, and in that large sense the cultural pattern remained a unity; yet within that frame, the ecclesiastical order was definitely split, east opposed to west. When one remembers how central in the life of that society was the church, and how about it were organized concepts that have immense implications for American social history, this division becomes truly momentous, not to say prophetic.[6]

In opposition to the scholasticism of John Cotton and others in Boston, for example, Thomas Hooker ("the Greate Hooker," Taylor called him) betook himself and his followers to the mouth of the Konekitakat River to exemplify a more individual piety than they had known in the east. To the chagrin of the Boston fathers, Hooker's communities of believers became more and more antiintellectual, emotionally introspective, and aggressively evangelical. When Edward Taylor went to the valley in 1671 he was a friend of Boston's Mathers and to some extent remained under their intellectual influence all his days, but his work shows a difference as well. He appears not to have been long in the valley when he became extremely defensive of covenant theology, developed an obsession with emotional preparationism, and turned to the writing of private, emotional verse. In large measure his meditative poetry is a product of the valley itself. In a number of ways, in fact, it is a description of a man's religious life in the valley.

The difference of the valley from Boston and Cambridge is seen primarily in Hookeresque preparationism, in the ways that Yale and Dartmouth (and later Amherst College) acted as antidotes to the liberalism of Boston and Harvard, in the ease with which Stoddard moved the churches to accept open communion, in Jonathan Edwards' insistence in opposition to Charles Chauncy and other Boston rationalists that religious experience engage all of a person's faculties and not merely the intellect, and in the ways in which the various Awakenings battled the intellectualism, the Arminianism, the "Unitarian Departure," and the growing Transcendentalism.

Taylor's poetry also represents this difference. Though he would not go as far toward pragmatism as Stoddard and could not go as far into esthetics as Edwards was to do and would have been horrified at the recurring mass hysteria over sin and salvation in the area, still he is part of an antirationalistic movement within Puritanism identified primarily with the valley.

He has Hooker's emphasis on an introspective piety and Edwards' emphasis on total involvement in religious experience. Where his friend Increase Mather would argue a man's "effectual calling" coldly in such a work as his *Awakening Soul-Saving Truths* (1720), Taylor could become ecstatic: "A Crown, Lord, yea, a Crown of Righteousness./Oh! what a Gift is this?" (1.44) Where his friend Samuel Sewall had reconciled his piety to his political and mercantile interests and ended up a moralist, Taylor centered his thought and poetry on the moved affections and has another kind of power as a result of that emphasis. Over against his colleagues in the east, Taylor was much more emotional, evangelical, sensuous. It is necessary to see him in the light of the more emotionally developed western orthodoxy rather than in the context of Puritanism as a whole. His life's work was in a way a defense of that difference, the Connecticut Valley Way.

In time that Way came to give a dark cast to the Puritan myth-structure. We can look back and see that there developed a Hooker-Taylor-Edwards tradition of the long, deep journey into the self which contained an energy that inevitably produced art in each—and later in others: Emily Dickinson, Hawthorne, and Melville. Taylor is important to that emerging tradition for the exemplary way in which he used language to move himself deeper into himself. We can also look back and see the development of a concept of tragedy in the valley, a concept always latent in Puritan thought but seldom admitted to or explored. The Connecticut Valley writers seemed much less able to ignore the realities of human experience than their less introspective brethren and much readier to face the possible inhumanity of the cosmos. The weight of empirical evidence of his and his world's worthlessness easily moved a writer like Taylor to anxiety about his state and anxiety about being rescued from it. In addition, in a short time a tradition of conversion emerged in the valley that emphasized emotions as the primary directors of the will, sanctioned visionary perception, and tended to dramatize religious experience. All of these came to a head, of course, in Edwards' thought. Taylor's poetry could hardly have been what it was without these same emphases.

It is not so much that Taylor fell into this tradition and found himself responsive to it, though, as that he assisted in its creation. He helped to bear the myth-structure into the area and found ways of giving it further life by means of a new sensationalism. When Taylor writes, for instance,

> Worldly Wisdom . . . is but a mock Wisdom, compared to
> Spirituall Wisdom. It is Such a Wisdom, that Christ meddled
> not with, nor traded in. . . . This Wealth, and Wisdom is little
> comepared with Christs,[7]

and at the same time wallows in anxiety over the human condition and his own helpless state ("My Sin! my Sin, My God, these Cursed Dregs . . . set my Soule a Cramp" [1.39]), he shows the extent to which he was in the antirationalist Connecticut Valley Puritan tradition. The rational in his poems has been replaced by the services of religious emotion in moving the human will. Because his poems show how he knew that the senses can serve the spirit, they therefore have the purpose of drama in trying to stir the affections. In these ways, they can be seen as counterparts to the theology of argument, definition, explication, and right reason that prevailed generally in Puritan thinking elsewhere. Though they were meant for his excitement alone, his poems can easily be compared with the revivalist sermons of Edwards and others. They are small awakenings in a tradition that in time would easily absorb the Great Awakening, though in the process would lose many of its sacramental and intellectual qualities.[8] This is not to say that the skeletal structure of the Puritan myth was changed by Connecticut Valley emotions, only that it was fleshed out by feelings that would give it the means of sure survival well into the nineteenth century. Without the many Taylors of the area, Calvinism would have died sooner.[9]

To identify that which is mythic in Taylor it is necessary to note the ways in which in any thorough consideration of Taylor the Puritan system of thought is juxtaposed against the man himself, or rather the man against the system, the man against the myth, even as he is part of it. In the Taylor of the *Preparatory Meditations*, for instance, we have a man arguing his guilt of sin *while* enjoying a sense of grace (so that one may feel he is merely playing at being a fallen individual yet all the while fairly sure of heavenly approval); the security of the structure is there even as he imagines his freedom from it. There is also for him in his theology always the possibility of sanctification *and* justification, that is, a feeling of freedom allowed by the structure itself, a liberating knowledge that his actions, conduct, and thought are independent of his fundamental worth. The very practice of poetry itself *alongside* the practice of piety is a structural juxtaposition; on the one hand, there is the theology that demanded the preparationist verse and on the other the use of that demand as an excuse to practice a life of his own, the primary world of reality leading to despair and the secondary world of imagination encouraging hope.

Even in his style the juxtaposition of man and system is revealed. The stanza form is conventional and rigid in Taylor, yet a personality moves and breathes *within* it; quatrain and couplet, like the faith, dominate completely, yet he pushes and pulls against their restrictions. Too, the iambic meter in the discipline of his lines is constant (even often maintained at great cost to the quality of his verse), yet with caesuras and compound stresses he tries to bend it to his will. The resorting to offrhyme is also evidence of working within a system but allowing one's individuality its expression as well. In the form of Taylor's verse, therefore, the choice of a rigid system of belief is always present and he becomes a poet by virtue of the rigid system *and* as he violates it enough to make room for himself in it.

It is in the disparity between mythic *language* and individual *speech*, better than anywhere else, where one may discover the mythic in Taylor. The distance between the two describes his poetic sensibility. As a theologian Taylor necessarily thinks and writes in the language of the structure, for it is the necessary condition of his speaking. The language of his ideology very nearly surfaces in many of his poems. Some poems are little more than versified dogma. In other poems there is only a thin veneer of imagery covering the doctrine. Though the poems seldom degenerate into sermons, either explicatory or minatory, and though few technical terms of the theology crop up in the poetry, still the poetic diction is chosen in defense of the myth-structure as Taylor understood and believed in it rather than in defense of his understanding of and belief in himself.

The provocative power in Taylor's poetry is not so much in the speech he actually uses as it is in the myth-structure, the theology, behind it. Yet the theology in it does not qualify his writing as literature. The forms that the language of the myth take do that. It is the system of belief in his poems that ultimately gives them their significance and not the personality of the author or the significance of the speech he uses in the individual poems. The bald appearance of the theology in even his best work is evidence that Taylor recognized that even though his is the thought and his the speech in his work, it is the theology which allows, even encourages, him to do it and by virtue of which he can deliver his meanings.

To be sure, in Taylor we find the standard tropes with which Puritans represented salvation: coronation, white robes, marriage, bread and wine, and many others that appear in almost everyone's verse, everyone's sermons. The standard uses of Biblical and patristic imagery are there (for example, his scatological and erotic metaphors), as are the standard types and antitype. For the most part he expropriates his speech from a theological context. Yet there is in most of his verse almost always something added, something of the man himself. Sometimes it is no more than the sound of his own voice. At other times it is the interposition of himself between the subject and the reader: "I am here. I live and breathe. I long for God's love," he seems to be saying over and over again in his Meditations. And then, for the most part, his better poems become his better poems when the individuality of his speech has taken us away from the doctrine he espouses and has focussed our attention on himself instead. The fresher, more unique, even more eccentric his speech becomes, the better poetry he writes, for he has freed himself within the system of his beliefs.

His words have values of their own, of course, but do not so much thereby escape the structure as bring to it the richness of these new values, values determined by the semantic associations of the image- ry. The nontheological associations then add to the theology a range that includes his own personality and experience. The tendency of his words to expand cumulatively is of course limited by the system; they will not take on meanings outside or beyond that system. But by writing poetry as he does, with wit and sensuousness and allusions and ingenuity of sound and syntax, he expands the system into something large enough to include even himself, fallen and yearning for acceptance.

In Meditation 1.1, as an example, even though the first part of the poem (quoted above) is bald doctrine, it becomes interesting first when Taylor picks up the phrase "Cannot bee . . . Confinde" and extends it with some rather unusual analogies. He does so in order to make a place for himself within the formal scheme of salvation that he is describing. God's unconfined love becomes a flood filling heaven and all hell, filling mankind's veins and flowing out as blood at Christ's crucifixion, and finally "overflow[ing] my Heart!" The myth of salvation is still intact but the metaphors have run loose. Tied to the tetherpole of the theology, they have swung fairly wide, wide enough to include "my Heart." They communicate because of the myth behind them, but in their wild, one might even say *passionate*, variety, they admit of an individuality that the language of the theology did not. By virtue of his speech, then, Taylor has a kind of individuality within the system of his beliefs.

Similarly, behind a poem like "Huswifery," as Norman Grabo has shown, there is an extremely elaborate theology.[10] The language of the theology appears, in fact, in most lines of the poem: "Covenant of Grace," "Holy Spirit," "Ordinances," "Understanding, Affections, Will, Judgment, Conscience," "Glory." Still none of this makes it a poem. It becomes poetry by virtue of the witty manipulation of the dominant metaphor (making the glory robes), the ingenious allegory (spinning wheel and loom as God making a tool out of man), and the unique tone of voice. Phrases occur which imply the theology but move away from it wittily: "Heavenly Colours Choice,/All pinkt [with Christ's blood, of course]" and "my Soule thy holy Spoole" (full of sound puns). But more important to the issue of making an individuality through the speech is the recurrent syntax, "[You] Make me . . . [You] make mine . . . [You] cloathe therewith mine," implying the extension of the myth to include Taylor, and the emphasis on first-person pronouns in the position of the object (*me/my/mine* occur 12 times), suggesting that his subject is his individual worth and the acceptability of his individuality:

> mine apparell shall display before yee
> That I am Cloathd in Holy robes for glory.

The individuality of the imagery of the poem represents well the freedom Taylor seeks within the forms of his belief. Or perhaps one should say that such imagery was a way that Taylor found of reconciling his language and his speech, his beliefs and his desires, his theology and his experience.

Who can doubt that Taylor has made an individual speech out of a cold theology when he reads in other poems of his attractive lines like these:

> When I wore Angells Glory in each part
>   And all my skirts wore flashes of rich die
>   Of Heavenly Colour, hedg'd in with rosie Reechs,
>   A spider spit its Vomit on my Cheeks.
>
> $$(1.47)$$

> Black Imps, young Divells, snap, bite, drag to bring
> And pick mee headlong hells dread Whirle Poole in.
>
> $$(1.39)$$

>   spirituall food doth spirituall life require.
> The Dead don't eate.
>
> $$(2.106)$$

What shall an Eagle t'catch a Fly thus run?
Or Angell Dive after a Mote ith'Sun?

(1.24)

Joseph was cast into the jayle awhile
And so was thou. Sweet apples mellow so.

(2.7)

That little Grain within my golden Bowle,
. . . stands amaizd, and doth adore. . . .

(1.13)

One should see how hard Taylor was trying to find an individual speech within the language of the myth. To make an individuality for himself within the rigidities of his thought and form, Taylor often had to resort to poetic devices like frivolous conceits, puns, rapid shifts in dominant metaphors, mixed metaphors, extremely far-fetched analogies, eccentricities of sound and syntax, and a whole bag of Elizabethan rhetorical devices—all of which became means for adding to the divine scheme of things something of his own personality. His meditative poems inevitably move from the quotation of (or allusion to) scripture to the search for an individual imagery and end with an emphasis on his own needs, his own existence. Oddly enough, this represents, as it does with a poet like Emily Dickinson, his struggle to be himself within the system. Indeed, only when thus read mythically is there any poet Taylor in the theology of his poems!

Taylor is very worried, however, about the distance between the language of the theology and the individual speech necessary for his poetry. His complaint about his writing in Meditation 2.138 is typical:

But though I can but stut and blur what I
    Do go about and so indeed much marre
Do thy bright Shine: I fain would slick up high
    Although I foul it by my pen's harsh jar.
    Pardon my faults: they're all against my Will.
    I would do Well but have too little Skill.

His "Jarring Pen," he complains further (2.132), only makes "a ragged line [that is] Unfit" to describe that which he has faith in. Still he forces himself "to speake of thee" even though his speech is inadequate to his subject: "If I had better thou shouldst better have."

It is not so much any disparity between *the* faith and *his* faith that torments him as it is the disparity between *the* Word and *his* words, that is, between his ideology and his poetry:

> Speeches Bloomery can't from the Ore
> Of Reasons mine, melt words for to define
> Thy Deity. . . .
>
> (2.43)

Taylor appears to know that his speech must be eccentric enough to be noticed but not so eccentric as to be outside the circle of the faith. Noticed, it can then be offered as an individual gift of praise. Faithful, it can be imagined by Taylor to be close to God's word. He is apologetic of his human speech yet paradoxically finds it a valuably individual means of praise:

> Then while I eye the Place thou hast prepar'de
> For such as I, I'le sing thy glory out
> Untill thou welcome me. . . .
>
> (1.41)

In its eccentric condition his speech is his individual gift, like the gift of his individual self. He lives in the hope that it is acceptable and in the anxiety that it is not.

Taylor also seems to be aware that the freedom of his range of speech does not in any way change the myth-structure he holds to but only actualizes it. In fact, without the fresh and free speech he uses, the theology would for him be nearly dead. The extent to which he creates an individual speech is the extent to which he is keeping the theology alive in his life. His freedom of speech is therefore in no way destructive of the faith but revives it constantly. In its way, his little wildness defends and promotes the faith. His poems are true "application."

Putting himself repeatedly in the same literary situation (preparation for communion) and disciplining himself to use the same format for his poems (meiosis, amplification, and a plea for grace), he puts his ability with language to an extremely severe test. Given such restrictions—the pull of the theology, the narrow literary theory, the limited ability with language—it is amazing that he is as free as he is. His vocabulary is much richer than any other American poet in the early period;[11] he was thereby much freer within the system.

Poetry as a *liberating* art in Puritan culture may be an important, neglected idea. In Taylor's hands it became a way of extending the range of the myth that bound him. The ideology was perhaps livable without such a device, though perhaps not yet alive in *him* until he wrote. Perhaps Taylor came to the writing of poetry out of the discovery that whereas the prose of his sermons justified the theology, it was the nature of poetry, the nature of the speech necessary for adequate expression, to justify his individual existence. The distance between the qualities of his language and the qualities of his speech shows how he accepted the system and tried to find a place within it.

Ironically, though, by writing poetry, Taylor actually created a new myth, one that would have been instructive to another puritan poet, Emily Dickinson. The Puritan theology was of course primary in Taylor's thinking—and therefore latent in him. As he wrote his poetry, however—stretching metaphors to include himself, using his own person and voice as the substance of his poems, manipulating the rhythms of his lines to represent his personal feelings—his art (merely a secondary system of action) developed a new myth, the myth of The Puritan Liberated by Art. Reality, in writing the way he did, became not what the theology called reality but what his art made it take: a construct of freedom within form.

The disparity between myth-language and individual speech (that is, the freedom within form) is itself mythic in still another way: it derives from and parallels the biography Taylor gives of himself in his Meditations. There, he is the individual struggling for acceptance into the system, knowing that he is not acceptable until he has discovered his worth as an alienated individual. The structure that he loves and yearns for lies behind all he says but all he says represents the individuality, the distinction, the alienation that he experiences. In the individuality of his poems he of course feels that he fulfills the requirements of the myth. His practice of poetry therefore has mythic importance for him. The fact of being a poet created a reality that he could believe and live in. This is the value poetry had for him.

To have created such a myth is no mean achievement: the very power of his picture of The Puritan Freed Through Language is impressive as a new construct. We credit Emily Dickinson in American literature as the creator of and embodiment of this myth, but Taylor participates in its making, too. The model of the Puritan artist, as Taylor could have shown her, provides for freedom within form.

Chapter 10

Rough Feet for Smooth Praises

What Vean can e're Divine? Or Poet sing?
  Doubtless most Rich. For such shew God most
    Wise.
  I will adore the same although my quill
  Can't hit the String that's tun'd by such right
    Skill.

In the final analysis, perhaps the most fruitful way of talking about Edward Taylor's poetry honestly and at the same time claiming for it an integral place in American literature is to see how it is *primitive*. It is the primitive character of his style which, better than anything else, makes his an indigenous American poetry. "A naive original, an intermittently inspired Primitive," Austin Warren calls him, and the title honors him for his uniqueness and his relation to American culture.[1]

The roughness of the form of Taylor's poetry is the best evidence of this primitivism. "Occasionally, the outside of the poem, so to speak, is left so rough, so rude, that the art seems to have faltered. But there is apparent to reflection the fact that the artist meant just this harsh exterior to remain, and that no grace of smoothness could have imparted her intention as it does. . . ."[2] This is William Dean Howells writing about Emily Dickinson. But it also identifies the style of Taylor, with its awkwardness for effect, its fragmentation and disparate improvisation, its unbalanced detail and functional distortion, its uniquely awkward way of revealing personality. With the roughness of his form it is possible that Taylor, like Emily Dickinson, was expressing himself, not flawed, but best.

The term "primitive" need not suggest the manner of the work of a simple man with no academic or technical training and little book learning, nor merely an everyday competence in writing or an innocence of vision and simplicity of expression, an incorruptible honesty and freedom, a quaintness. Nor should it suggest work proceeding from someone who is self-taught and therefore outside important critical criteria, nor, as Yvor Winters suggests, an inferior artist, a "major poet on a smaller scale."[3] This is another sort of primitivism, one dealing with the ideas that went into literary romanticism and naturalism rather than a description of the primitive as a formal artistic technique. As an idea, it describes a native creativity, a naturalness and naivete and spontaneity, or sometimes a reaction against technology and mechanization, a simple romantic remoteness from society. But as a technique, it has to do with the mastery of a narrow range of expression yet a lack of formal correctness, the use of those features of one's personality excluded by form and rule and convention, the involvement of the naive in one's sophistication, the artistic use of one's own individual human insufficiency.

The sort of primitivism that one finds in Taylor's poetry is available in early American art. Though there are dangers in comparing literature with painting, the way in which individual personality and the features of early American culture appear in the forms of the primitive in both is instructive. The qualities that identify the intrinsic style of primitivism in art, as art critic Jean Lipman explains,[4] do not necessarily include that which is early, provincial, crude, untutored, nor a deliberate childlike simplicity. Instead primitivism is a kind of independence from the real appearance of things. This is not a convention but the result of an individual's "primitive memory image," an imaginative faculty by which he selects those aspects of his idea which do not represent it with any visual accuracy yet which present it in its clearest and most complete form. He works from memory rather than with the pictures that reality presents to the eye. This can be a very sophisticated process, as we see in modern abstract painting. Fidelity to memory (as opposed to fidelity to the eye) distorts visual reality, and, Miss Lipman writes, "it is thus that 'primitive' or 'archaic' arts are invariably distinguished by a unique freedom to develop the purely aesthetic qualities of abstract design."[5] What to the realist appears crude, uncouth, stiff, distorted, or poorly executed in the primitive becomes in this light original, individual, lucid, and abstract.

Simplicity of memory image, when uncoordinated with visual plausibility, results in perspectives with considerable distortion (angles and lines in portraits and landscapes do not correspond with that which the eye sees in reality) and arrangements that could not have been juxtaposed in real life (objects and figures appear almost at random as they substantiate an idea in the mind of the painter). Where the academic painter optically unifies a whole scene and gives the spectator the scene he chooses to represent just as he saw it, the primitive painter will not approximate the appearance of observed reality. The perspective is not unified. The lighting is not natural. The content must be accumulated bit by bit from different parts of the picture. The natural elements of the picture are simplified and highly stylized, even calculable. There is little in the picture that resembles actual appearance.

The compositional means used by the artist to clearly and forcibly set down the mental pictures upon which he based his representation resulted, unconsciously, in the enhancement of abstract design at the expense of illusionistic realism. Individual objects were most often represented in profile or in full face, form was abbreviated and flattened, movement was restricted, contour lines were emphasized, and colors were sharpened. All the compositional aspects of a primitive picture reveal a non-optical attitude. Each unit of the painting seems to exit separately as it did in the form of a series of memory images in the artist's mind, and these images appear to have been combined rather than synthesized in the final representation. The non-optical attitude explains not only the single departures from visible reality in the primitive pictures, but also the so-called inconsistencies—considered from the point of view of visual plausibility—sure to exist between various aspects of a picture. As the primitive limner did not conceive his portrait as an optically consistent whole he did not consider it objectionable to attach a relatively realistic head to a decoratively planned torso. A landscape painter saw nothing amiss with placing in his sky a geometrically rayed sun and a scattering of stencilled stars and then including cast shadows in his representation of trees and houses.[6]

Based on essentially nonoptical vision, primitive painting therefore depends on the personality of the artist, for all the facts that go into his work are first filtered through his mind and personality. Much more than with representational/naturalist painting, his individuality appears on his canvas—and, oddly enough, appears in the very distortions of visual reality that result. In his "flaws" his personality becomes evident, for in the disparity between observed reality and memory image there is, as in modern abstract painting, room for the expression of himself, even if it is an unconscious expression. The primitive delights by the unconscious sincerity with which private fantasies are expressed. The excellence of the primitive's work therefore depends more on his force of personality than on the beauty or interest inherent in his subject matter, more in fact on his instinctive sense of abstract design than on his technical facility for representing observed reality, more on his personality than on any concern for public appreciation.

For all of the optical eccentricity of a primitive painting there is much that is highly stylized and conventional. The primitive painter of the seventeenth century was an ordinary craftsman—a sign and coach and house painter, a housewife occupying her leisure hours with tinsel and watercolor pictures, a young lady in a seminary whose curriculum included painting on velvet, or an itinerant limner or house decorator—who tried to do what was passably "correct." He knew certain conventional formulae for portraits and landscapes. He used stock figures, standard poses, stencilled designs, repetitions of suitable settings and scenes. He worked within his severely limited knowledge of technique, believing that those limits could make his art. Yet it is not the conventions that make the primitive interesting but the disparity between the formal correctness and the ways an artist creates his own esthetic experiences in his own way unhampered by external requirements. In this conflict between the conventional and the individual lies humor, freshness, and originality; in other words, something of the personality of the painter.

The emergence of personality from the disparity between convention and optical distortion—this is the distinctiveness of the primitive in American art. This is to admit, of course, that what one finds of interest about the primitive is often different from what was intended. What the artist did not do right according to his own formal standards is what makes him an interesting artist, for his individuality expresses itself in the "flaws" honestly and goes unwittingly beyond his own mediocre abilities to produce something new, fresh, surprising. He is an artist by virtue of instinct and accident rather than experience and intent. His sheer joy of expression is what he expresses best. That these are identifying characteristics of the poetry of Taylor I would like to try to show.

How this individuality emerges in primitive technique may be seen in several examples. The portrait *Henry Gibbs*, painted by the so-called Freake limner about 1670, has its primitive value in its "flaws." The boy has a curiously stiff quality. His features are that of a doll cut from wood. There is trouble with roundness of the anatomy. Eyes and mouth are rigid and frozen. The pose is static and flat. Hands and feet are placed awkwardly at unlikely angles. He holds a bird of only two dimensions. The clothes are done in meticulous detail but in simplistic perspective. He is far too stumpy and fat for his figure. In fact, the perspective of the whole is warped. The floor is almost on the same plane as the wall behind the boy. He stands upon a severely slanting checkerboard. Shadows do not fall quite right and there is a displacement of foreground and background. The color is limited and exaggerated. The contrasts of light and dark are simplistic. But because of the lack of optical reality, the picture has an individuality. Whatever conventions the limner had in mind (and if he was like most limners of the period, he did scores of standard paintings during winter months at home and then filled in the faces when he could get out and find buyers), these are done according to *his* imagination and *his* memory, and the result is a unique stylization, a sharply simple form that could only be his own, a bold distinctiveness, and the important (though perhaps unintended) factors of humor and play-fulness. The painting delights because it is formally wrong, but esthetically *right*. In this disparity is its individuality.

Moses Marcy in a Landscape (anonymous, ca. 1760) delights one in the same "flawed" way. In it Marcy stands stiffly facing the front crowded by the symbols of his success—large house, fertile fields, trading ship, uniform, massive account book, pipe and punch bowl. Perspective, proportion, and organization of detail are sacrificed to this one idea. The wind in the trees, the waves on the ocean, smoke from house and ship, and a bird on a branch are all frozen stiffly in place. Marcy stands in a fertile field that is oddly bare except for a single tree (with bird) and, strangely enough, a large table. There is little just proportion: bird and cup are enormous; green fields hang over the ocean; the bird is cut in two by the shoreline; the ship sails up to the inland house. The house faces us squarely, and the table in front of Marcy tips obliquely toward us to show its contents plainly. The geometry is inaccurate, and there is a lack of emphasis. The painting is in an incongruous mixture of styles. The detailed decora-tiveness stands in strange contrast to the flatness of the objects. The pastel shading conflicts with the harsh angles of the objects. The stenciled foliage is inconsistent with the caricatured face of Marcy. Nothing fits (what is the house doing so isolated and almost floating in the air? what is the ship doing along the shore churning up water and smoke the way it is? what is Marcy doing out in the middle of a field with punch bowl and bird?), and yet it all seems fit—fit because the distortion delights. The conventions of painting of the period are alluded to but the individuality of the painter intervenes and the result is, as in almost all primitive art of the period, a unique personality, humor, playfulness, and witty abstraction of recognizably representative reality. Again, in the "inability" to get things formally right and out of an instinct for freshness and surprise, the painter gives us something unique.

In our own time, perhaps Grandma Moses illustrates best the techniques of American primitivism of the colonial variety. The delightfulness of her work lies not so much in its serious moral intent or in its nostalgic and antitechnological usages, but in its "flaws," that is, its naivete, its predictable, stylized distortions of optic reality. This is often the overlooked factor of her fame.[7] Her *Quilting Bee* (1950), for example, is primitive by virtue of the humorous disparity between the perspective that is promised and the flatness that results from naively filling space to make a joyful design. Optical reality is distorted as the quilting room is distended to the size of a gymnasium and then filled with awkwardly tilted tables, mis-sized chairs, and many brightly colored figures at oblique angles. Objects are not in positions on their proper planes but are factors in a colorful design. The delight lies in the lack of faithfulness—in the three successive windows, each showing a different scene outside; in the uncoordinated sizes of people; in the frozen quality of the scene's busyness; in the steaming dinner that's spread out to look at but goes unattended. The innocence, naivete, and technical flaws are of course not intended but are nonetheless the qualities that make one's response.

The primitivism in Grandma Moses is, frankly, an incongruent and therefore humorous sense of space. She said her work was not done from nature but was from memory and was for decorative purposes.[8] "I like to paint old-timey things. . . . I do them from memory, most of them are day dreams, as it were. . . ."[9] She could not do optical illusions and so she did her own patterns of scenes. Her primitivism is also a humorously crude use of the colors that delighted her—often a child's boldest colors, simply placed, against plain white. Too, her primitivism is simply a pictorial representation of her enthusiasm, her private joy, her strong feeling almost always overwhelming any convention of design or form. Because limited in technique, her works are highly stylized and predictably repetitious, even self-imitating. But in the quality of their very limitations one finds an artfulness that was not intended. As with most primitive colonial art, the delight comes from the disparity between intent and response.

A comparison of Grandma Moses' work with the Currier and Ives prints she sometimes "copied" (like her *Home for Thanksgiving,* 1939) shows how it is her naivete, simplistic geometry, predictable stylization, warped perspective, trouble with depth of figure, simple colors, flatness—in other words, her flaws—that when brought together are delightful. Where in Currier and Ives we have almost a machine-produced optical reality highly romanticized, in Grandma Moses we have a child's work that is fresh because either instinctive or accidental, but certainly unexpected and successfully naive. It is her *misrepresentations* of Currier and Ives that delight. Through her distortions, the focus of her work changes from the objects she paints to her own joyous vision. She succeeds in painting her vision of things, but it is in spite of the conventions she feels she is following. What is "wrong" turns out esthetically right.

In being unfaithful to reality, inept at form, and consistently herself within conventions, she becomes interesting. She has therefore become an easy symbol of *hope* in American art, for her work shows the human spirit succeeding delightfully despite its alleged insufficiency. In delighting in what was not intended and what is flawed, we discover about ourselves the ability to identify ourselves with the innocence, goodness, and joy of childhood in the accidental, flawed, fallen world.

Edward Taylor is the Grandma Moses of American literature. In his meditative poems he works hard at imitating accepted poetic conventions and is most interesting when he "fails"—that is, when his conceits go too far and become embarrassingly entertaining, when his passion over his depravity or his love of God makes his rhythms and rhymes rough and alive, when he mixes metaphors and thereby reveals something of his own personaility, when his syntax collapses and surprises. He becomes an individual at such times and probably had no intention of revealing himself thus. Mainly in his flawed exterior he becomes a poet of that which he wanted to be a poet—his passionate need for love of God.

I am not suggesting that there is much in Taylor that parallels American primitive painting, but suggesting that, like a primitive painter, Taylor becomes an interesting artist through his flaws. Perhaps he was, simply, a poet in spite of himself—or simply *naturally* a poet.

In Taylor the roughness of form that makes it necessary to consider his work as primitive is itself important to his being a poet. He comments often on the "rough feet" that he has for singing "smooth praises" to his maker.

> They Onely do produce a Lisping stut,
> A piece of Sorry Non-Sense in a Rhyme
> That none can read, Construe, scan or decline.[10]

It is an obsession with him:

> My tatter'd Fancy; and my Ragged Rymes
>   Teeme leaden Metaphors: which yet might serve
> To hum a little touching terrene Shines.
>   But Spirituall Life doth better fare deserve.
>   This thought on, sets my heart upon the Rack.
>   I fain would have this Life but han't its knack.
>
> Reason stands for it, moving to persue't.
>   But Flesh and Blood, are Elementall things
> That sink me down, dulling my Spirits fruit.
>
>   (2.82)

He admits the insufficiency of his poetry and fears that it symbolizes his own:

> Am I bid to this Feast? Sure Angells stare,
>   Such Rugged looks, and Ragged robes I ware.
>
>   (2.62)

He prays God to look beneath the harsh exterior to the intent, the worth beneath. Yet in his sufficiency he detects the lowliness, the humility that God insists on. As Christian poet, the roughness of form therefore becomes him, and the power of his verse comes from the tension between the desire to be formally acceptable and the recognition that it is not his abilities but his insufficiency, his humility, that is demanded. His verse is, from this point of view, good verse only when flawed and his life a humbly acceptable one only when part of a fallen condition. "Thy Grace, Dear Lord," he writes, "[is] my golden Wrack, I finde/Screwing my Phancy into ragged Rhimes. . . ." (1.32) In his lowliness, his "depravity," he is God's servant, and with his "rough feet" he *does* sing God's praises, as desired. That is, ironically, God's grace in him.

This does not mean that he is striving for anything short of the highest standards of the few poetic conventions he has in his ear, but only that the flaws of his writing are constant reminders of his fallen individuality. As such, they are, ironically, important to his consciousness of his own brave struggling and varied personality. Otherwise his poetry would be all convention, his life merely laws, rules, order. Where his meditative poems, like his life, have their liveliness is, as with the primitive painter, where he falls short of or exceeds conventions and shows his real, though perhaps "unintended," humanity and individuality. Though the church gave Taylor his poetic interest, it could not give him his poetry. Only his flawed feelings could make his rough feet sing at all. It was therefore unwittingly his best praise. As with a primitive painter, his individual instinct (quite against his will, against his desire to obey the rules and conventions) made his poems of worth.

The primitive painter gets his proportions fascinatingly "wrong" from a sense of abstract design instead of the reproducing eye. And like that, the structure of many of Taylor's poems follows feeling rather than formal convention or logic. They fall apart and fly apart and have their coherence in factors that have little or nothing to do with the conventions attempted: the tone of voice, the color of the images, the consistent botching of syntax, rhythm, and metaphor. In the flawed structure Taylor's personality pokes out.

Meditation 1.2, for an example, has the trappings of a conventional preparatory meditation—beginning and ending with statements of dependence on God for his life, with meiotic and amplified illustrations in between. It is a replay of the standard contrast between All and Nothing. Yet things do not fit so neatly in it, and its interest comes from such. The theme of the preciousness of God comes from the poem's text: Canticles 1:3, "Thy name is an ointment poured out," but Taylor's metaphor for this preciousness is at first not ointment but jewels that are "above all price." Taylor interjects himself into the metaphoric scheme by insisting that the jewels need a box (himself as a wicker cage made by "Heavens Workmanship") and the box in turn needs a "sweet Perfume" (God's grace). All of this makes a playful dominant metaphor for the poem. But the unity is disturbed by some oddly mixed metaphors underway: birds are in the box, the box becomes an eggshell, the egg can be sold, and so Taylor ends up as a purse with God's grace as his money. It's a fairly long way from ointment to purse and money, even though the jumps can perhaps be justified in Puritan theology. Apparently anything that comes to Taylor's mind as being precious can be put into the picture. (There is also the matter of eating the sacramental Christ—Taylor's real subject—and so the imagery must be moved, even if awkwardly, from precious jewels to birds and edible eggs and back to precious money.) Though lack of focus and emphasis results, the result is also color, variety, freshness of image, naive logic, and humor—that is, the unity coming not from any convention but from Taylor's own personality. The usual structure of a meditation is there but flawed into a better poem, better because its design is dictated by personal feeling more than by rigid rule.

This is not to say that the awkwardness of the organization of Taylor's poems is always successful after a primitive manner. A poem like Meditation 2.34, for example, is ruined by the lack of control over the proliferating metaphors. Taylor's allegory in the poem makes the earth a coconut and the advent of Christ is "The richest Carbunckle" in it for a kernel. He apologizes for this comparison ("Should I, my Lord, call thee this nut?") and shifts to what may have seemed a more appropriate one, a pearl within an oyster. Unaccountably he gets the pearl ground up to make sacramental bread ("kneaded up in Love/To Manna in Gods moulding trough above") which when eaten fills mankind with grace. But this metaphor of pearl-like sacramental bread is dropped in order to get to the sacramental wine. Shell of nut and oyster remind him of a cask of wine in a tavern; hence, "Love steps in [and] turns by the Conduit Cock" so that man may drink of salvation. Christ's atonement, in a theologically appropriate but nonetheless silly, surrealistic metaphor, is the payment for this wine: his "Veans full payment on the Counter drop." And then Taylor inserts a stanza describing how Christ's

humanity (*our* humanity) is scoured, bleached, and purified for glory.
Man's veins are made as white as a rose-of-sharon lily (a pun on
risen) and ready for judgment. The metaphors in this Meditation
jump by free association but make no happy design, no single effect.
It is not worth the energy needed to put them all together and they are
fairly embarrassing side by side. The breaks, shifts, and distortions
reveal a personality at work on the poem, but the result is incoherent.

But in most of the poems, Taylor creates (quite against his will, one
could reasonably feel) a new and delightful effect when he violates
structural conventions and lets his passion for his subject create a
design that is appropriate to his inveterate hope. Whether organized
around a metaphor turned into many ingenious analogies or around
shifts in metaphors occasioned by remote logic or linguistic accident,
the proportion is askew and surprising. The result is rough but
entertaining. The structure is conventional as intended but much
more interesting in the "flawed" result. The personality of the one
who thus flaws his work and yet whose instinct makes an entertaining arrangement is remembered long after the intent of the structure
is forgotten. Perhaps this is why Taylor's poems seem to be much
more about Taylor himself as a poet/singer than about his ostensible
subjects of theanthropy, atonement, grace. It is mainly his joy in
expressing himself that Taylor ends up expressing best.

There is also a difficulty with levels of diction in Taylor's poetry.
Styles are often oddly mixed—theological terms spiced with homeli-
ness ("I/Under the Wrath of God must ever fry"), archaic diction with
coinages ("O that I could . . . dart my dulness through with glouts
that stroy!"), elaborate amplifications of the divine mixed with puns
("A King, a King, a King indeed, a King/Writh up in Glory!")—and in
the disjuncture there is a humor, a freshness, a surprise that results.
What color there is in a Taylor poem may often come from the very
ineptness of handling the tone of his diction.

Meditation 1.29 illustrates the fortunate naivete of this practice.
The poem begins with the dignity of scriptural quotation: "My
Father, and your Father, to my God, and your God," but Taylor's
first lines are homely: his imagination, he says, "stole away" from
him and runs "a Wooling" over the idea of the fall of man. "Gods
Garden" he then describes in trite and vague glorifying terms but the
process of man's salvation in very earthy terms: man is "A Chat"
burning in a fire, a fruit threatened by "a nipping Eastwinde";

Christ's saving hand is "Milke white-Gracious"; the devils are "Hells Nymphs" that "ding" at the fruit to knock it down. Conventional Biblical typology ("Fruits of the Tree of Life") is intermixed with ingenious conceits ("I being grafft in thee"), and honorific lists ("Thou art my Priest, Physician, Prophet, King,/Lord, Brother, Bridegroom, Father, Ev'ry thing") are intermixed with humble prayer ("But, Lord, as burnish't Sun Beams forth out fly/Let Angell-Shine forth in my Life out flame.") Although there are disparities here, the variety itself makes a consistent tone. The shift from one level of diction to another in a poem like this one is ironically appropriate to the subject of man's earthbound dependence and God's munificence. Instinct may have made a unity out of the poem where Taylor's conscious poetic ability could not.

His belief in a miraculous universe and the need for a variety of language corresponding to that miraculousness may be the source of this "difficulty." Or it may result simply from a delight and enthusiasm over his subject that overwhelms consistency, proportion, and sophistication. Perhaps this disjuncture in his language is what Taylor meant by his "Ragged Faculties, alas!/ And Blunted Tongue." Whatever "Carbuncle-Stayes/Studded with Pretious Stones [and] Carv'd with rich Curles/Of Polisht Art" he offers for his poetry of praise, it is "to thy Throne [but] a dirty thing." (1.21) He looks at his language and finds that in it "Thy Bits of Glory" have been rather sorrily "packt in shreds of Praise." (1.28)

> What shall I say? Such rich rich Fullness would
>   Make stammering Tongues speake smoothly, and Enshrine
> The Dumb mans mouth with Silver streams like gold
>   Of Eloquence making the Aire to Chime.
>   Yet I am Tonguetide stupid, sensless stand,
>   And Drier drain'd than is my pen I hand.
>
> (1.27)

In any case, this mixing of styles parallels the mixture of styles one often finds in primitive painting. It is part of the primitive in Taylor. If Taylor had recognized the disparity, it must have simply represented to him the chaotic character of his fallen nature. And if he did not recognize it, it represents, when the humor and surprise are right, an instinct for design through variety of language. Though

Taylor may have been unaware of the stratifications of his vocabulary, they are in their "primitivism" not without an effect. His style is not eclectic but a farrago of misunderstood styles. But that may be its advantage, for it is, as a result, without some previous boundaries.

His "trouble" with metaphorical consistency is also a mark of the primitive in Taylor. "My Quaintest Metaphors are ragged Stuff," he confesses. (1.22)

> My Metaphors are but dull Tacklings tag'd
>> With ragged Non-sense. Can such draw to thee
> My stund affections all with Cinders clag'd,
>> If thy bright beaming headship touch not mee?
>
> (2.36)

The admitted raggedness appears when Taylor conceives of his poem as a gathering of many images—not always complementing each other, some squarely in the middle of his canvas, other items crowded off the edges, some minor metaphors up front and large, some major analogies in the background and small. The raggedness also appears when an image in a poem goes unfinished in detail; since proportion is often unimportant to Taylor, only the outline and color of the image are given and then he moves on to another one. There are other kinds of roughness in his mixing of conceits ("My wound/Shall sing thy praises"), his doubled metaphors made from phonic puns ("me dub . . . with Saints Johns Wort good"), his irrelevant metaphors ("My ravisht Soule [will] sing with angells Quire.") Taylor's use of metaphor is in fact often so crude that a different poem than was intended seems sometimes to have been made by his awkwardness.

What is amazing about Taylor's apparently accidental or at best careless uses of metaphor is the successful poetry that this roughness sometimes makes. His mixed metaphors, for instance, usually work out rather well. The line "my rough Feet shall thy smooth praises sing" (1.39) has a pun on "feet" suggesting the drudgery of man's travail and the making of acceptably rhythmic verse; feet do not normally sing but perhaps here in this context they do. The exclamation that "Dry Dust eate[s] Living Bread" (1.9), though on the surface inconceivable, is actually an apt synecdoche for the relationship of spiritually dead man and his savior. Even such sensuously mixed-up lines as "My Songs of Praise too Sweeten'd with this fume/Shall scale thine Eares in Spicknardisick Tune" (2.19) have an accuracy when it is realized that in his sacramental ecstasy Taylor is perhaps experiencing something close to synesthesia.

Many of Taylor's concoctions for metaphors turn out rather appropriate as well. When he writes, "the Spirits winde/Scarce blows my mill about. I little grinde," there is an etymological pun (spiritus = breath) and a theological reference (the spiritual making of real flour for sacramental bread) which make the picture of a still windmill appropriate to the characterization of a lifeless soul. Or when he writes such mixed and excessive metaphors as "Oh! that my Love, was rowld all ore and ore/In thine, and Candi'd in 't, and so refin'd/More bright than gold" (2.17), he can catch in one metaphor, "refin'd," how the sweetness of his regard for the majesty of God (the candy and the "gold") may amount to grace.

Even the metaphors that result from phonetic accidents add substantial interest to a poem. In a combination like "Guarded, Engarden'd" (1.3), the sweetness of prevenient grace is nicely caught. In a combination like "One All-Might/A Mite the other" (2.44), he can catch the contrast between God and man. When he speaks of the "breadth and length [which] meate out Eternity" (1.36), he can combine thoughts of the sacrament of the Lord's Supper and sacramental universe by punning.[11] Or when he writes, "thy quick'ning Love might make [my spirits] spring/With its Warm Sun Shine till like birds they sing" (2.32), with puns Taylor can turn Christ into the muse of his poetry.

It is possible that this roughness of the exterior of his writing was not accidental or careless but deliberate in order to show man in his fallen condition working to succeed at understanding himself and praising God. With his roughness of metaphor, as with the other features of his style that make it primitive, Taylor can play the game of being both bad (that is, in need of grace) and good (worthy of grace). When it succeeds, his primitivism actually shows his personality best: acceptable, on occasion delightfully acceptable, even in its fallen insufficiency. As in the case of a successfully naive painting, something beyond the human abilities that Taylor is aware of makes his work interesting: something comes out of the man to make good out of poor, meat out of the eater, grace out of the fallen. What in another poet is flaws, in Taylor therefore may mean salvation!

Perhaps most noticeably though, the exterior of Taylor's poems is

made rough by the aberrant rhythm and rhyme. "My Rhymes do
better suite/Mine own Dispraise," he notices, "than tune forth praise
to thee." (1.22) Though the roughness of rhythm is often themati-
cally functional (as in the heavy stresses of "My Sin! my sin, My God,
these Cursed Dregs,/Green, Yellow, Blew streakt Poyson hellish,
ranck" and "Joy, joy, Gods Son's the Sinners Advocate" [1.39]), it
more often appears simply careless or rigid. He will sacrifice almost
anything in the form of a poem to maintain the discipline of rhythmic
convention. Where Taylor's individuality emerges in the rhythm,
however, is in the polyphonic contrast between (a) the metrical
discipline behind a line of verse and (b) the actual rhythm of the
speech of the line:

(a) Yee Angells, help: This fill would to the brim
   Heav'ns whelm'd-down Chrystall meele Bowle, yea and
      higher.
   This Bread of Life dropt in thy mouth, doth Cry.
   Eate, Eate me, Soul, and thou shalt never dy.

(b) Yee Angells, help: This fill would to the brim
   Heav'ns whelm'd-down Christall meele Bowle, yea and
      higher.
   This Bread of Life dropt in thy mouth, doth Cry.
   Eate, Eate me, Soul, and thou shalt never dy.

                                                    (1.8)

In such a contrast between the iambic pentameter discipline and the
almost accentual reading, there is opportunity for the recognition of
an individual voice. The "roughness" makes this possible.

But again, the roughness of rhythm is less important in either its
thematic function or its polyphonic revelation of personal voice than
in its function as metaphor: the rough rhythm, along with awkward
rhymes and contorted syntax, represents Taylor's human
insufficiency. The form that his verse is in imitates (and perhaps
esthetically fallaciously imitates) the state he is in. The perhaps
unintended exterior best represents Taylor's fears about the awful
state of his spiritual interior.

The rhymes, often obtained at the cost of the syntax, are slightly
impure in most of Taylor's Meditations: whatere/clear, flower/pour,
thy wealth/thyself, which/sticks, would/hold, ashore/under,
goeth/loaf, thing/brim, bread/had, this/dish, like/light, in/sing,

seas/rays, and many others.[12] Some of Taylor's rhymes, as the *Taylor Concordance* shows,[13] are, within his Leicestershire dialect, pure rather than slant. Taylor experimented nonetheless with assonance and consonance, accepting either for a rhymed pair of words. Yet he appears to have deliberately roughened his rhymes for a primitive effect rather than keeping them within the conventions of rhyming of the time.

For another matter, the syntax in Taylor's lines is often barely recognizable as English ("We'l Nightingaile sing like/When pearcht on high/ In Glories Cage, thy glory, bright,/And thankfully,/For joy.") The grammar is often forced ("Begracde with Glory [and] gloried with Grace"; "Tumbling thy Joy, Lord, ore, it rounds me up"; "My Spirit then engaged and pomegranat'de.") A poor poeticizer's liberties are taken with the language (*opes* for *opens*, *extract* for *extracted*, *in'ts* for *in its*, *th'way* for *the way*, *bent* for *be/are not*; *physicianwise*, *Larklike*, *Weddenwise*, *Angell kinde*). Also, the spelling, punctuation, and capitalization are creatively irregular and disruptive. Some stanzas are so rough in structure, metaphor, and mechanics as to suggest indifference to communication:

> Thou pry'st thou screw'st my sincking Soul up to,
>   Lord th'Highest Vane amazements Summit Wears
> Seeing thy Love ten thousand wonders do
>   Breaking Sins Back that blockt it up: us snares.
>
> (2.8)

Still one other way in which Taylor's poetry is primitive is in the unintended humor. His tendency is to write that which he condemns—"Wits Wantonings, and Fancies frollicks." (2.57) One has to smile at some of the things that result from both Taylor's flippancy with divine matters and his extreme seriousness over poetic forms. While I think his humor is a natural expression of his personal spiritual joy and his delight in writing about his serious beliefs, his writing is often humorous in a way that he would not have noticed. As with primitive painting, there is a disparity between intention and apprehension that makes the work of interest. One can easily enjoy finding fun where one had expected dry piety.

There is humor when at the end of a poem like Meditation 2.39 Taylor finds he needs to tie the poem's idea and dominant metaphors up together for a climax, no matter how incongruent they are: "My

Tunes shall rap thy prayses then good Store/In death upon the
Resurrection Doore." There is humor when he is unconscious of the
connotations of some of his metaphors, as in Meditation 2.65, in
which he is talking about being included in God's garden bed of grace
but slips into the erotic with the lines "If thou dost stud my heart with
graces thus/My heart shall beare thee fruits perfumed flush." There is
humor, too, when he lets a metaphor get out of hand, as he does with
the pomegranate in Meditations 2.139–40; it is first "Thy Golden
Vessel filld with Graces Wine," then a heart full of love and a face full
of the beauty of the sacramental red and white, and finally it develops
into a temple full of atoning blood that can gush out to save all
mankind. And then there are of course the many unintended puns,
mixed metaphors, far-fetched analogies, incongruent conceits,
stumbling rhythms and syntax. But ironically, with such awkward,
unintended humor, Taylor's verse is turned into the joyous expression of his faith that he wanted it to be. This is an important
consideration and justifies regard for the primitive quality of his style.
Again, too, this ineptness (the grace in him?) seems to accomplish
what his formal knowledge of technique (his fallenness?) cannot do.
In his insufficiency, his humility, lies his quality, his salvation.

All of this primitive roughness of execution represents Taylor's
honesty about himself:

> My Gracious Lord, I would thee glory doe:
>   But find my Garden over grown with weeds:
> My Soile is sandy; brambles o're it grow;
>   My Stock is stunted; branch no good Fruits breeds.
>
> .   .   .   .
>
> Though I desire so much, I can't o're doe.
>   All that my Can contains, to nothing comes[.]
> When summed up, it only Cyphers grows
>   Unless thou set thy Figures to my Sums.
>
>   (2.4)

As he writes he is frustrated, he knows, by "these Words, which by my
Fall were spoild." (1.7) The Fall to him excuses the primitivist
disparity in his work between the desire for formal acceptability and
the individuality of the execution.

There are further implications of the primitive character of

Taylor's poetry. This discussion has tried to make it evident that
Taylor is a poet who is exceedingly self-conscious of his style and
technique. He knows he is "lacking highest Art." (2.106) He writes
about his style almost as much as he does about his God. Perhaps this
is because he takes his success with poetic technique as a sign of his
grace, his failure as a sign of his fears. He is sure that working with
language—both as minister and a poet—is his earthly calling. And in
his obsession with divine things, he is naturally very self-conscious of
his performance.

> My Deare Deare Lord, I know not what to say:
>   Speech is too Course a web for me to cloath
> My Love to thee in or it to array,
>   Or make a mantle. Wouldst thou not such loath?
>   Thy Loves to mee's too great, for mee to shape
>   A Vesture for the Same at any rate.
>
> (2.146)

This self-consciousness, of course, wastes words. The time he uses to
talk about his technique detracts from his call to service and worship.
Only rarely in his better poetry does he get outside himself. Preparatory meditation gave him a self to talk about without giving him the
ability to talk well. He seldom rises above his prepossessive humility.
But for this reason his consistently primitive style with all of its
entertaining solecisms is fully appropriate. It is personally appropriate because it parallels the low regard he is supposed to have of
himself and it is theologically important because in its belabored
insufficiency it necessitates the intervention of the Holy Spirit. It is
God-dependent verse, made (if it is good verse) out of a coupling of
Taylor's intent and (Taylor would believe) God's power. A flawed
style is therefore best.

It is best in still another way. The result of distortion in art,
whether primitive or expressionist art and whether painting or
poetry, is to change the focus from the object to the artist and his
vision. It is a form that individuality takes. In Taylor his primitive
style works precisely this way. His ostensible subject in almost all of
the meditative poetry he wrote is Christ's role in the work of grace
—and it is interesting to watch him give that subject the variety of
expression that he does. But because of his blunders with some of the
narrower conventions of poetic structure, tone, imagery, rhythm,

and other matters of his delivery, his subject becomes himself and his *view* of his grace. The focus changes with the distortion. It centers not so much on the cosmology or theology that it promises to but on the psychology of a man formed by the art of writing about other things. "Spoild" by the Fall, his language reveals a human being at work.

This fact dictates that one's discussion of Taylor should begin and end with the picture of the man that is created by his poetry. The man is made more interesting, I think we can be fairly sure, by his verse. "I'm not/Pleasd with my mud," Taylor exclaims, and yet it is the human being that the flaws of his poems create that is interesting to us. The proscriptions of Taylor's theology prevented him from singing himself and celebrating himself after the order of any Whitmania, of course, but the form that his poetry is in does it nonetheless. Either this was an ingenious trick on his part to get sympathy and help from the divine or the natural result of a poeticizing mind that *was* self-obsessed. In any event, like a colonial limner, he comes across as an individual in spite of his efforts to fit a narrow pattern of conventions—in Taylor's case, fit the pattern of the savable or saved.

Taylor's is a deliberately indecorous language. A living language is always a little bit unsettling. The mildly surprising and mildly sensuous language he uses is necessary to moving himself, to keeping his religious sensibilities from fossilizing into the *forms* of religion.

Though in a discussion of so orthodox a man as Taylor it may seem cynical to suggest that the primitive in his style is evidence of an unconscious reaction against the formalities of Puritanism, it may nonetheless be the case. A poet's work with thought and language, if it is not mere versified thought or thought-shocking stylistics, quite naturally sets him on a liberated course. The rigid organization of a typical Taylor poem parallels Taylor's inclination to absolute conformity to all features of the structure of his faith. But so may his excesses and divergence from his ideal represent an artist reaching for a variety, a naturalness, a colorfulness, a delight beyond (though never in conflict with) the rudiments of orthodox convention. He intends no rebelliousness at all, yet because of his inability to do well as he wishes, he finds his style amounts to such:

> My Heart, my Lord, 's a naughty thing all o're:
>   Yet if renew'd, the best in mee, 't would fain
> Find Words to waft thy praises in, ashore,

> Suited unto the Excellence in thee.
> But easier 't is to hide the Sun up under
> Th'black of my naile, than words to weald this Wonder.
>
> (2.51)

With his solecisms he manages to extend the boundaries of his belief wide enough to include something of himself. The extent to which his practice of poetry and his piety actually correspond is the extent to which his individuality is giving the formal religion a life and a liveliness. Quite naturally the more he ends up writing about himself in a style that represents his individual personality, the more he is giving to legalistic Puritanism an added dimension. *It* begins to take, if only to himself, some of the shape of his imagination. Ironically, it therefore profits from his fallen state.

Even as the roughness in his style functions as a description of his faith, it serves also as an identification of his work as part of an American way in poetry. Both an American painting and an American poetry begin at that point when colonial limners and versifiers alike begin to violate the European conventions they intend to emulate by imitation. The extent to which they fail in this is the extent to which they succeed as *American* painters and writers. When their own experiences and personalities, their own eccentric vision and flaws of hand and ear, their own invented techniques and touches enter their work, they are breaking with tradition, if only at first in small and unnoticed ways, and making a new one. The primitive tendency is, as art critic Lloyd Goodrich sees it, to discard traditional forms and rebuild one's art on its basis in memory and the senses:

> An essential factor in the growth of American art has been the interaction—sometimes the conflict—between native creativity, relatively primitive but original and vital, and the powerful pull of European knowledge and skills.[14]

Primitive art in the seventeenth century was an expression of the settlers' desires to break ties with European tradition and begin anew from the facts of their own local lives. In the tradition of American literature, Taylor's primitive poetry functions in this same way.

Even though Taylor despairs of the sound of his own insufficient, unbegraced voice, in that human failing there is a break with tradition and a use of his own sensed experience. This is a way in which

Taylor did not realize that his soul-wracked blottings were appropriate to the New England Way of religion that he spent his days writing and preaching to defend. In his poetry, that defense is nicely personalized. The roughness of his feet that he seems ashamed of was appropriately New England praise for his God. Edward Taylor created better than he knew.

Chapter 11

A Puritan Humanist

This Orbe is emblem of the Sphere of Grace

(2.122)

For all of the ways in which Edward Taylor is a part of American traditions lasting into the twentieth century, he still has all the appearance of the last writer of covenant theology, the last Puritan. Though in our literary history the last part of the seventeenth century and the first part of the eighteenth clearly belongs to him, he most certainly is limited to *it*.

Even as the first three generations of settlers were writing themselves dry of defenses and hopes—Solomon Stoddard (and a handful of sentimental reformists like him) was starting to change the terms of Puritan ontology, and the vulnerable Cotton Mather (and a score of enraged and enthused chiliasts like him) was accommodating himself to deism and the American tragedy, and Jonathan Edwards (with other animators) was soon to rewrite the faith as a pretranscendentalism—even as the winds changed in other directions, moving ideas toward our own time, Taylor appears to have been our one major writer to have held the ground of his beliefs and to have brought New England Puritanism to a sufficient climax with his poetry. The American thirst for the irrevocable was easily expanding the world beyond him. His poetry has all the appearance of an apt symbol of the end of a movement.

Perhaps because he was the first important American poet and one of the last ardent Puritan defenders, Taylor has never been fully justified as belonging to the tradition of humane letters that we associate with the modern world. Taylor does not yet figure significantly in the transition from Calvinist perfectionism to American humanism and romanticism. He has not been seen as one of the thinkers and writers who, in Perry Miller's words describing the movement from colony to province, "carried us from the medieval universe of Protestant scholasticism to the very threshold of the Age of Reason."[1] If his many poems and his few ideas are never in doubt as givens of a climax of autonomous convictions of a significant place and time, his humanism is. The justification of any postmedieval admission of man's hand in the Creation has always been rather thin in the criticism of his poetry.

I use humanism in its classical sense here, meaning a belief in man's ability to perfect himself, rather than in its Christian sense. Christian humanist Taylor most certainly is, for at the heart of all he writes is a belief in the dignity and worth of man achieved by Christ. But classical humanism is incompatible with this sense and is the tradition of almost the whole of American letters (Edwards, Eliot, and Flannery O'Connor are distinct exceptions), in contradistinction to the apologetics of Christian humanism. Taylor's thinking about man is most certainly humanist in the Christian sense. But, as I would like to show, his thinking about *writing* puts him squarely in the center of our classical humanist tradition. Then we can have him firmly in mind as the first significant *poet* among American writers.

We have not found it difficult to know how Mather, as diarist and historian, managed God's contingency on human history or made a style to give the divine a worldly form. And we have not found it difficult to know how Edwards included mankind among the media of God's will and thereby made man absolute. But we have not known very well how Taylor belongs to humane traditions. We have not yet named that which warrants his canonization at the head of American letters.

If Taylor's humanism is located in his persistent theanthropism, an argument of the last two decades,[2] it needs severe qualification, as I have tried to show through this entire study, by a reminder of his equally persistent misanthropism. In an overwhelming number of his Meditations and in his *Christographia* sermon series, Taylor emphasizes a humanistic argument he feels he can make on behalf of Puritan theology: man's participation in divine nature through a half-human Christ, the Incarnation. It is a belief that excites him on mankind's behalf:

Gods onely Son doth hug Humanity,
Into his very person. By which Union
His Humane Veans its golden gutters ly.
And rather than my Soule should dy by thirst,
These Golden Pipes, to give me a drink, did burst.

(1.10)

This he calls the "blessed Theanthropie." It is a concept which is one of the primary sources of Taylor's unusual delight in Calvinism and a considerable stimulus behind his writing his meditative poetry. In the two series of his Meditations he is the rather flamboyant artist of a doctrine which, he feels, throws light into the dark corners of man's condition. Taylor feels that as he concentrates on the physical Christ, he is concentrating on man: the Incarnation is a form of humanism.

By careful definition, Taylor works in his writings with scripture (mainly Paul) and church fathers (mainly Origen and Calvin) to describe colorfully a dignity for New England man which he felt other ages and other persuasions had not found so well. In the lacunae of a special dualistic christology Taylor describes the place for man. No one else in early America was to devote himself to this task quiet so ardently.

As Taylor understands the doctrine of the Incarnation, the idea forms Christ out of God's nature (but without subtracting from God's essence or person) and out of mankind's nature (but without the addition of individual human traits of depravity). Taylor's "theandricall" Christ is a person of two distinct natures but without a personality of his own; from God he gets the power to save and from man the ability to feel, suffer, and die. Taylor calls this a "Personall Union," for he is struck by the personal relationship of two natures combined in one being. This use of the uniquely dark side of human nature in forming the person of Christ is, for Taylor, God's answer to Satan's attempt to "draw man into Sin . . . and ruine man eternally . . . and shew him to be weake and shallow." Theanthropy "brings out of this Stinking thing Sweetness."[3]

The idea makes man's nature an important half of a divinely schizophrenic Christ, and mankind is raised to Taylor's esteem thereby:

A Physicall Union of God and Man, is absolutely impossible.
But now for God to assume in the Second person, Human

nature into a personall Union to his Godhead, will do the thing.
It advances Humane Nature into the greatest proximity to God
that Created nature is Capable of, out of the greatest distance
from God possible, and makes it so much more Glorious than
ever by how much it was fallen from Glory. . . . It is the Won-
derfullst advancement given to our Nature that created nature
is, or Can be capable of: it lifts it up almost into Deity itselfe. It
makes it partaker of Divine Efficiency, partaker in Divine Honour, and a Partner also of Divine Adoration.[4]

This theanthropic lust of Taylor's is genuine. He wants to describe the
dignity of fallen man and he is excited by the point of conjunction of
human and divine natures in Christ. In one of his poems defining this
conjunction, he exults:

> Two Natures distance-standing, infinite,
> Are Onifide, in person, and Unite.

> In Essence two, in Properties each are
>   Unlike, as unlike can be. One All-Might
> A Mite the other; One Immortall fair.
>   One mortall, this all Glory, that all night.
>   One Infinite, One finite. So for ever:
>   Yet ONED are in Person; part'd never.

> The Godhead personated in Gods Son
>   Assum'd the Manhood to its Person known,
> When that the Manhoods essence first begun
>   That it did never Humane person own.
>   Each natures Essence e're abides the same.
>   In person joynd, one person each do claim.

> Oh! Dignifide Humanity indeed:
>   Divinely person'd: almost Deifide.
> Nameing one Godhead person, in our Creed,
>   The Word-made-Flesh. Here's Grace's 'maizing stride.
>   The vilst design, that villany e're hatcht
>   Hath tap't such Grace in God, that can't be matcht.

> Our Nature spoild: under all Curses groans
>   Is purg'd, tooke, grac'd with grace, united to

A Godhead person, Godhead-person owns
    Its onely person. Angells, Lord its so.
    This Union ever lasts, if not relate
    Which Cov'nant claims Christs Manhood, separate.

                                    (2.44)

Through Christ's humanity, fallen mankind has taken a " 'maizing
stride." His definition of Christ's person in terms of the divine use of
man's "spoild" nature provides Taylor with relief from the oppres-
siveness of the doctrine of the Fall.

Taylor's initial motive, however, is not to honor humanity so much
as to encourage in his congregation (and elsewhere) an unwavering
conviction of the absolute necessity of (and absolute dependence of
man on) Christ. He can only think of man's dignity in this sense.
Taylor wishes to prevent, as he puts it, "many Hereticall notions
touching Christ" and to make an earthy Christ man's example:[5]

> It is impossible for the Slighter of the Body of Christ ever to be
> Saved. . . . God hath prepared it for him: its therefore an Excel-
> lent piece. Its not to be Spit upon, though it was Spit upon: Its
> not to be buffeted, tho' buffeted it was. Its the Glory of all the
> Creation: it is to the astonishment of Reason, its for the Exalt-
> ment of Man. . . .[6]

This "Exaltment" is more in praise of God than of man, for it is not
out of any merit on man's part that he is linked with the divine in
Christ, nor because man is thereby raised to any higher level than his
low estate by the conjunction, but simply because of God's loving
condescension (through Christ). Theanthropy celebrates human nature without honoring that which is unique to human nature, only
that which is superadded to it, the divine side of Christ. Worthless, it
is given worth. Man is not accepted by Taylor as he is; only in a
refined form is he admissible to the hypostatic union Taylor envi-
sions:

> The Nature of the Godhead cannot admitt Sinfull Manhood
> into Personall Union unto it. For then the Person of the
> Godhead would be render'd Sinfull, by the Sin of the Persons
> Manhood: but this is impossible. Hence there must be great
> Work laid out upon the Materialls Provided to fit them for their

> Personall Union to the Son of God. . . . The Godhead . . . do
> utterly deny all Union unless there be then a preparation passed
> upon the Manhood to fit it for this Union.[7]

Except for certain workings of God, human nature would normally "offer Violence to [Jesus'] Personality."[8]

In spite of his exclamations to the contrary, Taylor is not celebrating all of humanity in his doctrine but only Christ's humanity (and man's only by extension) when he exclaims:

> In this Union lieth the Highest advancement that ever God gave,
> giveth, or can give, or that Created nature can receive, for it is
> brought as nigh to Godhead nature: as is possible. Its brought to
> have its being and Essence in the midst of the Trinity. And that
> this Should be granted to Sinfull Humane nature. What Grace is
> here? oh! it is not onely Such as carries along with it eternall
> Glory, and Happiness to all the Elect, but advanceth this Indi-
> viduall Manhood assumed by the Son of God into his person:
> [and] also our nature in it out of the most wretched State, into
> the most transcendent preferment that is possible.[9]

It is a Pyrrhic victory for man, really little more than an illusion of grandeur. For Taylor it is an honor that human nature was chosen as God's device for creating an independent God in Jesus, but from a classically humanistic point of view it is an empty honor, for it does not change the nature or lot of man any but leaves him in his low estate—and is therefore a mere compliment to a worm.

As was underscored earlier, Taylor is easily given to an ecstasy over his doctrine that sounds like the spontaneous mysticism of the Jesus-freak: he is easily made happy over the remote, impersonal, historical fact of Christ as man:

> The Feast of Tabernacles makes me sing
>   Out thy Theanthropy, my Lord, I'le spare
> No Musick here.

>   (2.24)

But Taylor knows it to be "A Union Not Artificiall"—that is, man's relationship to God is a conjunction, not a fusion, not a combination or superimposition—in order to keep man in his place and prevent arrogance of the race through identification with the example of a theanthropic Christ:

Now this Union is Such a Uniting of things together as makes no
essentiall alteration in the things thus United, but Constitutes a
Speciall Relation between them.[10]

This Taylor calls "a Mysticall Union," the understanding of which
Taylor feels can come to us through understanding the nature of
metaphor: through simile (the divine is accessible to man when man
is *like* Christ), through synecdoche (Christ is representative of all
mankind), and through symbol (communion as a substitute for
actual union). Though continually ecstatic over the relief this union
provides an eschatology dominated by the doctrine of original sin,
Taylor hedges when it comes to the actual practical effect on man
himself: "His assuming Holy Humanity . . . cannot reward
[mankind] with Glory, because its fallen Nature, not redeem'd."[11]
Taylor's excitement is over an elaborate idea Christian apologists
construct with language. It is for him a most fortunate epistemology.

Taylor's definitional skill here is not a heresy, not a divergence or
an eccentricity, but most certainly an extravagance, a luxury. It is an
emphasis Calvinism in New England could not afford, however
rampant. If it was important to him personally, as it most certainly
was, then over against other rigors of covenant theology this was
sentimental, romantic. Taylor's celebration of man's dignity was
subversive of the hell the Puritan needed for stimulus; man could rest
content under Taylor's ecstatic optimism, for he was elevated above
the angels without lifting his own hand. Taylor is a much better
dramatizer of the hell he develops his own hopes out of than he is a
poet of the security of a theanthropy, which gives him some of the
blandest rhetoric in his poems and some of his silliest metaphors.

The two points at which Taylor is most doctrinally extravagant
and sentimental are in his equating of theanthropy with common
grace:

> Oh! what Grace is here? Unheard of the like! Unparalleld
> Grace! the Grace that is the Grace of the Onely true God in
> truth. Shall our nature not onely finde Grace to Save it, but to
> advance it into Personall Union to that God, who is the onely
> true God, that is offended and dishonoured by it; whereby it is
> as much advanced above its first Glory in innocency, in bright-
> ness of Honour, and highness of excellency, as it was cast below
> that State in darkness of Sin, and dolefulness of Sorrow. Oh!
> what Grace is here?[12]

and also in his attempt to apply personally an abstract concept. He assured his congregation in 1701:

> Godhead Nature is in him, and his nature is in thee. His Nature is not without thine that thy nature might not be without him. He Honours thy Nature: do not thou dishonour his. Thy Nature is in his Person: His Nature is in thy person, that thy Person, and his person might make an Union of persons by his personal Union.[13]

It is at these points that the logic behind Taylor's Christian humanism is seen for its desperate personal basis: the Incarnation as he dramatizes it in his poems gave him an outlet for his elaborate hope and it made a place for him personally as a man in a cosmic scheme that threatened to exclude him.

> I'm Thine, Thou Mine! Mutuall propriety:
>   Thou giv'st thyselfe. And for this gift takst mee
> To be thine own.
>
> (2.79)

His Christian humanism is so secure a rock to him that it may seem wrong to fault him for failing to see that any other dignity for man was possible.

Taylor is, in fact, a great deal more convincing as misanthropist. He is much more adept at interesting us in our torments, much more successful with the demoniacal than the divine. At one and the same time he can believe that "there is a rich treasure of Wisdom that Human Nature is the Storehouse of" and yet have little regard for man's arts and ideas:

> All the Wealth, and Wisdom of this World is not comparable to the Treasures of Wisdom in Christ. The Wealth of this World is such, as this Worlds Wisdom is exercised about. Hence it is but low, and little, and but of a little Concern and lasts but a little While, Cald thick Clay, and that flys away, as an Eagle. And they cannot be otherwise being onely the produce of Worldly Wisdom, Which is but a mock Wisdom, compared to Spirituall Wisdom. . . . The Pearles, and Carbuncles of Wor[l]dly treasures are but dirty boulders, or paltry Pebles Stones.[14]

Taylor has the conventional mistrust of man's mind: "Beward lest any man deceive you thro' Philosophy, and vain Deceit, after the traditions of men and rudiments of the world, and not after Christ."[15] He recognizes the desire for wisdom inherent in man ("There is a naturall desire of Wisdom, as an Essentiall Property of the Rationall Nature"),[16] yet for Taylor Christ is the only place to find such:

> It is domineering folly in you not to betake yourselves to the right wayes to become wise. Here is the way, and the Onely way to become Wise. All the treasures of Wisdom are in Christ. Hence no Wisdom out of him.[17]

It is a paradox in Taylor's poetry, as in much Christian poetry, that he should have been so warmed by his theanthropism to the end of his days and yet would base his faith so firmly on the rock of human depravity:

> The Properties of the Godhead are not inherent in the manhood: for then the Manhood in its Nature Would be the Subject recipient of Simplicity, Immutability, Infinity, Eternity, Omnipotency, Omnisciency, Omnipresence, etc. Which its impossible to be. . . . The Consequence of the proofe is false, viz, that the Allfulness of the Godhead dwells in the Manhood Everywhere.[18]

There is no goodness inherent in man. The hope for man (and Taylor's personal hope, especially) lies not in mankind but outside himself, often remote, in a saving Christ:

> If thou gets an Intrest in Christ, all things Come along with him. Thou wilt have the All-Fulness of the Godhead that dwells in him bodily for thy Enriching: Oh! then Strive for this intrest.[19]

Taylor's theanthropism provides the subject matter and tone for much of his meditative poetry, and his poetry, if seen in the light of secular traditions, is made insubstantial thereby, in fact, marvelously irrelevant, a superfetation.

But there is another feature of Taylor's poetry that I have pointed to in this discussion as evidence of a strong strain of humanism in him: the fact that his major poetry (as well as his *Treatise* sermons) is *preparatory* in its doctrine and psychology; that is, it celebrates preparatory meditation as a means of perfecting human behavior and through human behavior purifying church and state.[20] Like Augustine, Taylor held out for the ability of man to carry out "the function . . . of expectation." If Taylor could not raise mankind as far as classical humanists have by his device of a theanthropical christology, perhaps he thought he could do so by advancing active introspection to the level of a humanistic art.

We saw in his biography at the outset of this study that the preparationist ontology of Thomas Hooker was attractive to Taylor from about 1680 on for the reason that it allowed him to believe human works to have something to do, if only tentatively and weakly, with human justification. Better than the ecstatically argued but illusory optimism of his theanthropism, his ardent championing of preparationism reveals his humanistic bent. It was the closest thing to the humanistic ideals of Arminianism that New England orthodoxy would allow.[21]

> O let thy lovely streams of Love distill
> > Upon myselfe and spoute their spirits pure
> Into my Viall, and my Vessell fill
> > With liveliness, from dulness me secure.
>
> (2.32)

Taylor becomes excited in his *Treatise* sermons over the new possibility for the advancement of mankind ("a graft on nature's stock," he calls it) that preparationism made:

> All being under the call are to endeavor to be fitted to celebrate the wedden [of the Lord's Supper]. For it's a graft on nature's stock not to go slovenly and in dirty tattered rages, or naked, to celebrate choice feasts, but to prepare for such solemnities. So that this gospel wedden feast being presented unto all, and all under the gospel being invited to it, it is a strong motive to stir up all to prepare for it.[22]

By means of such preparatory meditation, Taylor finds in Puritanism the limits of natural ability greatly expanded, the ability of unregenerate man enlarged beyond what Christ alone could do for man through the Incarnation. The process makes "the New Man." In proper introspection, sanctification of a certain kind (the effort made to believe, whether predisposed or acquired) was evidence of justification: the ability to grovel is nonetheless an ability. It was a way of making faith active and encouraging in man a will and giving him something to do about his salvation. The Christian humanist in Taylor here almost becomes a classical humanist. The process of preparation honored man as man so that he might proceed to affirm himself as *only* man:

> His receiving [an ordinance] is his own act. His own precursive agency being necessary unto his conversion wrought in and by his receiving doth constitute him an agent, and active in his own conversion. So that hence it appears that the soul is first in act as a cause, and not in a second sense as an effect, of his conversion as in receiving Christ.[23]

Taylor describes preparation as "one of the greatest inducements" to self-regeneration and calls the result in men's lives "a visible glory": "Hence the method of divine wisdom hath set it as a motive to stir [man] up to the highest gospel qualifications in order thereunto."[24]

It is important to see what this inward-turning process did for Taylor himself, how this active stoicism was to him a regard for his humanity and an advancement of his bearing as a man in the world, especially since this is what we watch when we read the best of his poetry. Taylor defines the preparational process as one in which "My mental Eye . . . Did double back its Beams to light my Sphere/Making an inward Search, for what springs there." (2.27) In introspection Taylor cultivated the power of longing for a better man in himself, beginning by taking his ability to study his nature and faults thoroughly as a sign of his spiritual worth and continuing by undertaking self-improvement in the confidence of some spiritual results. Preparation made Taylor's faith active: there was something he could do, negative as its direction usually was in his poems, to prove his worth. Nonpreparationists could perhaps understand their worth, but a preparationist like Taylor felt he was *undertaking* the question of his worth by "Making an inward Search." In his preparatory poetry he plays the role of a worthless man working at humiliation and hope. There he is actively engaged in the question of his worth without actually determining it, yet all the while proving to himself that his ability to thus involve himself in the exercise of self-analysis is itself an exercise of his inherent worth. His ability to discover his need is the extent to which a special grace is perhaps already upon him. His

manliness is shown by his ability to make it into the hell in himself.
"If ye by the Spirit mortify the deeds of the flesh," he wrote in his
Treatise, "ye shall live. So that the work of mortifying sin is the work
the Spirit carrieth on in you."[25]

But Taylor's devotionalism is strongly masochistic—and that per-
verts much of its humanistic intent. The Christian virus of meditative
intensity which helped him escape passivity and dullness of spirit
—and which he saw as a means for keeping man's faculties alive,
engaging one's mind productively—also tormented him into verbal
self-flagellation. It refined his excruciations.

> Astonisht stand, my Soule; why dost not start
>   At this surprizing Sight shewn here below?
> Oh! let the twitch made by my bouncing Heart
>   Gust from my breast this Enterjection, Oh!
>   A Sight so Horrid, sure its Mercies Wonder
> Rocks rend not at't, nor Heavens split asunder.
>
> (1.18)

Preparationism gave him a jubilant despair that was stimulating but
which also perpetuated extravagances of his faith, its macerations
and will to suffer, its tragic desires and illusions. In theory, preparation has the look of a humanistic process (both Christian and classical) but in practice, as the example of the poetic Taylor demonstrates,
it was as full of hell as of simulations of salvation, as degrading as it
was activating.

Preparatory meditation in Taylor's hands, as in Hooker's and
Thomas Shepard's, made man's weaknesses both appalling and
appealing—a tension which organized Taylor's *Meditations* for him
and turned them dramatic almost against his will. As Taylor practices
it with his poems, preparatory meditation is a reinstatement of
oneself in hell for the ostensible motive of being reinvigorated by
one's sufferings and for reliving the sources of one's misery and
dreams of glory. But while probing the grounds of his own life and of
evil, the preparationist gets stuck, feasting on his tortures, enlivened
sensually by his humility, fascinated with the hellish preoccupation
of watching himself: while "Making an inward Search, for what
springs there, . . ." Taylor himself admits, "I finde myself
defild:/Issues and Leprosies all ore mee streame./Such have not En-
terance. I am beguild." (2.27) His pain gives him pleasure, and so he

comes to prefer the masochism of his counterfeit hell to the unsure possibility of the unknown glory he is supposed to be demonstrating his capacity for. In the Fall itself is his joy:

> this world doth eye thy brightness most
> When most in distance from thyselfe. . . .
>
> (2.21)

"Oh! I am so thronged with carnal thoughts, I know not what to make of myself," Taylor confesses in one of his *Treatise* sermons.

> I am overrun with evil and carnal thoughts. Where I have one thought of spiritual concerns, I have twenty laid out upon the things of the world. Truly this is the condition of God's children here in this life. . . . Of all the enjoyments of this world, the enjoyment of this temporary life is enjoyment of the choicest thing.[26]

Taylor found his fulfillment within the awful condition of the world, within his low estate. That undercuts his preparational attitude seriously as a classically humanistic one.

For all of its introspective quality, Taylor's is not a kind of poetry that advances the writer's self-knowledge; it does not move him beyond itself. Self-consciousness was awareness of himself, to be sure, but mainly understanding of the reality of impossibility. His effort in most of his poetry is to keep reminding himself that he is Man: he broods over himself and over the species with the zeal of a fanatic. He indulges his whim of masticating his ego and he generalizes the disadvantages of man's condition, transforming his perplexities into a norm. In Taylor's hands, preparationism is pathology.

The location of Taylor's humanism in his theanthropism or his preparationism, while proving the humane sympathies inherent in his Christian humanism, may only substantiate Philip Hobsbaum's complaint, "Whenever you find Calvinism, you find an impoverishment of human experience."[27] These theosophical enthusiasms of Taylor's, whether inherited from Augustine and Calvin or dramatized by himself, degrade man even as they attempt to affirm him. Any classical humanism does not appear to lie in the content of his works, where *he* would have us look for it, but in his relationship to the act of writing itself. Herein lies the third critical concern over Taylor's contribution to humane letters and the one which makes it possible to see him in a classical tradition. I would like to suggest that the forms themselves of Taylor's expression worked a miracle: in willing words, he made for himself a singularity, a voice, an affinity with the world and a tie with his God, a freedom, a greater affirmation of his humanity than the conventions of Christian humanism could. In other words, in his reliance on poetry he made an organism that, like his desires for himself, transcends itself. This is the central argument of this study.

Though Taylor felt he was most easily made spiritually alive by his concentration on the worldly Chirst and his worldly self, we can know from the fact of his writing so much and so well that it was *words* that made a world for him to be a man in. It is instructive to observe again that in large part the subject of Taylor's poetry is Taylor's poetry. In his poems he is obsessed with the need for words and the power of words over his well-being. He cannot stop writing about writing. In most of his Meditations, Taylor takes on the persona of a poet exulting in, worried about, and dependent on his poems. The dominant imagery of his poetry is the imagery of writing/speaking/singing.[28]

> I am this Crumb of Dust which is design'd
> To make my Pen unto thy Praise alone,
> And my dull Phancy I would gladly grinde
> Unto an Edge on Zions pretious Stone.
> And Write in Liquid Gold upon thy Name
> My Letters till thy glory forth doth flame.
>
> ("Prologue")

So prevalent is Taylor's concern in his poems over his ability to write that it is as if on a literal level Taylor's poetry symbolizes his fallen condition, for only because he is fallen does he write about his condition. His verse is what he makes as a man in the face of the Fall. He is made an individual of humble significance as he writes. His ability to express well his inability to express himself is the Puritan paradox of being justified yet human:

> Untun'de, my Lord. My Cankard brassy wire
> 'S unfit to harp thee Musick. Angells pipes

Are squeaking things: soon out of breath. Desires
    Exceed them; yet screwd highst up are but mites
    To meddle with the Musicking thy glory.
    What then's my jews trump meet to tune thy Story?

File off the rust: forgive my Sin, and make
    My Heart thy Harp: and mine Affections brac'de
With gracious Grace thy Golden Strings to shake
    With Quavers of thy glory well begrac'de.
    Though small's my mite, its dusty Wings e're will
    Sprindg out thy fame tun'de by thy Spirits Skill.

                    (2.54)

Through writing Taylor is determined to turn the insufficiency of his
humanity into something considerable: "My rough Feet shall thy
smooth praises sing." (1.39) Like any other poet, Taylor wrote in
order to be a person within the impersonal system of his beliefs.
    Throughout his poems Taylor, like any other poet, sees writing as
necessary to his value, his salvation: "I fain would something
say:/Lest Silence should indict me." (1.21) He feels condemned if he is
"but an empty Sound." (2.16) "Duty," he claims, "raps upon her
doore for Verse." (2.30) This appears to be the case because he senses
a "glory" within himself when he writes:

And shall I gag my mouth, and ty my Tongue,
    When such bright Glory glorifies within?
    That makes my Heart leape, dancing to thy Lute?

                    (1.21)

As expected, Taylor plays the Puritan writer's conventional role of
being afraid that his "desire [to write] be Pride" and the role of
acknowledging that he will perform poorly as a writer ("My Rhymes
do better suite/Mine own Dispraise," 1.22), and yet, as we have seen
throughout this entire study of Taylor, he enjoys attempting the
equation of his human abilities as a writer with his spiritual worth:

Let him in Whom all Fulness Dwells, dwell, Lord
    Within my Heart [a pun on art]: this Treasure therein lay.
    I then shall sweetly tune thy Praise, When hee
    In whom all Fulness dwells, doth dwell in mee.

                    (1.27)[29]

His ability to write he tries to take as a form of grace in his earth-
bound life:

> Thy joyes in mee will make my Pipes to play
> For joy thy Praise while teather'd to my clay.

(1.48)

This is an illusion that it is safe for him to entertain—even an illusion
he feels confident *living* in—as long as he qualifies his declamations of
hope with equally strong disclaimers of his poetry's, and his own,
worth. As in the tone of his theanthropic and preparational yearn-
ings, he can imagine his writing, and himself, begraced if kept
humble.[30]

It is interesting to observe how easy it is for Taylor to delight in his
humanity at those times when he concentrates on himself as writer,
as manipulator of worldly materials, as self at work, as maker.
Writing is an enlargement of his life:

> My Glory is that thou my king maist bee.
> That I may be thy Subject thee to sing
> And thou may'st have thy kingdoms reign in mee.

(2.16)

He easily relates writing well to being a "better man":

> Words and their Sense within thy bounds are kept
> And richer Fruits my Vintage cannot raise.
> I can no better thing bring, do what I can:
> Accept thereof and make me better man.

(2.106)

Writing poetry is a means of self-betterment:

> as my Life thy lines do parallell,
> My Harp shall play.

(2.118)

The emphasis in such imagery is on himself and his possibilities as a
man:

> all my Growth to thee shall bud with blooms
> Of Praises Whistling in Angelick Tunes.

(2.68)

Writing apparently encouraged this hope-filled self-consciousness in him: there is a "Harp within" with "bright golden Wyers" ready to "sing thy Praise in better Strain."(2.17,23,25)

One could easily take Taylor's comments equating writing and his worth superficially—many of them tags at the beginnings and ends of poems or inserted as punctuation midway to remind us of his concern for his art—if it were not for the fact that he writes most of these apologia *after* he has finished writing the substance of a poem. His method is to complete his poem and *then* pray for the ability to write a poem—such as these lines at the end of Meditation 2.11:

And set me in thy Sunshine, make each flower
Of Grace in me thy Praise perfum'd out poure,

with the phrase "Grace in me" suggesting that he equates skill in writing with personal spiritual worth. His endings suggest that he saw his poems as means of stirring a fuller life in himself: although he has written his "Praise" already, he now must enlarge his life until it too is sufficient praise of God. "I will tune thy Praise," he writes, "with holy Breath." A poem is therefore a stimulus to an enlarged life. Writing is a device, he says, that will "fit me for thy Service, and thy Face" (2.14). Even as he finishes writing a piece, he seems to be praying for the ability to write. He is eager to get back to his pen as soon as he has set it down. Writing exhilarates him, moves him, motivates him, stimulates him, gives him the active participation in his worth that he (on his own, in this world, this "Sphere of Grace") does not normally have:

This little Voice feasts mee with fatter Sweets
Than all the Stars that pave the Heavens Streets.

(2.35)

To be sure, the sources of much of Taylor's good feeling about the stimulus his writing gives him are simply theanthropy ("I shall weare thy Nazarite like Crown/ In Glory bright with Songs of thy Renown," 2.15) and simple preparation ("this rich banquet makes me thus a Poet," 2.110). But there is an additional element: Taylor is determined to have a will to exercise in some fashion, and poetry is his attempt to express the fact that he does have a will, that he can will, that he is willing. That is, as Edwards would have it, during the act of writing he can discover the extent to which his nature is an *inclined* nature:

> Will thy Will, I must, or must
> From Heavens sweet Shine to Hells hot flame be thrust.
>
> . . . .
>
> I shall be grac'd withall for glory fit.
>
> (1.16)

In other words, if he can write well—that is, elaborately, baroquely (his hope for himself) and at the same time awkwardly, humanly (his humility)—he might consider himself elect. It *is* some evidence.[31] In neither theanthropism nor preparationism do Taylor's desires come to anything more than desire, but with writing, the action itself is its own end. The process itself is involving, enlivening, moving. The process itself is proof of his religious affections. The action is an accomplishment.

The act of writing confers reality and autonomy on the persona of Taylor's Meditations. Writing keeps him from the universal and ties him to the properties of the world: the little sensations of his poems—in the rhythm, rhyme, structure—are a bond with beings and objects. He clings to his poems, though they are themselves frail, worldly things, for they are his means of praise, his life.

Writing is so important to Taylor's concept of himself as a human, as my study has attempted to show, that he writes about poetry as not the beginning of his relationship with God but as the result. He wants grace *so that he can write*. Poetry for Taylor is in part theanthropic (the word is also the Word) and in part preparatory (language is action) but mainly it is existential, autonomous, self-sufficient; that is, it is a human action that affirms itself. While he is writing Taylor is something. His poetry gave him the role of aspiring believer to play; it gave him, through the sound of language, an involvement in time and movement; it gave him, through imagery, a unity with the abstract and ineffable. In it he is doing something: his faith is active. And made active, his beliefs confirm his humanity as something significant. Through art mankind is still merely mankind—irrelevant, marginal, insignificant—yet also affirmed because conscious, enduring, vigorous, animated, aggressive, colorful, even (though qualifiedly so) regenerated. The low estate of a mere maker of words defines man's active participation in his fears of his worthlessness and his hopes of his worth. Through the personal assertion of poetry, Taylor felt he could, as a man, appropriate a life for himself by means of the dregs of the Fall, language.

The most active part of a Taylor poem—that is, when Taylor describes himself actually participating in his spiritual desires—is when he writes about writing. Otherwise he describes himself as largely helpless and abjectly dependent. By writing, he does not presume to earn any value, or even mainly to impress God with his abilities as a man, and most certainly not to determine God's determinations about his salvation, but simply to have life ("I fain would have this Life but han't its knack," 2.82), to live intently ("Enlay my thoughts, my words, and Works with Grace," 2.99), to make the most of the Fall ("Might but my pen in natures Inventory/Its progress make," 2.57), indeed to glory in being human ("Thy Praise shall be *my Glory* sung in state," 2.53).[32] As my study has tried to show, writing made it possible for him to prove to himself his ability to be what it was his lot to be—human. His is therefore the first Puritan poetry—and perhaps also the last—to serve as an adequate symbol of a classical humanism within early American culture.

Notes

1: Introduction to a New Poet

1. *American Poets: From the Puritans to the Present* (Boston, 1968), pp. 22–23.

2. "Edward Taylor: A Revaluation," *New England Quarterly* 21 (1948), 519.

3. *Waiting for the End* (New York, 1964), pp. 209–10. Taylor's poetry has also contributed the title of a scholarly work, Ann Leighton's *Early American Gardens: "For Meate or Medicine"* (Boston, 1970).

4. *Upon the Sweeping Flood* (New York, 1966). The plot and point of Miss Oates' title story are derived from Taylor's poem of the same name. She shows a man "physicking" the heavens with his own arrogant emotions and the resulting "excrements" that fall upon the world.

5.   I don't know whether I am light or heavy.
I'm light as a dollar
—No, so heavy,
I can believe it's me, not Reverend Taylor,
who prayed
gazing cloudward,
"Oh Lord,
can this crumb of earth the Earth outweigh?"
Love,
only the shining of the sun is simple today.
At the burlesque show
you said,
"The girls are so
agonizingly slow."

> How do you, my dear, tolerate me
> when I always wish the one lovely girl to be
> dancing out of her fiesta dresses forever?. . .

From *Paper Airplane* by Allan Kaplan. Copyright 1971 by Allan Kaplan. The poem originally appeared in *Poetry* (April, 1970) and is reprinted by permission of Harper & Row, Publishers, Inc. Mr. Kaplan misquotes the first line from Taylor's "Prologue" to *Preparatory Meditations* for his poem: "Lord, Can a Crumb of Dust the Earth Outweigh?"

6. Except where the title of the poem is given, all references to Taylor's poetry in the text of this discussion are to the First and Second Series of the *Preparatory Meditations* and to the numbered meditations within those series (thus: 2.57), and to *Gods Determinations* (GD), as found in the Donald E. Stanford edition, *The Poems of Edward Taylor* (New Haven, 1960).

2: This Pilgrim Life of Mine

1. Stiles wrote of Taylor a number of times: "Memoir of Reverend Mr. Taylor" (1767), Stiles Papers, Yale University Library (New Haven, Conn.); "The Genealogy of the Revd. Mr. Edward Taylor Pastor of Westfield," Stiles Papers, Yale University Library; *Extracts from the Itineraries and Other Miscellanies of Ezra Stiles* (New Haven, 1918), pp. 81–83, 206; Stiles to Thomas Jefferson, 21 June 1784, and Stiles to Thomas Hutchinson, 25 March 1765, Stiles Papers, Massachusetts Historical Society (Boston, Mass.); Franklin B. Dexter, ed., *The Literary Diary of Ezra Stiles* (New York, 1901), 1: 366–67. The Stiles sketch of Taylor ("Memoir") is included in Abiel Holmes, *Life of President Stiles* (Boston, 1798), p. 381; in *The Westfield Jubilee* (Westfield, Mass., 1870), pp. 155–56; and in Charles W. Mignon, Jr., "Some Notes on the History of the Edward Taylor Manuscripts," *Yale University Library Gazette* 39 (1965), 169–70. Edmund Morgan has written of Stiles: "Ezra carefully saved the Taylor papers (using the blank pages of a commonplace book to record his own comments on the Stiles family) and thereby preserved the best poetry written in colonial America. But it is doubtful that Ezra ever fully appreciated the poetic genius of his maternal grandfather." *The Gentle Puritan: A Life of Ezra Stiles, 1727–1795* (New Haven, 1962), p. 4.

2. In *Annals of the American Pulpit*, ed. William B. Sprague (New York, 1857), 1: 180.

3. *Rev. Edward Taylor* (New York, 1891).

4. *A Sermon Commemorative of the Two-Hundredth Anniversary of the*

First Congregational Church of Westfield, Mass. (Westfield, 1879).

5. *Westfield and Its Historic Influences* (Springfield, Mass., 1922), 1: 126–29.

6. *Biographical Sketches of Graduates of Harvard University* (Boston, 1881), 2: 410.

7. Two events of historical interest to Taylor's biography between Sibley and Johnson are the publication of his diary in the *Proceedings of the Massachusetts Historical Society* 18 (1880–81), 4–18 and the account of the finding of a book of copies kept by Taylor, 13 (1899), 124–29; 14 (1900), 212–17.

8. *The Poetical Works of Edward Taylor* (Princeton, 1939), pp. 11–15.

9. Grabo, *Edward Taylor* (New York, 1961), pp. 17–83; Stanford, "An Edition of the Complete Poetical Works of Edward Taylor" (Ph.D. diss., Stanford University, 1953); Stanford, "Introduction," *The Poems of Edward Taylor* pp. xxxix–xlviii; second edition (New Haven, 1963), pp. xi–xvii; and Stanford, *Edward Taylor* (Minneapolis, 1965), pp. 5–14. We can perhaps expect Taylor biographies to take the two directions suggested by the general comments of Dwight W. Call, "Edward Taylor: Pastor and Poet," in *Westfield, Mass., 1669–1969,* ed. Edward C. Janes and Roscoe S. Scott (Westfield, 1968), pp. 10–76, and the specific, newly unearthed personal records about him, like the Diaries of Stephen Williams (*American Literature* 34 [1962], 270–74).

As Student

10. In Holmes, *Life of President Stiles*, p. 381.

11. Best on the subject of Puritan educational theory as a form of revolutionary activity is Richard L. Greaves, *The Puritan Revolution and Educational Thought* (New Brunswick, N. J., 1970).

12. The evidence is overwhelming that Taylor did not attend Cambridge or any other university, contrary to tradition, but one of the dissenting academies—either St. Andrew's or Coventry or perhaps Sheriffshales or Nettlebad in Oxfordshire. It has not been possible to ascertain when it was that he attended. See Charles W. Mignon, Jr., "The American Puritan and Private Qualities of Edward Taylor, the Poet" (Ph.D. diss., University of Connecticut, 1963), 209–15.

13. Norman S. Grabo, ed., *Edward Taylor's Christographia* (New Haven, 1962), pp. 132–34.

14. Francis E. X. Murphy, ed., *The Diary of Edward Taylor* (Springfield, Mass., 1964), pp. 37–38.

15. Ibid., p. 38.

16. Ibid., p. 39.

17. Lockwood, *Westfield*, 1: 138.

18. Alexander Medlicott, Jr., "Notes on Edward Taylor from the Diaries of Stephen Williams," pp. 270–74.

19. It was during such a stay at the home of the Rev. James Fitch of Norwich, Conn. that Taylor became acquainted with his first wife, Elizabeth. See Lockwood, *Westfield*, 1: 156.

20. H. W. Taylor, in *Annals of the American Pulpit*, p. 179.

21. "Possession of a library in the late seventeenth or early eighteenth century," writes Thomas H. Johnson, "was not uncommon in New England, but it is rare that one so large is encountered in such a remote settlement as Westfield." "Taylor's Library," *The Poetical Works*, pp. 201–20. That Taylor's library was quite a bit more extensive than the inventory indicates has been suggested by Donald E. Stanford, "Edward Taylor's Library," *Early American Literature* 6 (1971), 89–90, and by Thomas Davis and Virginia Davis, 'Edward Taylor's Library: Another Note," *Early American Literature* 6 (1972), 271–73.

22. Two recently discovered manuscript books not included in Johnson's list are copies of parts of *The History of the Council of Trent* and Origen's *Contra Celsus* and *De Principiis*. Francis E. X. Murphy, "An Edward Taylor Manuscript Book, " *American Literature* 31 (1959), 188–89.

23. The letter is in Taylor's Commonplace Book and has been transcribed for me by Thomas M. Davis.

24. H. W. Taylor, in *Annals of the American Pulpit*, p. 179.

25. *Anti-Intellectualism in American Life* (New York, 1963), pp. 58–61.

26. In Donald K. Junkins' tabulation of Taylor's images ("An Analytical Study of Edward Taylor's Preparatory Meditations" [Ph.D. diss., Boston University, 1963], pp. 257–408), we see how rich and specific the imagery is, without a great deal of dependence on technical language.

As Dissenter/Defender

27. H. W. Taylor in *Annals of the American Pulpit*, p. 177.

28. See B. B. Edward, "Complete List of the Congregational Ministers in the Old Country of Hampshire," *American Quarterly Register* 10 (1838), 384–401.

29. H. W. Taylor, in *Annals of the American Pulpit*, p. 177.

30. "The Lay-mans Lamentation," in Donald E. Stanford, "The Earliest Poems of Edward Taylor," *American Literature* 32 (1960), 138–43.

31. Taylor's association with Sewall is indicative of his proximity to the personalities and events at the heart of the life of the colonies. The two were life-long friends, having been roommates for two years at Harvard and corresponding with each other often thereafter. The strong affection that existed between them for many years is seen when Sewall writes in his Diary

on 24 May 1676: "Taylor came . . . and sat with me. God grant we may sit together in heaven." He must have seen Taylor off and on in Westfield, too, for he knew of his work and was acquainted with the Taylor children. He was strongly affected by Taylor's preaching in Boston, and was especially concerned about Taylor while old and enfeebled. At his death Sewall referred to him as "My Old Friend and Colleague . . . having diligently and Faithfully served the people of Westfield in the work of the Ministry 58 years." Shortly afterwards he wrote: "I humbly pray that Christ may be graciously present with us all Three [Samuel Mather, Taylor, and himself] both in Life and in Death, and then we shall safely and Comfortably walk through the shady valley that leads to Glory." *Diary*, 7 July 1729.

32. This Puritan ambiguity is now diffuse in American religious and political life, but it has survived almost whole in one form—among the Mormons, where covenant theology is maintained by the sacraments much as it was in the seventeenth century and yields a reactionary conservative political outlook. See Robert A. Rees, "Seeds of the Enlightenment: Public Testimony in the New England Congregational Churches, 1630–1750," *Early American Literature* 3 (1968), 22–29, and O. Kendall White, Jr., "The Transformation of Mormon Theology," *Dialogue: A Journal of Mormon Thought* 5 (1970), 9–24.

33. Norman S. Grabo, ed., *Edward Taylor's Treatise Concerning the Lord's Supper* (East Lansing, Mich., 1966), pp. 109–12.

34. "A Particular Church is God's House," Boston Public Library, Boston, Mass.

35. Ibid.

36. The manuscript of this sermon is in the Boston Public Library but was also copied by Taylor (with considerable change) into the Westfield Church Record (now in the Westfield Athenaeum). It and the other documents of Taylor's participation in the Stoddardean Controversy are discussed by Norman S. Grabo, "Edward Taylor on the Lord's Supper," *Boston Public Library Quarterly* 12 (1960), 22–36; "The Poet to the Pope: Edward Taylor to Solomon Stoddard," *American Literature* 52 (1960), 197–201; *Edward Taylor*, pp. 31–39; and in his introduction to Taylor's *Treatise*, pp. xix–xxxii.

37. Edwards to Benjamin Colman, 30 May 1735, in *Works of Jonathan Edwards*, 4 (New Haven, 1972), 102; repeated in *A Faithful Narrative of the Surprising Work of God*, ibid., p. 153; and in Benjamin Colman's abridgment of same, ibid., p. 119.

38. Lockwood, *Westfield*, 1: 168–69.

39. The manuscript of the letter is in the Massachusetts Historical Society. It is included in Grabo, "The Poet to the Pope," pp. 199–200. Stoddard wrote a direct answer to Taylor's epical indictment in his book *An Appeal to*

the Learned (Boston, 1709): "I consider that it would be a doleful thing to Propagate an Errour, and lay a Foundation of the Corruption of the Land; to spread and diffuse Poison that may have a malignant influence from Generation to Generation."

40. The manuscript of the letter, dated 4 June 1688, is in the Massachusetts Historical Society. It is also printed in Grabo, "The Poet to the Pope," p. 102.

41. The major documents in the controversy are: Increase Mather, *The Order of the Gospel* (1700); Increase and Cotton Mather, *Defense of Evangelical Churches* (1700); Stoddard, *The Inexcusableness of Neglecting the Worship of God* (1708); Increase Mather, *A Dissertation, wherein The Strange Doctrine . . . is Examined and Refuted* (1708); Stoddard, *An Appeal to the Learned* (1709); and *An Appeal, of Some of the Unlearned, both to the Learned and Unlearned* (1709) by an unknown writer.

42. *An Appeal to the Learned . . . Against the Exceptions of Mr. Mather*, p. 53.

43. The minister that followed Taylor in the Westfield pulpit, Nehemiah Bull, moved the congregation fairly easily toward Stoddardeanism. It was therefore appropriate that after the congregation moved to a second, larger meeting house in 1720, Taylor's old log church (where he preached for 48 years) should have been taken over by a group called the Separates, a group dedicated to, among other fundamentalist practices, a strict interpretation of the doctrine of the Lord's Supper.

44. *Treatise*, p. 197.

45. Ibid., p. 126.

46. The manuscript of his two sermons on church discipline is in the Boston Public Library. Along with the 1679 sermon and some notes, these were to have been Taylor's major published work on the Stoddardean controversy. They came into the hands of Thomas Prince, who was planning to use them as the basis for a work of his own on the subject, but they were never published. These are being prepared for publication now by Professor Thomas M. Davis.

As Minister

47. From Taylor's "Publick Records of the Church at Westfield Together With a brief account of or proceeding in order to our entrance into that State," Westfield Athenaeum, hereafter referred to as Church Record. This portion of the record is quoted in Lockwood, *Westfield*, 1: 107–8. The entire document is being edited for publication by Professor Thomas M. Davis.

48. *Diary*, p. 38.

49. Ibid., pp. 38–39.

50. Ibid., p. 39.

51. Lockwood, *Westfield*, 1: 139. In addition to the fifteen acres given him by the town in 1671, in 1691 Taylor inherited from a nephew, William Arms, a plantation of a hundred acres on the Back River in Virginia, which property Taylor asked his friend Samuel Sewall to secure for him but which he apparently eventually lost. Dexter, *Extracts from the Itineraries*, p. 89.

52. Taylor, "Church Record."

53. Letters between George Phelps, Joseph Whiting, and Samuel Loomis of Westfield and Solomon Stoddard and John Strong of Northampton, 5 January, 3 May, 29 July, and 21 August 1673, Westfield Athenaeum.

54. "Church Record."

55. Lockwood, *Westfield*, 1: 103.

56. "A Particular Church."

57. "Church Record," and in Lockwood, 1:110

58. Ibid., pp. 108–9.

59. Ibid., p. 116.

60. Ibid., p. 117.

61. Ibid., p. 143.

62. Ibid., pp. 54–55.

63. "A Particular Church."

64. "The Letter Book of Samuel Sewall," *Collections of the Massachusetts Historical Society*, 6th ser., 2 (1886–88), 274.

65. This is seen in Taylor's two sermons on church discipline in 1713.

66. The order of composition of sermon and poem needs a thorough discussion. On the basis of the Christographia essays, Norman S. Grabo maintains that the poems followed of necessity from the sermons ("Introduction," *Christographia*, pp. xxxiv–xxxv; see also Junkins, pp. 188–219, and Robert M. Benton, "Edward Taylor's Use of His Text," *Amercian Literature* 34 [1967], 31–41.) This argument ignores the fact that few of Taylor's other Meditations are as doctrinal as these are, that there is a disparity between the tone of generalized "application" at the ends of the sermons and the confessional tone of "application" in his poems, and that no poems can be found to correspond with Taylor's other extant sermons. To be sure, most of the Preparatory Meditations were written, as Taylor's own title has it, "Chiefly upon the Doctrin preached upon the Day of administration," but this says only that Taylor had a general subject in mind when he wrote some of his poems, not that the sermons moved him to writing them. It would appear to have been the *occasion* that turned him to preparatory meditation more than the subject or the form of his preaching. It was a matter of temperament with him that he should turn to his God and turn within himself *before* he presumed to convey the Word of God to his congregation.

67. The regular occurrence of rhetorical terms in his poems also suggests

that many of them may have served as prayers for assistance preparatory to his writing and preaching. This may account especially for Taylor's constant reference to his writing as an oral/aural creation.

68. Such is most certainly the case with the Prologues to his two collections of poems; the elegies on the death of his wife (1.34) and a son (2.40); miscellaneous meditative poems like "The Ebb and Flow," "Huswifery," and "Upon a Spider Catching a Fly"; the whole of *Gods Determinations*; and others. It is also difficult to conceive of Taylor delivering sermons on poetic theory (1.21, 22) or on the anatomy of Jesus (2.115–27) to his congregation. Though it may be largely the case, the sermons were not always "the occasion, the reason, the impulse, and the source of the poems," as Grabo argues. It cannot be the case that "Taylor completed *all* the poems after the sermons." Thomas M. Davis makes a valuable case for the idea that the poems were not always connected with the doctrine of the sermons preached, Taylor's claim to the contrary ("Edward Taylor and the Traditions of Puritan Typology," *Early American Literature* 4 [1969], 45–46). We must therefore admit a variety of reasons behind his meditative poetry, most of them having to do with personal preparation for divine acceptability.

As Family Man

69. *Diary*, p. 38.

70. Ibid., pp. 37–38.

71. Lockwood, *Sermon*, p. 11.

72. *Diary of Samuel Sewall, Collections of the Massachusetts Historical Society*, 5th ser., 1 (1878), 481–82.

73. See William B. Goodman, "Edward Taylor Writes His Love," *New England Quarterly* 27 (1954), 510–15.

74. *Diary*, 1:6.

75. Donald E. Stanford, "The Parentage of Edward Taylor," *American Literature* 32 (1961), 215–21.

76. Emma C. Nason, "Ruth Taylor and Her Five Daughters," in John Taylor Terry, *Rev. Edward Taylor*. Taylor wrote no verse about his second wife or their children.

77. My information on Taylor's dates and those of his descendants is confirmed by the records of the Genealogical Society of the Church of Jesus Christ of Latter-Day Saints. I express my gratitude to Mrs. Naomi Harker of Salt Lake City for the research.

78. It has been claimed that Oliver Wendell Holmes (himself a doctor-poet) was a descendant of Taylor. But this is an error. His father's first wife, Mary Stiles, was the granddaughter of Ezra Stiles, but this was not Holmes' own mother. It is interesting, nonetheless, to see how close Holmes came to

discovering Taylor. His father, Abiel Holmes, knew Stiles' records of Taylor along with the Taylor manuscripts. In an essay "The Pulpit and the Pew" (1881) Oliver Wendell Holmes tells of reading Sprague's *Annals of the American Pulpit* and being moved by the interests of the Puritan clergy:

> The objects about me, as I am writing, call to mind the varied accomplishments of some of the New England clergy. The face of the Revolutionary preacher, Samuel Cooper, as Copley painted it, looks upon me with the pleasantest of smiles and a liveliness of expression which makes him seem a contemporary after a hundred years' experience of eternity. The Plato on this lower shelf bears the inscription: "Ezrae Stiles, 1766, Olim e libris Rev. Jaredis Eliot de Killingworth." Both were noted scholars and philosophers. The hand-lens before me was imported, with other philosophical instruments, by the Reverend John Prince of Salem, an earlier student of science in the town since distinguished by the labors of the Essex Institute. . . . These reminiscences from surrounding objects came up unexpectedly of themselves, and have a right here, as showing how wide is the range of intelligence in the clerical body thus accidentally represented in a single library making no special pretensions. *Pages from an Old Volume of Life* (Boston, 1891), 408–9.

It is a temptation to speculate that it is also Taylor to whom he is referring. It would have been appropriate for Taylor, who lost five children and a wife within one year of having or giving birth, to have had a poet-doctor great-great-grandson who would discover a cure for puerperal fever.

79. *Christographia*, p. 14.

80. Ibid., p. 15. This does not mean, however, that Taylor's view of women was high. They were to his mind consistently "the weaker sex" in his sermons and have few rights. "It is not likely that any converting ordinance should be left to the administration of women, and not be fixt in the hand of the sacred function." *Treatise*, p. 98.

81. *Christographia*, pp. 132, 23, 393–94.

As Frontiersman

82. Lockwood, *Westfield*, 1: 218.

83. Ibid., pp. 229–30.

84. Ibid., pp. 226–28.

85. *Treatise*, pp. 153–54.

86. The New World references and the American qualities in Taylor's poetry have been documented and discussed inadequately. Louis Martz, for instance, found "almost nothing (except for an occasional canoe or rattlesnake) that one could single out to suggest a specifically American allusion" ("Foreword" to *Poems*, p. xxxv). Norman Grabo writes: "The history of the

New World was too recent and too little to provide the 'stuff' of poetry. And his major poems almost never allude to his American locale. But these facts in no way minimized the influence of his American experience. Taylor transcended his frontier circumstances not by leaving them behind, but by transforming them into intellectual, aesthetic, and spiritual universals." *Edward Taylor*, p. 173.

88. Most of these figures are from Donald Junkins, "An Analytical Study," pp. 110–87.

88. Junkins has cataloged 1,749 references to nature in Taylor's *Preparatory Meditations* alone. This is unmatched by any English poet between Shakespeare and James Thomson.

As Doctor/Scientist

89. Regarding the science curriculum Taylor would have had at Harvard, see Theodore Hornberger, *Scientific Thought in the American Colleges, 1638–1800* (Austin, Texas, 1946).

90. Taylor to Increase Mather, 22 March 1683, *Collections of the Massachusetts Historical Society*, 4th ser., 8 (1868), 629–30.

91. *Poems*, p. 519.

92. Taylor reported the discovery to Mather, who then communicated the discovery to Dr. John Woodward of the Royal Society in 1712. Woodward was a Newtonian realist and pioneer geologist who for his *Natural History of the Earth* had used geological facts as proofs of the divine will. Mather's account is in the *Philosophical Transactions of the Royal Society of London* 29 (1714), 62–63. The claim that "some of [Taylor's] compositions were published in the scientific literature of the day" is erroneous (*The Westfield Jubilee*, p. 152). Except for his report of the Claverack bones, which he communicated privately to Mather, Taylor did not consider writing anything of a scientific nature.

93. Donald E. Stanford, "The Giant Bones of Claverack, New York, 1705," *New York History* 40(1959), 47–61. For a fuller discussion of Taylor's interest in the discovery see L. Lan Sluder, "God in the Background: Edward Taylor as Naturalist," *Early American Literature* 7 (Winter 1973), 265–71.

94. For Ezra Stiles' account of his grandfather's interest in the bones, see Dexter, ed., *Extracts from the Itineraries*, pp. 81–83, 206, and the Boyd edition of *The Papers of Jefferson*, 7: 312. Taylor's account may have contributed (through Stiles) to Jefferson's interest in the remains of ancient animals. See Jefferson, *Notes on the State of Virginia* (Paris, 1785), p. 77, and Brooke Hindle, *The Pursuit of Science in Revolutionary America, 1735–1789* (Chapel Hill, 1959), p. 323.

95. *A Briefe Exposition . . . upon . . . Ecclesiastes* (London, 1654), pp. 13, 22.

96. *The Works of President Edwards*, 2 (New York, 1808), 321–22.

97. Taylor's preaching and poetry are full of medical metaphors. These were used for effect and perhaps should not be misunderstood as showing his confusion of the two areas. Compare his more pathological poems, for example, with a Cotton Mather sermon of 1700:

> Every sinner has many Diseases. He has the Palsey of an unsteady Mind; He has the Feavour of Unchastity; He has the Dropsy of Covetousness; He has the Erisypelas of Anger;. . . He has the Cancer of Envy; He has the Tympany of Pride; He has the Apoplexy of Slothfulness: And what not?. . . We are but a Congregation of Sick Souls: Where am I preaching, Sirs, but in an Hospital?"

The Great Physician, Inviting Them that are Sensible of their Internal Maladies To Repair Unto Him for His Heavenly Remedies (Boston, 1700), pp. 9–10, 26.

98. There is a parallel in a sermon of Cotton Mather's delivered in 1717:

> But are not His People Distempered? Yes: But our SAVIOUR is a Shepherd who cures the distempers of his People. Sheep are liable to a Variety of Diseases. A Shepherd has his Medicines. He doth what we read in Ezek. XXIV.4. "Heal that which is sick, and bind up that which is broken." Tis what our SAVIOUR does for His People, how Effectually, how Gloriously. . . . In Him we have, the Grand Physician of Souls. What is He but, the Lord our Healer?

Ms. in the American Antiquarian Society, quoted in Otho T. Beall, Jr. and Richard H. Shryock, *Cotton Mather: First Significant Figure in American Medicine* (Baltimore, 1954), p. 77.

99. In Taylor's library were the following medical works: Nicholas Culpeper, *A Physicall Directory* (1649) and *Medicaments for the Poor* (1670); Josephus Galeanus, *Epistola Medica* (1648); Hendrick Gutberleth, *Pathologia* (1615); Johannes Magirus, *Physiologiae Peripateticae* (1610); Johann Schroeder, *Pharmacopoeia Medico-Chymica* (1644); Caspar Hoffman, *De Medicamentis Officinalibus* (1649); and John Woodall, *The Surgian's Mate* (1617). He also had access to medical works by Riverius, Origen, and Cotton Mather, but Taylor appears not to have known the few medical works published in the New World—Thacher's *Brief Rule to Guide the Common People of New England how to Order Themselves and theirs in the Small Pocks or Measels* (1677) or Cotton Mather's pamphlet of 1713 on measles.

100. See Raymond Phineas Stearns, *Science in the British Colonies of America* (Urbana, 1970), p. 425 to compare Taylor with serious scientists of the time. Of Mather, Stearns writes: "He had become recognized as a natural philosopher in many parts of the western world" and yet he "was a transitional figure in colonial life, poised between the old theological interpretation of natural phenomena and the new scientific explanation."

101. On this doctrine of signatures, Stearns writes:

Several New England physicians had had medical training in European universities. But the poverty of European drugs, together with the plethora of fascinating "Indian remedies," led them to experiment with native New England herbs and other remedies, often falling into the trap of the Doctrine of Signatures. The early Puritan theory of disease was anti-scientific (disease was a visitation of the wrath of God for the victim's sins) and this choked out more scientific practice in some cases. Even so, they were not basically unscientific for their day. . . . Clearly, the first generation of New England Puritans was cognizant of aspects of the new science although not actively engaged in its furtherance. Pp. 82–83.

102. In Agnes Arber, *Herbals: Their Origin and Evolution . . . 1470–1670* (Cambridge, 1938), pp. 250–51.

103. Taylor provides Ann Leighton with the best example (and the title) for her discussion, *Early American Gardens: "For Meate or Medicine"* (Boston, 1970), pp. 222–23.

As Poet

104. In Stanford, "The Earliest Poems of Edward Taylor," pp. 138–43.

105. Ibid., pp. 143–44.

106. Ibid., pp. 148–51. There are two other poems of this period that are thought to be Taylor's, "A Dialogue between the writer and a Maypole Dresser" and "This in a Letter I sent to my schoolfellow. W. M.," both bound in the manuscript of "Poetical Works" at Yale University Library and attributed to Taylor by Stanford. But Taylor was never elsewhere so didactic as the Maypole poem ("hee that takes delight in heathens games/Shall be pertaker of the heathen paines") nor so cryptic as the poem to W. M. (part of the poem is in Latin and over half of it in shorthand or code). Neither the language nor the ideas suggest Taylor's hand.

107. Johnson, "The Topical Verses of Edward Taylor," pp. 514–16, 516–18, 527–28.

108. Ibid., pp. 532–34.

109. *Treatise*, pp. 159–60.

110. Taylor did not write as dutifully as he might have liked, for he produced only 217 Meditations in 43 years, about two-thirds the number

that could have resulted from the exercises at six-week intervals. Or perhaps a number were discarded or lost.

111. For a discussion of the influence of the tradition of preparatory meditation on Taylor, see Louis L. Martz, "Foreword," *Poems*, pp. xiii–xxvii, and Stephen Fender, "Edward Taylor and 'The Application of Redemption,' " *Modern Language Review* 59 (1964), 331–34.

112. From Biblical numerology Taylor had the belief that the number 7 symbolizes completeness and perfection. ("What secret Sweet Mysterie under the Wing/Of this so much Elect number lies?") He thus stopped the series at 49, though there is little intrinsic reason for doing so.

113. Thomas M. Davis, "Edward Taylor's 'Valedictory' Poems," *Early American Literature* 7 (Spring 1972), 38–63.

114. Ibid., p. 51.

115. Ibid., p. 55.

3: Emergence of an American Poet

1. H. W. Taylor, in *Annals of the American Pulpit*, 1: 177–81; and in Sibley, *Biographical Sketches*, 2: 397–412, 534–36.

2. Cotton Mather, *Right Thoughts in Sad Hours* (London, 1689) includes a portion of one of Taylor's poems "Upon Wedlock and Death of Children." Other sources prior to 1937 where one might have discovered that Taylor had been a poet are: Sprague, *Annals of the American Pulpit*, and Sibley, *Biographical Sketches;* Lockwood, *A Sermon*, and *Westfield;* H. W. Taylor, in *Westfield Jubilee;* and Thomas G. Wright, *Literary Culture in Early New England* (New Haven, 1920).

3. H. W. Taylor, in *Annals of the American Pulpit*, p. 180.

4. However, the work was never published. "An Extract of Several Letters from Cotton Mather, D.D., . . ." *Philosophical Transactions of the Royal Society of London* 29 (1714), 62–63.

5. H. W. Taylor, in *Annals of the American Pulpit*, p. 179.

6. Donald Junkins, "Edward Taylor's Revisions," *American Literature* 37 (1965), 135–52. The argument here is about Taylor's craftsmanship, but in spite of the few revisions in diction, the poems for the most part do not seem prepared for publication.

7. Those who argue thus are: Johnson, *The Poetical Works*, pp. 11–15; Emma Shepherd, "Edward Taylor's Injunction Against Publication," *American Literature* 33 (1962), 512–13; and Donald E. Stanford, cited in *Early American Literature* 1 (1966), 4.

8. C. W. Mignon argues this point in "The American Puritan and Private Qualities of Edward Taylor"; in "Diction in Edward Taylor's *Preparatory Meditations*," *American Speech* 41 (1966), 243–53; and "Edward Taylor's

Preparatory Meditations: A Decorum of Imperfection," *PMLA* 82 (1968), 1423–28.

9. The debate over Taylor's orthodoxy between Thomas H. Johnson, Donald E. Stanford, Norman S. Grabo, and Michael J. Colacurcio on the one hand and Perry Miller, Kenneth B. Murdock, Roy Harvey Pearce, Nathalia Wright, Mindele Black, Willie T. Weathers, and Sidney E. Lind on the other hand seems to have been fairly decided in favor of orthodoxy, the argument of the former.

10. Mignon, "Edward Taylor's *Preparatory Meditations*: A Decorum of Imperfection." In addition, Professor Mignon shows how there is something about the meiotic and hyperbolic character of Taylor's conceits which makes him substantially different from the English metaphysicals and perhaps peculiarly American.

11. *The Continuity of American Poetry* (Princeton, 1961), pp. 45–54. Pearce gets only a glimpse of the importance of process to the poetry of Taylor, however. He says that Taylor's "eloquence lay immanent in what he knew, not in the telling of it—in the object of his discovery, not in the act of discovering the object."

12. The key work on the subject of Puritan meditation as a process is Norman Pettit, *The Heart Prepared: Grace and Conversion in Puritan Spiritual Life* (New Haven, 1966).

13. John A. Kouwenhoven, "What is American about America?" in *American Literary Essays*, ed. Lewis Leary (New York, 1960).

14. See Peter Thorpe's discussion of the justification of such "flaws." "Edward Taylor as Poet," *New England Quarterly* 39 (1966), 356–72.

4: Art's Cramping Task

1. William J. Scheick has convincingly argued the connection between Taylor's writing of poetry and the energizing of his will to live and believe: "The saint's ability to verbalize rightly depends on this act of grace conveyed by the Spirit. When the heart is transformed into the Spirit's instrument, the Word's art instructs the will how to tune graceful words of praise to God." "Nonsense from a Lisping Child: Edward Taylor on the Word as Piety," *Texas Studies in Literature & Language* 13 (1971), 46.

2. *The New England Mind: The Seventeenth Century* (New York, 1939), p. 42.

3. Taylor's example makes necessary a severe modification of Perry Miller's conclusion that "Poetry in Puritan eyes . . . was a species of rhetoric, a dress for great truths, a sugar for the pill." Ibid., p. 361.

4. The sermon is published in full in Donald E. Stanford, "Edward Taylor's 'Spiritual Relation,' " *American Literature* 35 (1964), 468–75.

5. Twenty-eight sermons have survived: his 1679 testimonies, "A Particular Church is God's House" (1679), eight sermons on the Lord's Supper (1693–94), fourteen sermons on Christ (1701–3), and two sermons on church discipline (1713). A twenty-ninth sermon has been identified by Professor Thomas M. Davis and Virginia L. Davis in the Westfield Church Record, but the date of it remains unknown; see "Edward Taylor on the Day of Judgment," *American Literature* 43 (1972), 525–47. In addition, there are fragments of a number of Taylor's sermons interspersed with scripture in the unpublished manuscript "Harmony of the Gospels" at the Redwood Library and Athenaeum. With only one of these works, the 1679 sermon "A Particular Church," did Taylor make an effort to get something published; it was rejected by a Boston printer.

6. "Profession of Faith," manuscript in Westfield Athenaeum.

7. Ibid., p. 67.

8. These have been edited attractively by Grabo as *Edward Taylor's Treatise Concerning the Lord's Supper*.

9. Ibid., pp. 153–54.

10. Grabo, *Edward Taylor's Christographia*.

11. Ibid., pp. 259, 254, 163, 259, 392, 394, 461, 134.

12. Taylor, "Two Sermons on Church Discipline," Prince Library, Boston Public Library, p. 3.

13. Ibid., p. 5.

14. Ibid., p. 37.

15. *Christographia*, p. 128.

16. Ibid., pp. 467–68.

17. Ibid., p. 239.

18. Ibid., p. 253.

19. Taylor, "A Particular Church is Gods House," in the "Church Record," Westfield Athenaeum, p. 5. This serious reservation about the value of art is even more explicit in a comment he makes in *Gods Determinations:*

The Reasonable Soule doth much delight
A Pickpack t'ride o' th' Sensuall Appitite.
And hence the heart is hardened and toyes,
With Love, Delight, and Joy, yea Vanities. (GD 409–10)

20. *Christographia*, pp. 19–20.

21. Ibid., pp. 77–78.

22. "A Particular Church," p. 56.

23. *Christographia*, p. 273.

24. A valuable discussion on this point is Kathleen Blake, "Edward Taylor's Protestant Poetic: Nontransubstantiating Metaphor," *American Literature* 43 (1971), 1–24.

25. *Treatise*, pp. 43–44.
26. "A Particular Church," pp. 56–57.
27. *Christographia*, p. 192.

5: *Gods Determinations*

1. The full title of the collection is *Gods Determinations touching his Elect: and The Elects Combat in their Conversion, and Coming up to Christ together with the Comfortable Effects thereof*. In this case "determinations" refers to the will of God, God desirous of the progress of the saints. The fact that Taylor had numbered the pages of the manuscript of *Gods Determinations*, but not any other pages of his poems in manuscript when he bound his poetical works together, suggests that he had at one point considered them for publication. We know that Ezra Stiles knew at least *Gods Determinations*, for on its first page he wrote: "This [is] a MS of the Revd. Edward Taylor of Westfield, who died there A.D. 1728 or 1729. Aetat. circa 88, vel supra. Attest. Ezra Stiles His Grandson, 1786." Beneath the signature of Stiles is written "Henry W. Taylor his Great Grandson 1868." There is the possibility that it is *Gods Determinations* and the funeral elegies and topical verses that are bound in front of it, rather than the Meditations, that H. W. Taylor was referring to when he wrote of Taylor: "Mr. Taylor cannot be said to have possessed a poetic genius of a very high order." It is also of interest that Thomas H. Johnson placed *Gods Determinations* first in his *Poetical Works* (1939), perhaps thinking it closer to the norm of known Puritan poetry; he admitted in his introduction to that edition that he preferred it to the Meditations. The early reviews of Taylor's poems followed suit, initially giving more consideration to it than to the Meditations. Most critical attention given Taylor between 1939 and 1960 is based on *Gods Determinations*, but since then, perhaps in part because Stanford's edition of *The Poems* (1960) puts *Gods Determinations* at the back of the book, the emphasis has shifted to the Meditations. See Constance J. Gefvert, *Edward Taylor: An Annotated Bibliography, 1668–1970* (Kent, Ohio, 1971) and Norman S. Grabo, "Edward Taylor," in *Fifteen American Authors*, ed. Robert A. Rees and Earl N. Harbert (Madison, Wisconsin, 1971), pp. 333–56.

2. Martz, "Foreword" to *Poems*; Norman S. Grabo, "*Gods Determinations*: Touching Taylor's Critics," *Seventeenth-Century News* 27, no. 2 (1970), 22–24. Grabo's essay is a survey of the criticism of the work; he concludes, "*Gods Determinations* is almost completely excluded from [any] vital kind of criticism."

3. Much attention has been given to the form (and the sources of the

form) of *Gods Determinations*, as if that is where its meaning lies. The conjectures as to its form run from morality play (Nathalia Wright, "The Morality Tradition in the Poetry of Edward Taylor," *American Literature* 18 [1946], 1–17), to allegory (Jean L. Thomas, "Drama and Doctrine in *Gods Determinations*," *American Literature* 36 [1965], 452–62), to literary meditation (Grabo, *Edward Taylor*), to epic (Dennis Barbour, "*Gods Determinations* as Epic Poem," [master's thesis, Indiana State, 1972]), to liturgical drama (Robert D. Arner, "Notes on the Structure of Edward Taylor's *Gods Determinations*," *Studies in the Humanities* 3 [June 1973], 27–29). Also, whether *Gods Determinations* is tripartite as Colacurcio suggests (three arguments for and against pride and despair by Satan and Christ) or tetrapartite as Grabo suggests (four conflicts in man's life: fall vs. redemption, temptation vs. conversion, mercy vs. justice, grace vs. worthiness) or pentpartite as Wright suggests (dialogues regarding the salvation of man) is ultimately not of great significance to the work. That it has a single direction in which the whole of it moves and a single, unifying tone would have been for Taylor a sufficient organization.

4. Taylor's consciousness of an audience and the ways in which he tries to appeal to it are discussed by Michael J. Colacurcio, "*Gods Determinations* Touching Half-Way Membership: Occasion and Audience in Edward Taylor," *American Literature* 39 (1967), 298–314.

5. *Gods Determinations* is suffused with the language of the church, far more than any other poetry Taylor wrote. He speaks, for instance, of "Inherent Grace," "speciall Grace," and "Call," and he refers to the ministry as "Watchmen Watching day, and night,/And Porters at each Gate, who have Command/To open onely to the right." Of value to the tone of his argument is the legal language of covenant theology current in the church at the time:

Desire Converts to joy: joy Conquours Fear.

They now enCovenant With God: and His:
   They thus indent.
The Charters Seals belonging unto this
   The Sacrament
So God is theirs avoucht, they his in Christ.
In whom all things they have, with Grace are splic'te. (GD 455–56)

6. *Contra* Grabo, "Gods Determinations: Touching Taylor's Critics," p. 23.

7. *Contra* Martz, "Foreword."

8. The topical character of *Gods Determinations* is seen in the fact that Taylor may be making a specific reference in his work to the Anne Hutchinsons and Roger Williamses of the colony when he writes:

Some few not in; and some whose Time, and Place
　　Block up this Coaches way to goe
As Travellers afoot. . . . (GD 458–59)

But it is difficult to know who in the area Taylor might be referring to when he speaks of a "corruptor" in their midst—Solomon Stoddard, perhaps?

　　the Lyons Carkass secretly
　　Lies lapt up in a Lamblike skin
　　Which Holy seems yet's full of sin. (GD 454)

9. For Taylor's role in the defense of covenant theology, see Robert G. Pope, *The Half-Way Covenant: Church Membership in Puritan New England* (Princeton, 1969), pp. 190–91, 254–55.

6: *A Metrical History*

1. Donald E. Stanford describes the history and characteristics of the manuscript in "Edward Taylor's Metrical History of Christianity," *American Literature* 33 (1961), 279–95. Professor Stanford transcribed the manuscript in 1957–61 and it is available in typescript at the Stanford, Yale, Louisiana State, and Redwood Libraries, and from Micro-Photo Inc., Old Mansfield Road, P.O. Box 774, Wooster, Ohio, 44691.

2. A note, not in Taylor's hand, has been inserted in the manuscript, naming it "A metrical history of the world from the beginning to 1558" —which it is not. Professor Stanford used this as reason enough to name the work *A Metrical History of Christianity*—which, if we are being precise about the type of material included, it also is not.

3. The poem ends with the year 1101 and begins again with the reign of Queen Mary. It may be that the leaves for this missing period are lost, but it is more likely that, lacking the final volume of the *Magdeburg Centuries*, Taylor did not have the material to versify that he wanted. The final brief section on the sixteenth century (31 ms. pages) is paraphrased from Foxe. It is unfortunate that we do not have material from Taylor on this intervening period, for it leaves us without his comments on the Reformation and specifically on Luther and Calvin.

4. In his essay on the *Metrical History*, Professor Stanford demonstrates how closely Taylor's lines resemble his sources. His method is not that of the plagiarist, however, but that of the simple versifier of prose stories. For a discussion of the influence of Foxe on English and New England Puritan historiography, see William Haller, *The Elect Nation: The Meaning and Relevance of Foxe's "Book of Martyrs"* (New York, 1963) and Peter Gay, "The Struggle for the Christian Past," *A Loss of Mastery: Puritan Historians in Colonial America* (Berkeley, 1966).

5. "A Particular Church", pp. 21–25, 59.

6. Taylor should not be faulted in this. Peter Gay writes: "The best seventeenth-century historians were, for the most part, clerics who exploited and refined the techniques of the fifteenth- and sixteenth-century scholars to glorify their God and confound rival sects. . . . Far from being radical, the Puritans' historical writings looked to the past, not merely for their subject matter, . . . but for their method, their style of thinking. . . . After stirring beginnings, both the course and the writing of Puritan history descended into a glacial age." Pp. 21, 24–25.

7. It is not a long way from this concept to Melville's horologicals and chronometricals, which may have as much of a base in a Puritan historiography like Taylor's as it does in his gnostic reading. Melville could never go the additional step that Taylor does, however, and accept the satanic as a form that God's grace takes.

8. Urian Oakes defined special providences in much the same way that Taylor does: "Yet sometimes there is in his Providence a Variation and Digression. . . . Herein the absolute Soveraignty and Dominion of God appears." *The Sovereign Efficacy of Divine Providence* (Boston, 1682), pp. 18–19.

9. This is suggested too by the way Flacius is used in his 1679 sermon "A Particular House" to discuss the heritage of ideas leading up to covenant theology in New England. (Pp. 21–25).

7: *Preparatory Meditations*

1. "Edward Taylor's Poetry: Colonial Baroque," *Kenyon Review* 3 (Summer 1941), 356. Harold S. Jantz was the first to recognize in early American poetry the dominance of a baroque style, as opposed to the plain style that Perry Miller, Kenneth B. Murdock, and Thomas H. Johnson had observed. In *The First Century of New England Verse* (New York, 1944), pp. 7, 12, 47, Jantz defines baroque in terms of a "tension" resulting from "a tightly packed form, broken lines and telescoped imagery" which "had no interest in being either smooth or romantic." This definition regards only the form, however, and to it must be added the factors of wit, surprise, and elaborate imagery. Besides Warren's and Jantz' studies, the most thorough study of the baroque aspects of seventeenth-century poetry is Calvin Israel, "American Puritan Literary Theory: 1620–1660" (Ph.D. diss., University of California, Davis, 1970).

Of the colonial acceptance of the baroque, Perry Miller writes:

Puritan hostility to the metaphysical style never became, among what we have called "orthodox" Puritans at any rate, hostility to stylistic cultivation or to the constant use of figures and tropes. In their most pious

moods the divines might call eloquence a carnal deceit, but they were
sufficiently of their times to believe that the faithful preaching which was
to enfold the grace of God should be constructed with all possible
"humane helps." They approved of sugaring bitter pills in order to
facilitate the cure of souls. *The New England Mind: The Seventeenth
Century*, p. 304.

Michael Wigglesworth is a case, however, of someone who voiced objec-
tions to the baroque. He damns it as being made up of "strained metaphors,
far fetch't allusions, audacious & lofty expressions" showing "meer ostenta-
tion of learning & empty flashes of a flourishing wit." Baroque writers
"daub over their speech with rhetorical paintments" and "winding, crocked,
periphrasticall circumlocutions, & dark Allegoric mysteries." "The Prayse
of Eloquence" (notebook in the New England Historical and Genealogical
Society).

2. "Edward Taylor's *Preparatory Meditations*: A Decorum of
Imperfection," 1423–28.

3. *The New England Mind: The Seventeenth Century*, pp. 60–63.

4. Taylor also refers to his poems as "worldly toyes" (1.24; 2.36, 42; GD
412).

5. Cotton Mather, *Johannes in Eremo* (Boston, 1695), p. 54. In similar
fashion Taylor says in his elegy on his wife that "The Doomsday Verses [of
Wigglesworth] much perfum'de her Breath."

6. Thomas H. Johnson, "The Topical Verses," 532.

7. Ibid., pp. 513–54.

8. Thomas H. Johnson, "Edward Taylor: A Puritan 'Sacred Poet,' " *New
England Quarterly* 10 (1937), 290–322; Austin Warren, "Edward Taylor's
Poetry: Colonial Baroque," *Kenyon Review* 3 (1941), 355–71; Wallace C.
Brown, "Edward Taylor: An American 'Metaphysical,' " *American
Literature* 16 (1944), 186–97; Mindele Black, "Edward Taylor: Heaven's
Sugar Cake," *New England Quarterly* 29 (1956), 159–81; Thomas G.
Wack, "The Imagery of Edward Taylor's *Preparatory Meditations*" (Ph.D.
diss., Notre Dame, 1961); Emma L. Shepherd, "The Metaphysical Conceit
in the Poetry of Edward Taylor" (Ph.D. diss., North Carolina, 1960);
Harvey Gilman, "From Sin to Song: Image Clusters and Patterns in Edward
Taylor's *Preparatory Meditations* (Ph.D. diss., Penn. State, 1967). This last
study is by far the best on the subject.

9. Gilman, p. 14.

10. Martz writes: "Taylor's place in literary history [is] as the last heir of
the great tradition of English meditative poetry that arose in the latter part of
the sixteenth century. . . ." "Foreword" to *Poems*, p. xxxv. See also William
R. Epperson's excellent essay "The Meditative Structure of Edward Taylor's
'Preparatory Meditations' " (Ph.D. diss., Kansas, 1965).

11. It is interesting to note in passing that Taylor did not think very highly of Loyola and his influence. In his *Christographia* Sermon 13, he calls him a "profane wicked person, and Treator." (P. 429).

12. Willard, pp. 29–30, 118.

13. *Elizabethan and Metaphysical Imagery* (Chicago, 1947). Those stimulated by this approach are Shepherd, Gilman, Black, Blau, Brown, and Wack—all cited above.

14. If Taylor was indeed a distant disciple of Herbert, it is instructive to compare him with a contemporary English disciple, Christopher Harvey, who published his *The Synagogue; or The Shadow of the Temple* in 1705 "in imitation of Mr. George Herbert." Compare the rough, excited, and primitively witty lines of Taylor's "The Reflexion" and Meditation 1.8 with Harvey's calm and gentlemanly lines on the Lord's Supper:

> 'Tis Dinner-time: and not I look
> For a full Meal. God send me a good Cook:
>   This is the Dresser-board, and here
>   I wait in expectation of good Cheer.
>   I'm sure the Master of the House
> Enough to entertain his Guest allows:
> And not enough of some one sort alone,
> But Choice of what best fitteth ev'ry one.
>
>   God grant me Taste and Stomack good:
> My feeding will diversify my Food;
>   Tis a good Appetite to eat.
> And good Digestion, that makes good Meat.
>   The best Food in it self will be,
> Not fed on well, Poison, not Food to me.
> Let him that speaks look to his words; my Ear
> Must careful be, both what and how I hear.
>
>   'Tis Manna that I look for here,
> The Bread of Heaven, Angels Food. I fear
>   No want of Plenty, where I know
> The Loaves by eating more, and greater, grow. (Pp. 17–18)

15. Cf. Stephen A. Fender, "Edward Taylor and the Sources of American Puritan Wit" (Ph.D. diss., Manchester University, England, 1962–63), and Morton Berkowitz, "Edward Taylor and the Seventeenth Century" (master's thesis, University of Massachusetts, 1968). Both studies show Taylor's differences from the English metaphysicals.

16. *Treatise*, pp. 47, 59.

17. Ibid., pp. 152, 21, 112, 221.

18. Ibid., p. 199.

19. Ibid., p. 48.

20. Ibid., p. 17.

21. *Christographia*, pp. xviii–xxxvii.

22. *Treatise*, pp. 153–54.

23. Ibid., p. 125.

24. Ibid., p. 170.

25. Ibid., pp. 159–60.

26. Ibid., p. 180.

27. "A Treatise on Grace," *Selections from the Unpublished Writings of Jonathan Edwards*, ed. A. B. Grosart (Edinburgh, 1865), p. 37.

28. *Christographia*, pp. 191, 258.

29. *Religious Affections*, ed. John E. Smith (New Haven, 1959), p. 394.

30. *Christographia*, pp. 19–20.

31. *Beauty and Sensibility in the Thought of Jonathan Edwards* (New Haven, 1968), pp. 23–24.

32. *Religious Affections*, pp. 253–54.

33. *The Nature of True Virtue* (Ann Arbor, 1960), pp. 27–28.

34. "Profession of Faith," p. 5.

35. "Miscellanies," Yale Collection of Edwards Manuscripts (Yale University Library), p. 489.

36. "A Divine and Supernatural Light," *The Works of President Edwards* (New York, 1843), 4:441–42.

37. Like "love" and "glory," the word "sweet" and its variants are recurrent in Taylor's poems to the point of a unifying motif in both series. In the two series, according to the Taylor concordance, they are used 500 times.

38. *Religious Affections*, p. 298.

8: *Preparatory Meditations*

1. Roland M. Frye, "Swift's Yahoo and the Christian Symbols for Sin," *Journal of the History of Ideas* 15 (1954), 201–17. Swift and Taylor were contemporary Christian apologists with much in common. Both artistically adapted Augustinian theology and normative Protestantism in defense of their orthodoxies—which led both of them to a use of the Biblical descriptions of filth and deformity that are symbolic of sin. But Taylor's is perhaps a more fully rounded Christian view of man—the sin and folly of man balanced by the image and purposes of God and the depths of man's excremental existence balanced by the victories of the spirit.

2. See Norman O. Brown, *Life Against Death: The Psychoanalytical Meaning of History* (Middletown, Conn., 1959), pp. 202–33, 308–22.

Brown's discussion of Swift provides insight into Taylor and other Puritan scatologists.

3. Leviticus 5–22. The Biblical references in this discussion are as rendered in the Geneva Bible of 1560, the version used by Taylor.

4. Titus 1:15; II Peter 2:10, 12; II Corinthians 7:1; Luke 14:35.

5. "On Original Sin," *The Nicean and Post-Nicean Fathers* (Grand Rapids, Mich., 1956), 5: 237–55.

6. Eugène Portalié, *A Guide to the Thought of St. Augustine* (Chicago, 1960), pp. 204–13.

7. Augustine's use of Ambrose (*Apologia Davidis*, 2: 56). See Portalié, p. 208.

8. *The Nicean and Post-Nicean Fathers*, 4:83, 18; 5:250, 253, 254.

9. Etienne Gilson, *The Christian Philosophy of St. Augustine* (New York, 1960), pp. 148–53.

10. *Institutes*, 1.xv.1–4; 2.i.5–11; ii.1, 16, 19; iii.2–3; 3.xii.1; xvi.2.

11. J. G. Walch, ed., *Sämmtliche Schriften* (St. Louis, 1881–1910), 1: 174; 2: 1514; 4: 1252; 5: 104, 118; 7: 43, 304; 9: 103, 825, 839, 1288; 12: 544, 1338; 13: 1259; 22: 232, 804, 1917. See also Hartmann Grisar, *Luther* (London, 1913–17), 5: 226, 229, 249, 315; 6: 132–33, 215.

12. *The Heart Prepared*, pp. 3, 101. See also Martz, "Foreword" to the Stanford edition of Taylor's poems.

13. II Corinthians 7:10.

14. *Works* (Edinburgh, 1862–64), 1: 47; 6: 33–34, 41, 44, 51. See Pettit, pp. 68–70.

15. *The Application of Redemption* (London, 1657), p. 271.

16. *The Souls Humiliation* (London, 1638), pp. 1, 5.

17. Quoted by Giles Firmin, in *The Real Christian* (London, 1670), p. 86.

18. *The Pilgrim's Progress* (New York, 1964), pp. 16, 31, 94, 98, 189, 255, 269, 270, 290, 320.

19. *Paradise Lost*, 10: 629–40; 11: 515–25. Donne, like many others in the Catholic-Anglican tradition, uses similar imagery: "Between that excremental jelly that thy body is made of at first, and that jelly which thy body dissolves to at last, there is not so noisome, so putrid a thing in nature." *Works* (London, 1839), 4: 231.

20. *Christographia*, pp. 11, 14, 20.

21. "Spiritual Relation," pp. 472–73.

22. Taylor's depressive obsession with dirt, like Calvin's and Luther's, confirms psychological analysis that has been made of the puritan type of personality: an obsessive fear of dirt and an almost surgical desire for cleanliness are associated typically with a feeling of remoteness from God. To such a purist as Taylor all things of the world are naturally impure. See G. Rattray Taylor, *Sex in History* (New York, 1954), pp. 161–67.

23. The use of scatological and erotic terms in the discussion of grace often results in such puns:

Offal: ordure; awful. ("The Return")
Sun of Righteousness . . . Upon such Dunghills: warmth making fertilizer
      produce; God the Son loving fallen man into new life. (2.67b)
thy Warm Sun: Christ as Lover. (1.14)
dying: death; intercourse; colored with Christ's blood. (1.14)
embraces: seductions; religious commitment. (2.6)
laying down [one's] life: atonement; intercourse. (2.32)
full of Spirits: drunk; pregnant; regenerate. (2.98)
walke . . . with Grace: female flirtation; communion with god. (2.148)

24. Taylor's imagery for this process is very much stronger than that in Samuel Willard's *Some Brief Sacramental Meditations* (Boston, 1711):

Bread is not made without *Grinding* of the grain to dust, and being
prepared with *Water* and *Fire*; and Christ became Food for Souls to live
on, by being bruised for our sins, and scorched in the fire of Gods wrath,
and so he is made fit for us to feed upon.

25. Grabo, *Edward Taylor*, pp. 49–66.
26. Compare with Herbert's poem "Miserie":

What strange pollutions doth he wed,
And make his own!

27. Robert H. Pfeiffer, *Introduction to the Old Testament* (New York, 1941), pp. 714–15; C. D. Ginzburg, *The Song of Songs* (London, 1857), pp. 20–102.
28. Taylor's affection for the Canticles was very much like John Saffin's. Saffin thought the Canticles had "more store of more sweet and precious, exquisite and amiable Resemblances, taken from the richest Jewels, the sweetest Spices, Gardens, Orchards, Vineyards, Winecellars, and the chiefest beauties of all the workes of God and Man." *John Saffin, His Book* (New York, 1928), ed. Caroline Hazard, p. 47.
29. Taylor's interest in Canticles was very much like John Cotton's:

[*For delights, or in delights*] it is an allusion to the marriage-bed, which
is the delights of the Bridegroom, and Bride. This marriage-bed is the
publick worship of God in the Congregation of the Church as *Cant.* 3.1.
      The publick Worship of God is the bed of loves: where, 1. Christ
embraceth the souls of his people, and casteth into their hearts the
immortal seed of his Word, and Spirit, *Gal.* 4.19. 2. The Church con-

ceiveth and bringeth forth fruits to Christ. *A Brief Exposition with Practical Observations upon the Whole Book of Canticles* (London, 1655), p. 209.

What Cotton uses to describe the institution of the church in its relation with God, however, Taylor personalizes considerably.

30. Evelyn Underhill, *Mysticism* (New York, 1955), pp. 136–40.

31. In fact, in none of the devotional poets is the erotic dominant the way it is in Taylor, unless of course Donne's love poems are really meditative exercises. It is with Donne rather than Herbert or Crashaw that Taylor has some affinity in this regard. Compare, for instance:

I . . . never shall be free,
Nor ever chast, except you ravish mee. (Holy Sonnets 14)

I enravished Climb into
The Godhead. . . . ("Upon a Wasp Child with Cold")

32. *Institutes*, 4: xvii. 1–10.

33. Miller, *The New England Mind: From Colony to Province*, p. 56.

34. Pettit, p. 17.

35. See particularly such writings as Thomas Hooker, *The Souls Implantation* (London, 1637), pp. 233, 253, and *The Souls Vocation or Effectual Calling* (London, 1638), pp. 238–39; and Richard Sibbes, *Works* (Edinburgh, 1862–1864), 1: 47, 59, 265; 4: 181, 198.

36. *The Puritan Family* (New York, 1944), pp. 161–68.

37. *A Compleat Body of Divinity* (Boston, 1726), pp. 876–79.

38. *The Heart of Christ* . . . (London, 1647).

39. *Christographia*, pp. 78–79.

40. "Spiritual Relation," 473–74.

41. Thus the shift in emphasis from the King to the maiden within poems in this series and the shift in reference after Meditation 148 to an interest primarily in the maiden.

42. This is different from the mystic's "dark night of the soul" and "Way of Purgation" (see Grabo, pp. 49–66) in affirming rather than denying one's necessary foulness and worldliness and unworthiness. Taylor's attitude is not one of self-denial and self-punishment but one of self-consciousness and fear of rejection by God. It is not so much self-discipline and self-formation, either, as it is a struggle with his spiritual desires in the face of his human limitations.

43. This pattern is seen explicitly in the title of a manuscript by Richard Denton of Stamford which Taylor liked very much and tried to get Increase Mather's help to publish—*A Divine Soliloquy; or, the Mirror of,* 1. *Created*

Purity, 2. *Contracted Deformity*, 3. *Restored Beauty*, & 4. *Celestiall Glory*. Letter to Increase Mather, 22 March 1683, *Collections of the Massachusetts Historical Society* 4th ser., 8 (1868), 629–30.

9: Taylor as a Myth-Maker

1. Introduction to *Diary*, p. 22.
2. *Poetical Works*, p. 14; *Emily Dickinson: An Interpretive Biography* (Cambridge, 1955), pp. vii, 20.
3. *Christographia*, p. 237.
4. Meditation 2.89; also in "A Particular Church," pp. 2–3, 9.
5. *Jonathan Edwards* (New York, 1949), pp. 4, 10–11.
6. *The New England Mind: From Colony to Province*, p. 230.
7. *Christographia*, p. 128.
8. It is in this regard that one may detect in Taylor a divided sensibility. In his sermons he inclines towards the eastern rationalism but in his poetry towards the western sensationalism. It may be that though he desired public recognition from the eastern intellectual center and preached and wrote his prose to catch their ears, in his heart he loved the western way of the emotions and could in private let his poetry emerge.
9. Joseph Haroutunian, *Piety Versus Moralism: The Passing of the New England Theology* (New York, 1932).
10. "Edward Taylor's Spiritual Huswifery," *PMLA* 74 (1964), 554–60.
11. See Mignon's study of Taylor's diction, "The American Puritan and Private Qualities of Edward Taylor, the Poet," pp. 187–203.

10: Rough Feet for Smooth Praises

1. "Edward Taylor's Poetry: Colonial Baroque," 370. Others who have commented on Taylor as a primitive poet are Roy Harvey Pearce, who finds it in Taylor an ignorance of technique ("Edward Taylor: The Poet as Puritan," *New England Quarterly* 23 [1950], 44–46), and Louis Martz, who feels that "Taylor is not a primitive" but "a subtle, learned man" ("Foreword" to *Poems*, p. xviii).
2. "Editor's Study," *Harper's* 82 (1891), 320.
3. *In Defense of Reason* (Denver, 1937), p. 93.
4. "A Critical Definition of the American Primitive," *Art in America* 26 (1938), 171–77. For additional definitions see Jean Lipman and Alice Winchester, *Primitive Painters in America, 1750–1950* (New York, 1950); Oto Bihalji-Merin, *Modern Primitives: Masters of Naive Painting* (New York, 1959); Mary Black and Jean Lipman, *American Folk Painting* (New

York, 1966). It is, of course, necessary to distinguish, as I think these critics do not, between a twentieth-century primitive like Henri Rousseau and colonial American primitives like, say, Edward Hicks and the other painters mentioned in this discussion. Hicks and the others are attempting to paint according to conventions—and failing—but in the process achieving new and delightful personal styles. Rousseau and many other twentieth-century painters of primitivism are deliberately attempting to recapture the techniques of the earlier primitives as a rebellion against modern standardization, intellectuality, and programmization of reality. Where the one is instinctive and mistaken, the other is deliberate and experimental.

5. "A Critical Definition," p. 171.

6. Ibid., p. 174.

7. For discussions of the primitive characteristics in Anna Mary Robertson Moses, see Otto Kallir, *Grandma Moses: American Primitive* (New York, 1946) and Kallir, ed., *The Art and Life of Grandma Moses* (New York, 1969).

8. Kallir, *The Art and Life*, pp. 20–21.

9. Bihalji-Merin, pp. 95–96.

10. Thomas M. Davis, "Edward Taylor's 'Valedictory' Poems," 61.

11. Taylor calls such puns "solicisms":

My Mite (if I such Solicisms might
    But use) would spend its mitie Strength for thee
Of Mightless might, of feeble strong delight. (2.48)

12. One exception to the general nonfunctionality of Taylor's impure rhymes is his poem "The Joy of Church Fellowship" from *Gods Determinations*, in which the rhymes become purer as the singing saints "Encoacht for Heaven" get closer to their goal.

13. Gene Russell, *Concordance to the Poems of Edward Taylor* (Washington, D. C., 1972); see also "Dialectal and Phonetic Features of Edward Taylor's Rhymes," *American Literature* 43 (1971), 165–80.

14. "What is American in American Art: Common Denominators from the Pilgrims to Pollack," *What is American in American Art?* ed. Jean Lipman (New York, 1963), pp. 8–23.

11: A Puritan Humanist

1. *The New England Mind: From Colony to Province*, p. 67.

2. This has been argued best by Grabo, *Edward Taylor*, pp. 69–83, and Introduction to *Christographia*, pp. xxiv–xxx.

3. *Christographia*, pp. 90, 96.

4. Ibid., pp. 91, 103.
5. Ibid., p. 141.
6. Ibid., pp. 28–29.
7. Ibid., pp. 12, 21.
8. Ibid., p. 66.
9. Ibid., p. 92.
10. Ibid., p. 78.
11. Ibid., p. 88.
12. Ibid., p. 95.
13. Ibid., p. 104.
14. Ibid., pp. 128–29.
15. Ibid., p. 139.
16. Ibid., p. 132.
17. Ibid.
18. Ibid., pp. 148–49, 151.
19. Ibid., p. 166.

20. The best discussion of preparationism (though Taylor is omitted) is Pettit, *The Heart Prepared.* Scheick has made the strongest argument for the connection between Taylor's meditative preparationism and the energizing of his will to live and believe, "Nonsense from a Lisping Child: Edward Taylor on the Word as Piety" (1971).

21. For the progressive influence of preparationism in New England, see Perry Miller, "The Expanding Limits of Natural Ability," *The New England Mind: From Colony to Province,* pp. 53–67.

22. *Treatise,* pp. 16–17.
23. Ibid., p. 106.
24. Ibid., pp. 143–44.
25. Ibid., p. 193.
26. Ibid., pp. 153–54.

27. "Calvinism in Action: The Super-ego Triumphant," *Hudson Review* 41 (Spring 1972), 23–50.

28. See the introductions by Gene Russell and myself in *A Concordance to the Poetry of Edward Taylor.*

29. Note Taylor's further use of the pun *heart/art* to connect his poetry and his spiritual worth:

> I strive to heave my heart to thee, but finde
> When striving, in my heart an heartless minde. (2.13)

> My Heart, my Lord, 's a naughty thing all o're:
> Yet if renew'd, the best in mee, 't would fain
> Find Words to waft thy praises in. . . . (2.51)

Taylor's claim to grace through the human activity of writing is also seen in his use of the pun *write/right* to represent the correspondence:

> Cleare up my Right, my Lord, in thee, and make
> Thy Name stand Dorst upon my Soule in print,
> In grace I mean, that so I may partake
> Of what I lost, in thee, and of thee in't.
> I'l take it then, Lord, at thy hand, and sing
> Out Hallelujah for thy Grace therein. (1:31)

30. In self-contempt and also in hope of grace, Taylor exclaims several times in his Meditations: "I eate my Word." To Taylor words contribute to "The Sweetness [that] makes my inward man revive." (2.84)

31. The following statement by Edwards should indicate to us that when he thought of himself as a writer, Taylor was much more of an enthusiast than Edwards:

> 'Tis no sign that affections are truly gracious affections, or that they are not, that they cause those who have them, to be fluent, fervent and abundant, in talking of the things of religion. . . . Especially are they captivated into a confident and undoubting persuasion that they are savingly wrought upon, if they are not only free and abundant, but very affectionate and earnest in their talk. . . . This is but the religion of the mouth and of the tongue. . . .
>
> That persons are disposed to be abundant in talking of things of religion, may be from a good cause, and it may be from a bad one. It may be because their hearts are very full of holy affections . . . and it may be because persons' hearts are very full of religious affection which is not holy; for still out of the abundance of the heart the mouth speaketh. . . . And therefore persons talking abundantly and very fervently about the things of religion, can be an evidence of no more than this, that they are very much affected with the things of religion; but this may be (as has been already shown), and there be no grace. *Religious Affections* (New Haven, 1969), pp. 135–36.

Taylor may have thought of his gift of writing as grace and to Edwards this would have been heresy.

32. My italics.

Index

87

.50

lor
can
hin
s-
mi-
the
n
is

les

it-
ty.